ROUSSEAU AND BURKE

ROUSSEAU AND BURKE

A STUDY OF THE IDEA OF LIBERTY
IN EIGHTEENTH-CENTURY POLITICAL
THOUGHT

ANNIE MARION OSBORN

NEW YORK

RUSSELL & RUSSELL · INC

1964

FIRST PUBLISHED IN 1940
REISSUED, 1964, BY RUSSELL & RUSSELL, INC.
L. C. CATALOG CARD NO: 64-20671

PRINTED IN THE UNITED STATES OF AMERICA

PREFACE

THE purpose of this study is to give a statement of the political thought of Jean Jacques Rousseau and of his bitterest contemporary English critic, Edmund Burke. From a comparison of their ideas it becomes evident that, in spite of Burke's scathing denunciations of Rousseau in the years of the French revolution when he regarded him as a false prophet who was leading a great empire to destruction, there was no important divergence of opinion on the question of fundamental principles. Indeed, when on occasion Burke presents a statement of abstract principle, he gives the best possible phrasing of Rousseau's doctrine. Thus when in the *Reflections on the French Revolution*, he states that 'He who gave our nature to be perfected by our virtue, willed also the necessary means of its perfection.—He willed therefore the state', he gives the fundamental tenet not only of his own political thought, but of Rousseau's as well. Elsewhere, as here, we find statements that illustrate a remarkable degree of harmony in their basic convictions. It is not necessary to conclude that Burke derived the essentials of his political philosophy from Rousseau, for he did not. He was entirely unaware of the fact that his sovereign principles were in accord with Rousseau's. But this was not surprising because the circumstances of their lives, their characteristic modes of thinking, and their approach to the problems of political philosophy led inevitably to methods of presentation that, in the main, had little in common with each other. Consequently it becomes intelligible why Burke should have regarded Rousseau as a false prophet and should have denounced him accordingly. But in the course of his denunciations of Rousseau and his disciples, Burke showed the essential weaknesses of Rousseau's doctrine, while at the same time he gave it its practical corrective. Thus as he pointed to the dangers and problems which confronted the state that was dedicated to liberty, he supplemented Rousseau's work.

Because this study covers such a wide range of thought, it

has been found necessary to limit it in several important directions. In the first place, the doctrine of the general will is too complex to be dealt with in all its important aspects within the scope of this study. A complete analysis of it and an examination of its strength and its defects from the point of view of political philosophy would require a volume to itself. Although fully aware that it is a two-edged weapon and that it can become, as Lemaître said, 'the most potent implement of tyranny that maniac ever forged', I have confined myself to that interpretation of it which seems to me to be in keeping with Rousseau's fundamental principles. Also, the student of Rousseau and Burke becomes increasingly conscious of the fact that their minds were cast in entirely different moulds and that he will therefore ignore the history of their development at his peril. Rousseau's mind grew in stature as his impact with life gave him a clearer understanding of its meaning and purpose. He began with the current concepts in political philosophy, but as his understanding of his central problem deepened and became clearer, he discarded much that was no longer of service to him and devoted his attention to the more significant idea of the general will. Moreover, following the publication of the *Contrat Social*, we find him devoting much attention to the application of his political principles. He was asked to give his ideas on a constitution for Corsica and on the government of Poland, and we find him deferring to expediency and circumstance in the best style of Montesquieu and Burke. Burke's mind, noble and luminous though it was, lacked the originality and the constructive capacity of Rousseau's. His ideas were more liberal in his earlier years, but his thought was so hedged in by fears in later years that he became uncompromisingly conservative in the works which, ironically enough, brought him enduring fame and showed most completely the mellowness of the intellect that had been accustomed to move and have its being in the rarer atmosphere of philosophic contemplation and wisdom that belongs to the statesman. It has not proved possible to discuss in detail the many statements of each which are in real or apparent contradiction to other pronouncements they have made. But bearing in mind the historical development of their thought, I have attempted, in the interests of clarity, to decide what their fundamental principles were and to present them. By following such a method it has been possible to show the fundamental agreement of the two men and the somewhat surprising harmony of their views on some of the most important issues confronting democracy.

While the principles that Rousseau and Burke expounded have always been of importance in the study of political thought, they are now of particular significance owing to the fact that they are the principles which are basic in the political structure of the great democracies of the world to-day—of Great Britain, France, and the United States of America—and are being challenged by the totalitarian states. The fundamental problems which confronted England and France in the eighteenth century, and which Rousseau and Burke attempted to resolve, are facing the modern world also. They have, of course, assumed a distinctive form for our age ; the question of the dominance of the state is the outstanding political problem of our time. In the hope that a statement of the fundamental principles which Rousseau and Burke presented to their age may not prove unprofitable to us in the consideration of our own problems, this study has been undertaken.

It is my very great privilege to acknowledge the special debt of gratitude I owe to Professor Ernest Hunter Wright, at whose suggestion this study was originally undertaken. Professor Wright very kindly placed his extensive Rousseau library at my disposal, and has helped me very considerably by his stimulating criticism of my efforts. I am just as deeply indebted to Professor Robert Morrison MacIver for his guidance, for his unfailing interest and for his kindly encouragement. I have also to acknowledge the helpful criticism of Professors Jefferson Butler Fletcher, George Sherburn, Hoxie Neale Fairchild, and Emery Neff. It is a very great pleasure to thank my colleagues and friends for their interest and their help. To my father, the Rev. Dr. Andrew Rule Osborn, who helped me to grasp the fundamental principles of Calvinism, I am deeply grateful.

CONTENTS

CHAPTER I

THE INSANE SOCRATES

'I HAVE read long since the *Contrat Social*', Edmund Burke replied when a young French friend, M. Dupont, asked him in the early days of the French revolution what he thought of the authors whose works were most influential in shaping the policies of the National Assembly. 'It has left very few traces upon my mind. I thought it a performance of little or no merit; and little did I conceive that it could ever make revolutions, and give law to nations. But so it is. . . .'[1]

Burke made no attempt to conceal his astonishment at the deference that was being paid to Rousseau's political doctrines in France, and at the amazing popularity of the *Contrat Social* in which Rousseau had given them classic expression. He did not question for one moment Rousseau's eloquence as a writer; neither did he deny Rousseau's claims to pre-eminence in the literary world. But it seemed to him that the views of an eloquent writer were being accepted enthusiastically without being subjected first of all to critical analysis which would divest them of their literary merits and show them in their true light. Burke was disturbed not only because the leaders of the French nation were deferring to the precepts of the *philosophes*, particularly of Voltaire and Rousseau, instead of heeding authors of greater authority whom Burke and all the world could respect without question, but also because of the whole aspect of the revolution. The wild enthusiasm which the course of events in France had aroused only served to alarm him profoundly. He feared greatly what the final outcome of it all would be.

M. Dupont, whom Burke had come to know and to admire when the young French advocate had visited England in the spring of 1788, had written enthusiastically to acquaint Burke with the progress of the revolution. He was particularly interested in its intellectual aspects, and for that reason he asked Burke for his opinion of the authors whose works were being studied assiduously by the members of the National Assembly. He anticipated a sympathetic response because he knew that Burke had invariably supported the cause of liberty throughout his long political career. Dupont had an intense admiration for the liberality of the views of the ageing English statesman, for the amazing range of his knowledge of men and affairs, and for the blending of practical wisdom and philosophical insight which had made Burke a dominating figure in politics for more than twenty years. He had taken it for granted that he would find Burke wholeheartedly on the side of the new régime, with its glowing assurance of liberty for the French nation, and its high hopes of inaugurating a glorious new era for all mankind.[2] But there was no enthusiasm in Burke's reply either for the revolution or for the authors who were admired so greatly by the National Assembly.

As he thought out his answer to M. Dupont's letter, Burke went back in memory to the days when Rousseau's works were being published, in an endeavour to recall as clearly as possible what his own impressions and reactions had been.[3] He recollected how each work from Rousseau's pen had in turn created a sensation in the literary world. The *Discours sur l'inégalité* (1755), translated into English, had brought Rousseau prominently before the reading public of England, and had enhanced the reputation he had already won in Paris as a writer of brilliant paradoxes. But it had also identified him with the cult of the 'noble savage', a fact that had immediately aroused Burke's antagonism. Burke had no love for the literature of the mid-century which gave expression to a desire to return to the simple life of the 'natural' man, away from the burdens and tribulations of civilized society. Indeed, his opposition to this type of literature had impelled him to attack it bitterly in an ironic *Vindication of Natural Society* (1756), because he detected in it a false attitude towards life and also the creation of a sentiment that could bring untold havoc to established institutions. In 1762, the *Contrat Social* had appeared, and Burke had read it, not so much because he genuinely expected to learn a great deal from Rousseau's exposition of political principles, but because he had made a point of keeping abreast of current literature, particularly that which touched upon political life and thought. Any hope he had of finding something of consequence within its pages, however, vanished quickly. He detected the handiwork of the author of the *Discours sur l'inégalité* in the opening pages of the work. Furthermore, he disapproved strongly of Rousseau's method of approach to his subject matter. He soon found that he was deep in a critical analysis of the foundations of political society, which the author was discussing from a purely speculative point of view. At no time would Burke himself enter into such a discussion willingly because he believed that it was fraught with infinite danger to the state. He regarded the social and political order as the product of a long period of slow growth. It was not a piece of machinery that could be taken to pieces, examined critically, and put together again at will. On the contrary, it was a delicate and exceedingly complex structure that had been moulded gradually into an organic whole. For this reason Burke believed that it should be regarded as a sacred heritage, and should be preserved intact. Above all, it had to be safeguarded from what he considered rash interference on the part of those who believed that they could improve upon the work of the ages. And because he sensed the challenge to the established order implicit in current speculative thought, he resented the fact that considerations of expediency had not deterred writers such as Rousseau from expounding their views regarding the fundamental nature of the state and the basis upon which the citizen owed to it his loyalty.

'But the social order is a sacred right which is the foundation of all other rights,' he read. 'Nevertheless, this right does not come from nature, and must therefore be founded on conventions. The essential thing is to know what these conventions are. Before coming to that, I have to prove what I have just asserted. . . .' [4]

Then came criticisms of the views of others regarding the basis of political obligation, which were followed by restatements leading to Rousseau's own version of the social contract. As the logical framework took shape, Burke was able to survey it critically. Rousseau had promised to construct the dwelling-place of liberty, but the edifice did not look very promising. On the contrary, its ominous aspect suggested that it was destined to become the stronghold of tyranny. Although the sweeping terms of the contract were designed to guarantee absolutely the liberty of the sovereign people, Burke noticed that the author was soon involved in limitations that looked perilously like retractions, and in contradictions that followed almost inevitably. But in spite of the jargon of the metaphysical school which could be called into service to cover up these weaknesses in his theory whenever necessary, and in spite of the attractions of a social geometry which not only gave Rousseau's fancy free rein, but also lent a touch of precision to the work as it progressed, Burke saw that eventually the author would find himself trapped in his maze of sophistry and logic. And in the chapter on Civil Religion he was ultimately caught. Here Burke found the sensational strictures upon Christianity for its defects from the point of view of the state, and Rousseau's version of the articles of faith for the 'purely civil confession of faith', which were to replace the Sermon on the Mount. Failure to subscribe to those articles carried the penalty of banishment from the state, while any one who after subscribing to them behaved as if he did not believe them was to be punished by death! [5]

Having read the *Contrat Social*, Burke put it aside without comment. It had proved to be the kind of work he felt was to be expected from the literary circles of Paris. Great as the claims of Rousseau and the Encyclopedists were to preeminence in literature, Burke would have preferred it if they had not regarded political thought as a suitable subject for metaphysical speculation. Their ignorance of the practical side of political life caused them to formulate theories which, for the greater part, were not even remotely connected with the world of practical affairs, and were therefore virtually worthless from the point of view of the statesman. Consequently criticism of their theories had to be limited to a question of their validity as consistent systems of thought. But Burke emphatically refused to undertake criticism of such a nature. For that reason, he had no comment to offer on the *Contrat Social* at the time of its publication. He felt that it would be quite time enough to think of criticizing Rousseau's doctrine when it began to play an active part in practical politics. He had not imagined that it would ever play any such part, because it was primarily an excursion into Utopia. It was visionary, and for that reason it was not very likely to impinge upon the world of reality. Neither did he find in it any of that insight which had characterized similar excursions by writers before Rousseau, some of whom had become exceedingly influential in moulding the course of history. Indeed, in the hope that he might discover in them elements of wisdom and truth, Burke was ever ready to examine the works of his contemporaries, even when their methods were most distasteful to him. But he had been unable to detect the presence of qualities in the *Contrat Social* that would have raised it out of the ordinary to a place among the classics. The doctrines that Rousseau had expounded in it belonged to the world of fancy rather than to that of imaginative insight. They were 'so inapplicable to real life and manners', he believed, 'that we never dream of drawing from them any rule for laws or conduct'.[6] Consequently he had no comment to offer until he found, to his amazement, that the unexpected had happened. For as he wrote his reply to M. Dupont in 1789, the visionary dreams of Jean Jacques Rousseau were moulding the destinies of Europe.

In itself, Burke had regarded the *Contrat Social* as of no particular consequence. But as he read it, he recognized that it was typical of an increasingly large number of works devoted to political speculation that were being published in France[7] and to a lesser degree in England also. The *Contrat Social* assumed significance, therefore, as a part of a movement of thought. But it seemed to Burke that it was of greater importance to devote his attention to criticism of that movement rather than to criticism of Rousseau in particular. At the time when Rousseau's work had been published, this movement had assumed vitality in two directions. On the one hand, there had been a marked increase in the number of writings devoted to the theory of politics. This had been due mainly to the desire on the part of thinkers and writers to bring the social sciences into line with the scientific philosophy that had been developed in the seventeenth century by Descartes and Locke, who in their turn had been inspired by the amazing development of the natural sciences that had culminated in the work of Newton. Descartes' method for the reorientation of philosophy had been to strike back to ultimate realities, and after establishing them as clear and self-consistent, to build upon them truths which followed as a logical consequence from his ultimate truths. The Cartesian method, however, was not primarily intended for speculative thought in either religion or politics. Nevertheless it had been extended to those fields by Fontenelle and other enthusiastic Cartesians in the early decades of the eighteenth century. Locke's method was distinguished from that of Descartes by his reference to the facts of experience as the basis of his philosophy. On the basis of this empiricism he had formulated a rationalistic psychology, upon which he had built a science of government. These two methods were used by the eighteenth-century theorists in their eager attempts to formulate a science of politics.

Together with this attempt to establish political philosophy on a scientific basis, there was a widespread awakening of public interest in political thought. It was this aspect of the movement that assumed special significance from Burke's point of view. Popular interest had veered from the endless controversies in the theological world to the greener fields of politics, where questions of an equally absorbing nature were being discussed. That interest grew steadily as men began to realize that they could play an active part in political life and that they were not confined, as they had been in theological discussions, to the role of interested spectators. Because of this new development, leading men began to make greater use of pamphlets and the columns of leading chronicles as a means of gaining the support of public opinion.

Burke was fully aware of the significance and of the dangers of this aspect of the movement. He knew that if the people realized the full extent of their power, they could force upon the government theories that appealed to them with sufficient vigour, whether those theories were politically sound or not. For that reason it seemed to him that it was of the greatest importance to guide the reading public out on to the broad highway of political philosophy. Consequently he took upon himself the task of teaching his readers the fundamental principles of politics so that they might distinguish between sound thought and the specious one-sided theories that were an almost inevitable accompaniment of any sustained attempt to formulate a science of politics. The essential task, as he saw it, was to teach and not to argue with people like Rousseau. With this in mind as he entered upon his life's work, Burke had set about making the reading public understand two important facts which seemed to him to be fundamental to a right approach to the problems of politics. In the first place, if politics was to achieve its end, it should be adjusted 'not to human reasonings, but to human nature; of which reason is but a part, and by no means the greatest part '.[8] It was essential to learn this lesson if the dangers of one-sided theories were to be avoided. At the same time, it was necessary for people to recognize that current theories, for the most part, were based upon assumptions and abstract propositions that belonged to the world of metaphysics, and that they were not grounded upon facts, which constituted the real basis for political questions. Ultimately, it was not the validity of the theory that counted, but the measure of success or failure that attended its application to a given set of circumstances. For that reason, theories always had to be brought to the touchstone of fact and experience. Actually it was the circumstances that rendered any scheme beneficial or noxious to mankind, or, in his well-known words, 'circumstances (which with some gentlemen pass for nothing) give in reality to every political principle its distinguishing colour, and discriminating effect'.[9]

The important French thinker, Montesquieu, whom Burke reverenced as the greatest genius of the age, had spent a lifetime demonstrating how the life of the individual was determined by his surroundings; by the past history of the society to which he belonged, which left its stamp upon his customs, beliefs, laws, and institutions, and his whole mode of living. If theory was to be of value, it could not afford to ignore these facts. In other words, theory had to give up its desire to find abstract principles that were true for all mankind, at all times and in all places. It had to make its principles relative

to the different peoples in the light of their circumstances.
But abstract speculation had not bowed to Montesquieu, and
the *Contrat Social* had appeared almost, it would seem, in
defiance of his teaching.

Dupont had declared to Burke that the members of the
National Assembly were disciples of Montesquieu also. 'You
say, my dear sir,' Burke wrote in reply, 'they read Montesquieu
—I believe not. If they do, they do not understand him. . . .
Sure it is that they have not followed him in any one thing
they have done.'[10] But with regard to the other writers to
whom Dupont had referred,

'I do believe the directors of the present system to be influenced by them!
Such masters! such scholars! Who ever dreamt of Voltaire and Rousseau
as legislators? The first has the merit of writing agreeably; and nobody
has ever united blasphemy and obscenity so happily together. The other
was not a little deranged in his intellects, to my almost certain knowledge.
But he saw things in bold and uncommon lights, and he was very
eloquent. . . .'[11]

And now the destinies of France were being moulded by the
visionary speculations, the substance of which Burke could
no longer recall very definitely, of an eloquent writer who
was 'deranged in his intellects'. It was the kind of tragedy that
Burke had spent his life trying to avert. But apparently neither
Montesquieu nor he had been able to impress upon men's
minds the weaknesses and dangers attaching to abstract theory.
But the time had come, not for giving way to utter discouragement, but for action. Thoughts of retirement from public life
had to be put aside entirely for the time being while he prepared for the most important and most desperate struggle of
his life. The scene of the drama had now changed from the
speculative movement to real life, where abstract thought was
attempting to dominate circumstances. Tragedy had attended
the shifting of the scene, even as he had often warned that it
would. But he could now demonstrate against the stormy
background of the French revolution the disastrous consequences that attended attempts to refashion the political life
of a nation in accordance with abstract theory. Rousseau's
doctrine of popular sovereignty had swept all before it and
France had been torn asunder so that the sovereign people

could enjoy ideal liberty. It did not surprise Burke that Rousseau was being acclaimed as the sponsor of a doctrine that implied an extreme form of individualism; during his lifetime, Rousseau had proclaimed his passionate hatred of the civilization that robbed man of his rightful liberty and warped his nature by putting him in chains. But while France would probably learn wisdom through suffering, Burke realized that he had to save his own country from the same kind of tragedy. 'Some people here,' he observed, were anxious to adopt Rousseau's doctrines and to 'reform our State on the French model. They have begun; and it is high time for those who wish to preserve *morem majorum* to look about them'.[12] The knowledge that England was not safe from the doctrines that had wrecked France spurred him on to begin his fight.

Liberty was fundamentally the main issue of the French revolution. Burke was not unsympathetic with the desire of a people to be free, but the trouble was that liberty, like other current abstract terms, was both vague and indefinite. It could be interpreted in many different ways, and there were moreover many false ideas attached to it. For Burke, liberty was a blessing and a benefit, not an abstract speculation, and, like other blessings to mankind, the nature and degree of liberty that a people could enjoy had to be determined by circumstances. 'The *extreme* of liberty (which is its abstract perfection, but its real fault) obtains nowhere, nor ought to obtain anywhere,' he had declared in his *Letter to the Sheriffs of Bristol* (1777), when taking issue with those who, at the time of the American revolution, had 'split and anatomized the doctrine of free government, as if it were an abstract question concerning metaphysical liberty and necessity, and not a matter of moral prudence and natural feeling'. 'Because extremes, as we all know, in every point which relates either to our duties or satisfactions in life, are destructive both to virtue and enjoyment. Liberty too must be limited in order to be possessed. . . .'[13] His views had not changed since that time, and he now regarded the abstract liberty for which the French had been willing to tear up their state as both absurd and outrageous. As far as the French were concerned, they not only had an entirely wrong conception of the nature of liberty, which Burke thought was only to be expected when they chose such an author as Rousseau to be their guide, but they had also gone the wrong way about achieving the liberty that had been within their reach.

Burke, however, was mistaken in regarding Rousseau's views of liberty as so diametrically opposed to his own. Because the revolutionary leaders had boasted that they were Rousseau's disciples, it did not necessarily follow that the extreme views to which they gave expression were a faithful reflection of the ideals of the author of the *Contrat Social*.

While it did not occur to Burke that there might be any injustice to Rousseau either in his own attitude to his work or in the interpretations the revolutionists were placing upon his doctrines, it seemed to him that it was of first importance to destroy Rousseau's influence by clearing away the misconceptions that existed in men's minds regarding liberty. Consequently he welcomed the opportunity M. Dupont had given him of outlining once more his own ideas on the subject. M. Dupont had asked him anxiously whether he thought the French deserved liberty.

'You hope, Sir,' Burke replied, 'that I think the French deserving of liberty. I certainly do. I certainly think that all men who desire it, deserve it. It is not the reward of our merit, or the acquisition of our industry. It is our inheritance. It is the birthright of our species. We cannot forfeit our right to it, but by what forfeits our title to the privileges of our kind, I mean the abuse, or oblivion, of our rational faculties, and a ferocious indocility which makes us prompt to wrong and violence, destroys our social nature, and transforms us into something little better than the description of wild beasts. . . .' [14]

Burke was entirely unaware of the fact that he was practically restating the main thought of the opening chapters of the *Contrat Social*. 'Man is born free,' Rousseau had asserted in the famous opening words of his treatise. Freedom was man's birthright. It was force, not nature, that had made the 'first' slaves. And if there were slaves 'by nature', it was because there were slaves 'against nature'. Their cowardice perpetuated their slavery, and thus they forfeited their title to the privileges of their kind. But, Rousseau argued, a man could not alienate his children's birthright even if he chose to become a slave himself. His children were born men and free; their liberty was their own, and no one else had any right to dispose of it. Indeed, it seemed to Rousseau that those who renounced liberty and those whose cowardly spirit led them to acquiesce in such a renunciation were in reality committing a crime against human nature. For a man

'to renounce his liberty means renouncing his quality of manhood, his rights as a human being, and even his duties. Such a renunciation is incompatible with the nature of man, because taking away all freedom from his will means taking away all morality from his actions.' [15]

In other words, man's moral nature was his distinctive possession; in virtue of it alone he could be free. For in man's nature Rousseau observed two principles, one which raised him to the study of eternal truths, to the love of justice and of true morality, to the regions of the world of thought which the wise delighted to contemplate; the other led him downwards to himself, made him the slave of his senses, of the passions which were their instruments, and thus opposed everything suggested to him by his higher nature.[16] To follow the former principle was to be free; to follow the latter was to be a slave. In moral freedom alone man could be master of himself, 'for the mere impulse of appetite is slavery, while obedience to a law which we have prescribed to ourselves is freedom'.[17] In a very real sense, therefore, 'liberty is not the reward of our merit, or the acquisition of our industry . . . it is the birthright of our species . . . we cannot forfeit our right to it, but by what forfeits our title to the privileges of our kind'.

Men so degraded as to merit the loss of privileges to which they were born, Burke believed, would have to be placed in a state of 'strong constraint' as a necessary substitute for freedom, to save them from 'the worst of all slavery, that is, the despotism of their own blind and brutal passions'.[18] Likewise, Rousseau told Mirabeau that he could see no possible alternative between the most austere democracy and the most complete and perfect Hobbism.[19] If men could not live in accordance with principles befitting free men, which were those of the *Contrat Social*, there was nothing for them but a Leviathan state.

'You have kindly said that you began to love freedom from your intercourse with me,' Burke continued to M. Dupont. 'Permit me then . . . to tell you what the freedom is that I love. It is not solitary, unconnected, individual, selfish liberty. It is social freedom. *It is that state of things in which the liberty of no man, and no body of men, is in a condition to trespass on the liberty of any person, or any description of persons, in society.* This kind of liberty is, indeed, but another name for justice, ascertained by wise laws, and secured by well-constructed institutions.' [20]

Fundamentally, Burke's chief objection to Rousseau as the prophet of liberty was that he believed Rousseau had advocated an extreme individualism that was incompatible with social freedom. Curiously enough, one of the principal objections raised by critics of the *Contrat Social* has been just the opposite. They have objected most strenuously to its absolutism, which they have regarded as inimical to individual liberty.

In point of fact, Rousseau's political theory held no brief for either extreme individualism or extreme collectivism. Historically, his political theory was evolved at a time when the weaknesses and inadequacies of the essentially individualistic doctrine of contract were becoming increasingly apparent. For that reason, Rousseau attempted to present the fundamental principles of the state that would resolve the contradictions implicit in the rival claims of individualism and collectivism. Although he did not completely succeed,[21] nevertheless through the doctrine of the general will in his *Contrat Social*, he was able to open up a sound and fruitful line of thought, the vitality of which has not yet been exhausted. Rousseau recognized the need for solidarity in the body politic, but he also recognized the right of the individual citizen to liberty, and he attempted to resolve the difficulties presented by the rights of the individual on the one hand and the claims of the state on the other. He built his whole political theory upon the view that liberty could be achieved only through the attainment of moral freedom on the part of the citizens, and through the embodiment of justice in the laws to which alone men could submit themselves and retain their freedom. In the *Contrat*

Social, he concerned himself exclusively with the exposition of the kind of association which could be founded upon the solidarity that came with the organic unity of a people, but which at the same time fostered the liberty of that people. When his treatise was denounced by J. R. Tronchin, the Procurator-General of the Swiss Republic, as tending to the subversion of all established governments, Rousseau wrote his *Lettres de la Montagne* (1764), in which he begged Tronchin to read the *Contrat Social* again.

'Read it, Sir,' he wrote, 'read this book which has been so much decried, but which is so necessary. . . . Everywhere in it you will see liberty asserted, yet always under the authority of law, without which liberty cannot exist, and under which we are always free, no mattèr what kind of government we have. Those who subordinate law to human passion are the people who really overthrow governments. . . .' [22] 'It is useless to attempt to identify liberty with independence,' he continued. 'These two things are so different that they are even mutually exclusive. . . . Liberty does not consist so much in acting in accordance with one's own will as in not being brought under the will of others. Then again, it consists in not bringing the will of others under subjection to our own . . . true liberty never destroys itself. For this reason, liberty without justice is a real contradiction. . . . There is then no liberty without law. Liberty is always affected by what happens to laws: it is supreme or it perishes together with them. I know nothing more certain than that. . . .' [23]

In terms of his doctrine of the general will, he declared that

'the only liberty possible is that which comes from observing the laws, that is, the general will, and it is no more in the nature of the general will to injure all than it is in the nature of an individual will to hurt itself. . . . The first and greatest public interest is always justice. All desire that conditions shall be equal for all, and what is justice but this equality? The citizen wishes nothing more than law and the keeping of law.' [24]

If this was really Rousseau's conception of liberty, then Burke's objection to him as the champion of extreme individualism and the advocate of an unsocial independence was not based on a knowledge of his actual doctrine. Although Burke had read the *Contrat Social,* he had clearly failed to see Rousseau's thought in its true light. He had disliked intensely the speculative method that Rousseau had used, and with the years that dislike had grown until it over-emphasized the form and lost all sight of the content of Rousseau's doctrine. In addition, Burke, like many another critic of Rousseau, had been misled by the rhetoric of the individualistic *Discours sur l'inégalité*, and his criticisms were applicable, not to Rousseau, but to the interpretation that had been read into a philosophical doctrine of the sovereignty of the people by revolutionary Frenchmen as well as by the radicals of England.

It was, in point of fact, the extreme individualism of the French revolution that caused Burke grave concern. The storming of the Bastille had given the signal for liberation from the oppression of the past, and the revolutionists had set to work to devise a constitution that would guarantee the imprescriptible rights of mankind to liberty and happiness. They were individualists, like the colonists of America who also had thrown off the yoke of oppression, and for the future they wanted their government to guarantee their freedom and they wanted to feel the weight of government as little as possible. The constitution they planned was to be up-to-date and scientific, and it was to be worked out in accordance with the most enlightened ideas of liberty and government that could be found. Unshaken in their confidence that they would ultimately succeed, even as the colonists in America were succeeding in building up a new nation dedicated to liberty, they faced courageously the disorders and the failures that brought ominous clouds into the sky in that dawn when it was bliss to be alive, and to be young was very heaven.

From across the Channel, Burke anxiously watched the course of events in France, but he was unable to see rhyme or reason in what the French were doing. Neither could he comprehend the attitude which made such a gigantic reorganization of their state appear rational. He watched with horror as they tore up the roots of the past, and dismembered their country, abolished privileges that had belonged to the nobility, levelled all ranks, and eventually removed their king from the throne. From France had come a 'new and pressing application' from Dupont for his sentiments on what was going forward. Dupont was clearly eager to keep up a correspondence with Burke on the subject of the French revolution and its doctrines. Burke began a detailed discussion of the French principles for him, but it was not long before he discovered that he had gone far beyond the limits of a letter. Nevertheless he continued, and gave his thoughts to the world in his famous *Reflections on the Revolution in France* (1790). In it he pointed out how grievously the French had injured their country in carrying out their desire for abstract liberty. If they did not change their policies soon he feared that their state would 'in a few generations, crumble away, be disconnected into the dust and powder of individuality',[25] and would at length be dispersed to all the winds of heaven. He even went so far as to express his belief that 'were Rousseau alive, and in one of his lucid intervals, he would be shocked at the practical frenzy of his scholars'.[26] It was possible that Rousseau had not meant his speculations to be carried quite so far. But in everything his 'scholars' had done, they had strayed out of the 'highway of nature', and as long as they were at war with nature they could never hope to find liberty. Burke believed that they would have to go back to the methods that had stood the test of time, and would have to use the materials they had at hand instead of discarding them in favour of metaphysical theories of the rights of man. Already the hard logic of facts had led them away from their objective. Instead of liberty, it seemed to Burke that tyranny had reared its ugly head. Their leaders, who had laid down 'metaphysic propositions which infer universal consequences' had been obliged to 'limit logic by despotism'.[27]

'When the peasants give you back that coin of sophistic reason, on which you have set your image and superscription,' he charged, 'you cry it down as base money, and tell them you will pay for the future with French guards, and dragoons, and hussars.' [28]

So instead of finding the Utopia of which Rousseau had dreamed, they had actually lost practically everything. Their ancient state was broken up, their property and their wealth were destroyed, the ancient orders existed no more. Men were reduced to loose counters 'merely for the sake of simple telling, and not to figures whose power is to arise from their place in the table'.[29] But worst of all, they had humiliated religion, which was their surest sanction for obedience in their state. For 'man is by his constitution a religious animal', and atheism, which had triumphed over religion, was against 'not only our

reason, but our instincts'.[3b] This destruction of the state was
the direct result of attempting to translate the individualistic
doctrine of the *Contrat Social* into fact.

The publication of the *Reflections* opened a heated controversy in England on the subject of the French principles, while
it also caused consternation among members of the National
Assembly. M. de Menonville, a member of the moderate party
in the Assembly, protested that Burke had been unjust to them
when he wrote: 'there they sit, after a gang of assassins had
driven away *all* the men of moderate minds and moderating
authority among them. . . .' Burke corrected this statement in
the next edition of the *Reflections*, and sent a corrected copy to
M. de Menonville. But the subject of the revolution agitated
him so profoundly that as he replied to M. de Menonville in the
Letter to a Member of the National Assembly (1791), he could
not resist expounding yet further his conviction that the desperate ills of France had been brought about because the French
had insisted upon following their so-called enlightened theories
instead of introducing reforms into the political system they
had inherited from their ancestors. The humiliating treatment
to which the king and queen were being subjected, the 'dis-
graceful' scenes that marked the celebration of July 14, the
anniversary of the fall of the Bastille, and the 'horrors' of the
days of October 5 and 6, haunted Burke's thoughts as he
protested to M. de Menonville against the pernicious doctrines
that had produced such disasters.

The letter was famous for its violent attack upon Rousseau,
who was anathematized as the originator of those doctrines. It
was particularly interesting because it indicated how profoundly shocked Burke had been by episodes in Rousseau's
life, which had been deliberately shown in their worst possible
light by malicious members of the Encyclopedist circle to
which Rousseau had once belonged. The astonishing episode
of Rousseau's quarrel with Hume during his famous visit to
England in 1766–7 seemed to lend confirmation to the un-
pleasantly bizarre picture of Rousseau's life that had gradually
pieced itself together. Burke had observed what was happening from close quarters, although he had made no effort to
meet Rousseau, and apparently had not come into direct touch

with him at all. Unfortunately, Rousseau himself provided ample material in his *Confessions* (1782) to shock Burke yet further. Consequently, it seemed a not unjust conclusion to reach that the man who had revealed so chequered a life and a soul that had fallen to depths so utterly degrading, no matter what redeeming features he might have possessed, was scarcely to be taken seriously in his philosophical role of moralist. In Burke's judgement, the *Nouvelle Héloïse* (1761), with its sickly sentimentality, and the *Confessions*, with their revolting details of Rousseau's sins, could scarcely have come from the pen of a man whose serious purpose in life was to uplift humanity. Yet, although Burke regarded these works as the product of a diseased imagination, it must be remembered that, unlike many of Rousseau's readers, he was prepared to see light and shade as well as sombre hues in them. At the same time, he was convinced that no possible good could come from studying Rousseau's works, which was what the members of the National Assembly were advocating, while there was much irretrievable harm that such a study could occasion.

From the point of view of political thought, Rousseau's method identified him with a movement that had invariably drawn fire from Burke. His *Discours sur l'inégalité* and his *Contrat Social* belonged to the speculative philosophy that had provided arguments for the radicals in England, and had furnished ideals for the revolutionary leaders in France. Obviously Burke had no conception of the time and thought that Rousseau had devoted to the problems of political philosophy, and he had no more idea of the nature of that thought than Voltaire had.[31] He had turned aside from Rousseau's writings, partly because he distrusted the author's reliance upon logic, and partly because he had no inkling of the trend of Rousseau's thought and therefore lacked the clue to its real significance. He thought of him as an advocate of the doctrine of the rights of man, with its individualistic assertion of the inalienable right of mankind to liberty, and as the writer who had done most, through his doctrine of popular sovereignty, to bring about the downfall of the French state. Thus while the passage in the *Letter to a Member of the National Assembly*, in which Burke gave unrestrained expression to his feelings regarding Rousseau, could not be accepted as a criticism of Rousseau's political philosophy, it was not without significance. It took into consideration the effect of Rousseau's life and writings upon the minds of young people, and it showed clearly the nature of the conclusions upon which Burke had based his criticisms of both Rousseau and the French revolution.

Burke hoped to impress upon M. de Menonville the nature of the evils he could foresee resulting from the policies of the radical majority in the National Assembly. He was hopeful that M. de Menonville and other moderate members would take some steps, before their power had gone completely, to restrain the 'irritable power', which had already done more than enough to horrify the outside world. While the recent outrages had agitated Burke profoundly, he was even more disturbed over the steps those in power were taking to engraft their system upon the life of the nation. By corrupting the youth of the nation, they were preparing the next generation to fit into the new order. Burke was particularly alarmed to observe that the young people were being encouraged to study Rousseau. Nothing, he declared, ought to be more carefully thought out than the nature of the books that were authorized for the education of the young. Certainly 'authors of mixed or ambiguous morality' ought not to be recommended, lest the students learn the 'humours of the professor' rather than the principles of the science. But the magistrate ought, above all, to be cautious in recommending any writer who carried marks of a deranged understanding, 'for where there is no sound reason, there can be no real virtue; and madness is ever vicious and malignant'.[32]

The Assembly apparently had no use for sound principles of education, for it recommended to its youth a study of the 'bold experimenters in morality'. Indeed, everybody knew that the leaders of the Assembly disputed as to which of them bore the best resemblance to Rousseau.

'In truth', Burke declared passionately, 'they all resemble him. His blood they transfuse into their minds and into their manners. Him they study; him they meditate; him they turn over in all the time they can spare from the laborious mischief of the day, or the debauches of the night.'[33]

Rousseau was their canon of holy writ. He was their 'standard figure of perfection', the modern canon of Polycletus. And to this author the 'foundries of Paris are now running for statues'. If Rousseau had been a great authority on geometry, no matter how vicious his 'practical and speculative' morals might have been, it might have been accepted that in planning a statue for him, they were honouring his genius for geometry. 'But Rousseau is a moralist, or he is nothing.' Therefore, putting all the circumstances together, it was impossible to escape the conviction that they were honouring Rousseau because he represented the ideal they wished to instil into the youth of the nation. They had to find a substitute for all 'the principles which hitherto have been employed to regulate the human will and action', in order to bring the moral system into line with their politics. For this purpose, they had chosen vanity, a 'selfish, flattering, seductive, ostentatious vice', in place of plain duty. Henceforth all natural and all social sentiment was to be merged in inordinate vanity, that vice which 'makes the whole man false. It leaves nothing sincere or trustworthy about him. His best qualities are poisoned and perverted by it, and operate exactly as the worst.' [34] And therefore out of all the 'infamous gang' from which they had to choose, they had selected Rousseau, because he was the most conspicuous example of vanity among them.

Rousseau, the 'great professor and founder of the *philosophy of vanity*', had been in England, and Burke, who had just become a member of Parliament, 'had good opportunities of knowing his proceedings almost from day to day'.[35] But the visitor had left no doubt on Burke's mind that 'he entertained no principle either to influence his heart, or to guide his understanding, but *vanity*. With this vice he was possessed to a degree little short of madness.' It was, in point of fact, the abuse and perversion which vanity made even of hypocrisy that had driven Rousseau, the 'insane Socrates' of the National Assembly, to 'record a life not so much as chequered, or spotted here and there, with virtues, or even distinguished by a single good action. It is such a life he chooses to offer to the attention of mankind.' [36] And it was such a life that, with a wild defiance, he had flung in the face of his Creator, whom he acknowledged only to brave. The Assembly had chosen this man, who by his own account was without a single virtue, as a model for their young people, and to him they erected their first statue.

It was that 'new invented virtue', which the Assembly had canonized, that had led their moral hero to exhaust the stores of his powerful rhetoric in the expression of universal benevolence, while his heart was incapable of harbouring one spark of 'common parental affection'. 'Benevolence to the whole species', Burke asserted, 'and want of feeling for every individual with whom the professors come in contact, form the character of the new philosophy.'[37] Setting up for an 'unsocial independence', their hero of vanity had refused the just price of common labour, as well as the tribute which 'opulence owes to genius', and then 'he pleads his beggary as an excuse for his crimes'. He melted with tenderness for those who 'only touch him by the remotest relation', but he sent his children to the foundling hospital. 'The bear loves, licks, and forms her young; but bears are not philosophers,'[38] Burke wrote in some of the sternest words ever directed to Rousseau.

The relationship of Rousseau's life to the political system of the revolution now became apparent. The system of government was as false as the system of education recommended by the Assembly. And to understand either, it was necessary to connect the morals with the politics of the legislators. Then it would be discovered that they had, in their systematic manner, begun by erecting statues to a 'wild, ferocious, low-minded, hard-hearted father, of fine general feelings; a lover of his kind, but a hater of his kindred'.[39] Paternal duties were rejected as 'contrary to liberty', as 'not founded in the social compact', and not binding 'according to the rights of men'.[40]

Furthermore, through the same instructor, by whom they corrupted the morals, they corrupted also the taste. 'Your masters,' Burke declared, 'who are his scholars, conceive that all refinement has an aristocratic character,' and therefore through Rousseau they were 'resolved to destroy these aristocratic prejudices'.[41] The way to this was through his 'famous work of philosophic gallantry, the *Nouvelle Héloïse*', where metaphysical speculations were to be found blended with 'the coarsest sensuality'. In addition, the *Nouvelle Héloïse* reflected an entirely false picture of the relationship of dancing-masters, fiddlers, and *valets-de-chambre* to the members of the households where they were employed. By a law, Burke pointed out, these people had become the 'equals' of their masters. And 'in this manner, these great legislators complete their plan of levelling, and establish their rights of men on a sure foundation'.[42]

There was not much more for Burke to add, beyond the statement that those who had studied the 'authors of sound antiquity', could find only transient amusement in the 'paradoxical morality' of Rousseau. But he tempered his remarks with the assertion that he did not consider Rousseau 'wholly destitute of just notions. Amongst his irregularities, it must be reckoned that he is sometimes moral, and moral in a very sublime strain.'[43] But it was still true that the general spirit and tendency of Rousseau's writings was mischievous, largely on account of this blending of a sublimely moral strain with depravity of sentiment.

Although Burke may not have been entirely wrong in his judgement of Rousseau's influence upon the minds of the young people who were instructed to read his works, it was nevertheless true from the nature of the references to liberty, the social compact, and the rights of man, that he was not criticizing the *Contrat Social*. As Sir Brooke Boothby angrily pointed out, the great prophet of liberty in France was being judged on a wrong basis.

'The author of this capuchinade', he declared, 'peremptorily decides against the character of a great man from the casual observation of a few days; looks for his virtues in the confession general of his sins, and determines upon the good or bad tendency of elaborate treatises on education and government written *ad rem*, from a few love letters in a novel.'[44]

Burke's attention was soon drawn from the scene across the Channel to the House of Commons, where he found that the doctrine of the sovereignty of the people was not regarded as at variance with orthodox Whig doctrine. His writings had been instrumental in bringing the issues of the French revolution into English party politics, but he could not endure to think that his colleagues, and among them his close friend, Charles James Fox, were calmly accepting doctrines that he had expected to hear preached only by the radicals who loudly proclaimed their sympathy with the doctrines of the revolution. Burke believed that it was deliberate mis-representation to compare the French revolution with the 'glorious' revolution of 1688, when the principles of the British constitution had been vindicated, and he turned upon his colleagues with as much asperity as he had shown in the *Reflections*, when he had vented his wrath upon Dr. Richard Price for presuming to make a similar comparison. To add weight to his contention that the principles of 1688 had nothing whatever in common with the Rousseau-inspired doctrines of the French revolution, Burke wrote his *Appeal from the New to the Old Whigs* (1791), in which he quoted extensively from documents relating to the English revolution of the previous century. He then took up the doctrine of the sovereignty of the people as he had found it expounded in Paine's *Rights of Man* (1791), and mercilessly criticized every flaw he could find in it. His conclusion was that no man who accepted the French doctrine could tolerate the British constitution in church or state.[45]

'They build their politics, not on convenience but on truth; and they profess to conduct men to certain happiness by the assertion of their undoubted rights. With them there is no compromise. . . . The whole scheme of our mixed constitution is to prevent any one of its principles from being carried as far as, taken by itself, and theoretically, it would go. Allow that to be the true policy of the British system, then most of the faults with which that system stands charged will appear to be, not imperfections into which it had inadvertently fallen, but excellencies which it has studiously sought.'

And the French, who had aimed at the 'abstract and unlimited perfection of power in the popular part' of their constitution, could be of no service whatever to the political arrangements of the English.[46]

Towards the end of 1793, Burke was beginning to feel the severity of the strain he had brought on himself. His stand against the French principles had caused him to break friend-ships of a lifetime, and his opposition had become almost an obsession. He had to keep on, however, because another and an equally sinister meaning was beginning to be read into the doctrine of the sovereignty of the people. It was no longer the extreme individualism of the doctrine that had to be attacked, but rather the extreme collectivism. As he addressed his *Observations on the Conduct of the Minority, particularly in the last session of parliament,* to the Duke of Portland and Lord Fitzwilliam, towards the close of 1793, he took exception to Fox's attitude on the French principles. Mr. Fox studiously, on all occasions, and indeed when no occasion called for it at all, Burke complained, brought forward and asserted 'their fundamental and fatal principle, pregnant with every mischief and every crime, namely, that "in every country the people is the legitimate sovereign", exactly conformable to the declaration of the French clubs and legislators' [47] that the sovereignty was one, indivisible, inalienable, and imprescriptible. It belonged to the nation. No section of the people and no individual could presume to exercise it. And this confounded 'in a manner equally mischievous and stupid, the origin of a government from the people with its continuance in their hands'.[48] While Burke accepted the doctrine that the government owed its 'origin' to the people, he denied that the people had retained their 'original' right over it. Indeed, he maintained that 'no such doctrine has ever been heard of in any public act of any government whatsoever' until it had been adopted, he thought from the writings of Rousseau, by the French National Assembly and had been made the basis of their constitution at home and of their propaganda abroad. 'These and other wild declarations of abstract principle, Mr. Fox says, are in themselves perfectly right and true; though in some cases he allows the French draw absurd consequences from them. But I conceive he is mistaken.' [49] The consequences the French drew were logical enough. The fault lay in the foundations of their principles.

The implications of collectivism, which could be seen unmistakably following a change of policy on the part of the leaders of the revolutionary system in France, were to Burke fraught with as much disaster to the individual as the extremes of individualism had been to the state. Now 'the will, the wish, the want, the liberty, the toil, the blood of individuals', counted for nothing. 'Individuality is left out of their scheme of government,' he pointed out in protesting against proposals to make peace with a nation of 'regicides'. 'The state is all in all.' [50] And even if saner counsels could prevail in France so that their politics could be established on more moderate lines, it would be impossible for those who had tasted of power to return to their rightful stations in life. 'Never can they who from the miserable servitude of the desk have been raised to empire, again submit to the bondage of a starving bureau, or', with an obvious reference to Rousseau, 'the profit of copying music. . . .' [51] Burke smiled in bitterness to hear talk of indemnity to such men, provided they returned to their allegiance.

He still held Rousseau responsible for the creed of the revolutionaries, although they had swung from one extreme to the other. He had unhesitatingly blamed him for the excesses arising from individualistic doctrine, and now just as unhesitatingly he laid the blame upon the same doctrine for the excesses of collectivism. From the doctrine that the people as individuals were sovereign, and therefore were at liberty to do as they pleased, the leaders of the revolutionary system turned to the contradictory doctrine that the people as an organic whole was sovereign. The nation could do as it pleased, but the individual and his wishes, instead of being of paramount importance, were now entirely subordinate to the pleasure of the nation. No individual and no group of people could claim the right to exercise sovereignty, because this right belonged to the nation as a whole, and sovereignty was by its nature indivisible, inalienable, and imprescriptible. Obviously the *Contrat Social* had not advocated extreme individualism and extreme collectivism at the same time, unless indeed the work was such a tissue of nonsense that it was really as devoid of merit as Burke had believed it to be. The revolution showed clearly that Rousseau's doctrine could be interpreted in different ways. Burke, however, made no attempt to resolve the contradictions implied in the varied part it played in the development of the French revolutionary policies. He made no effort to find out exactly what Rousseau had attempted to say in the *Contrat Social*. Indeed, it is more than probable that if he had taken Rousseau's treatise down from the shelves, he would have come to the conclusion once more that it was a 'performance of little or no merit'. For not only did Burke have a deep-rooted dislike for Rousseau's paradoxes, his logic and his abstract principles, but he also had the bitter knowledge that the *Contrat Social* could 'make revolutions, and give law to nations'. It would never have been possible for Burke to appreciate at its true value the contribution Rousseau had made towards a clearer understanding of political principles that were based upon the ideal of liberty.

Different methods of approach to political problems and differences in their social and intellectual backgrounds had inevitably made Burke the critic of Rousseau. Rousseau had been concerned primarily with establishing the principles of the modern state. Burke, on the other hand, was chiefly interested in historical process. The principles which he saw striving towards expression in the course of the French revolution, which he attributed to Rousseau instead of to Rousseau's disciples, seemed to him to be false and for that reason he criticized them unsparingly. Unfortunately, even in this he failed to make allowance for the vast difference between the political conditions of France and his own country, and consequently he did not sympathize with the revolutionary movement as otherwise he might have done.

Nevertheless, his role of critic of Rousseau's political principles was both important and instructive. His presentation of the practical considerations involved in the issues of the revolution was of particular significance because his conception of liberty was fundamentally in agreement with Rousseau's. Consequently, he was in a position to present truths complementary to those contained in the *Contrat Social*. Moreover, his arguments were especially instructive in view of the fact that he had devoted much time to reflection upon the philosophical aspects of the problems which confronted him as a statesman. Indeed his mind was so deeply steeped in political thought that he could not resist referring political issues of any kind back to the sovereign principles he had accepted as final, but which he refused to analyse or to fit into a system. Incidentally he did not see the beam in his own eye, for when he criticized Rousseau as a visionary theorist, he did not realize that his own thoughts were all too frequently far removed from the world of actualities. His philosophizing propensities, ironically enough, detracted from his own efficiency as a practical statesman.

Burke's misunderstanding of the author of the *Contrat Social* was not due to a fundamental divergence in their conception of liberty, upon which they had both based their political thought, for no such divergence existed. It was due to two main causes. The first of these was the difference in the circumstances under which Rousseau and Burke had lived and worked. Burke had failed to take into account the fact that Rousseau was a Genevan who lived in Paris at a time when the old social and political order was rapidly breaking down and when the problems involved in the reconstruction of French society challenged the best minds of France, whereas he was an Engishman, with a typically English outlook on life, who enjoyed the security of a relatively stable society. Closely allied to this were the temperamental differences which revealed themselves in the English statesman's reactions to Rousseau's characteristic mode of thinking, and to the literary form in which his thought found expression. Those differences were responsible ultimately for Burke's misunderstanding of what Rousseau meant by liberty, and for his complete failure to do justice to Rousseau through confusing his views with those of the radical extremists of the French revolution. Yet Burke agreed with Rousseau so often on points of fundamental importance that it was all the more unfortunate that he did not appreciate at its true value the contribution that Rousseau had made to political thought in his *Contrat Social*.

CHAPTER II

WHIG TRUSTEESHIP

THROUGH the 'glorious' revolution of 1688, England was able to introduce democratic methods of government in advance of all the important powers in Europe, where monarchies, although 'enlightened', were nevertheless absolute. Henceforth, however, as far as England was concerned, the constitution was to be recognized as supreme and was to be respected by King and subject alike. Its fundamental principle was government by consent of the governed, the ideal for which Parliament had fought desperately in the seventeenth century. Its functions were to regulate the powers of the Crown on the one hand and, on the other, to secure the liberties of the nation.

Because England had cut herself adrift from the political absolutism of European countries, she had to evolve her own constitutional machinery. Steadfast adherence to the principles of the revolution was consequently the sole criterion by which the statesmen of the eighteenth century could be guided. The goal of parliamentary leaders in 1688 had been the limitation by statute of the powers of the Crown, but when this task was accomplished, they found it necessary to formulate clearly and to develop their ideas of constitutional government. These ideas assumed the form of a doctrine of trusteeship, which in the eighteenth century became an important stepping-stone towards modern democratic ideals.

After the flight of James II in 1688, a Bill of Rights was drawn up as the first step towards constitutional government in the modern sense of the term. This Bill, which was passed in 1689 by the first Parliament of William and Mary, definitely limited the powers of the monarch. It did so by enumerating and specifically reasserting those rights and liberties of the people which had been violated by the Stuarts. With the exception of the statement that standing armies were illegal, the Bill of Rights made no changes in the constitution. When it stipulated that there could be no taxation without the consent of Parliament, that there should be frequent sessions of Parliament, that there should be freedom of electing members to Parliament and that members should enjoy freedom of speech in Parliament, it was merely setting forth in black and white the well-established rights of the people. But in future, all monarchs, when ascending the throne, would be required to subscribe to the Bill of Rights and would thereby be called upon to bind themselves to recognize and defend the traditional rights and liberties of their subjects. Thus through the Bill of Rights, Parliament sought to settle once and for all the dispute over the fundamental form of government in England and to guard effectively against any possible revival of an absolute monarchy such as the Stuarts had attempted to establish.

The Bill of Rights was followed by other important legislative measures, which not only consolidated the victorious principles of 1688, but also opened the way for the enjoyment of liberty in England. As a reward to the Dissenters, who had supported parliamentary leaders in their fight against the Stuarts, a Toleration Act was passed. This Act meant that Englishmen would no longer have to fear persecution for dissenting from the doctrines of the established Church.

'I doubt not you have heard before this', John Locke wrote to his friend Limborch in Amsterdam, on June 6, 1689, 'that toleration is now established among us by law; not with such breadth as you and true men like you, free from Christian arrogance and hatred, would desire; but 'tis something to get anything. With these small beginnings I hope the foundations will be laid on which the church of Christ can be built up. None are to be punished for their religious opinions, unless they are Catholics, if they will consent to take the oath of allegiance and to repudiate the doctrine of transubstantiation and certain other dogmas of the church of Rome. . . .'[1]

Liberty was conceded also to the press, and this, even more than the comparative freedom for religious opinion, made England an object of envy to such men as Voltaire and Montesquieu. The strictness of the censorship had been relaxed in 1688, when floods of pamphlets had appeared giving expression to all shades of opinion on the important issues of the moment. In 1695, Parliament, while proclaiming its right to serve summons on printers who published attacks on the government and also to levy a paper tax, allowed the Licensing Act to lapse, thus leaving England with something like a free press. It was left for subsequent champions of liberty to fight for the removal of the remaining reservations, but the main battle was won. When the bitterness and bigotry engendered by the struggles of the seventeenth century were allowed to die down, it was possible for Englishmen to enjoy freedom of thought and conscience, while they had but little to fear from the publication of works that would not find favour with the orthodox. More fortunate than the thinkers and writers of France, whose fight for such rights continued throughout the eighteenth century, Englishmen were now becoming safely entrenched behind constitutional government, and the 'principles of 1688'.

Their serenity, however, was rudely disturbed in 1701, when the revolution settlement was endangered through the deaths of Queen Mary and of the Duke of Gloucester, Anne's last child, which removed the immediate line of inheritance from the throne. These deaths meant that the government had to deal with the problem of the settlement with the Hanoverians, since it was quite conceivable that the exiled Stuarts might grasp any such opportunity to try to regain the throne, and it was highly desirable that there should be no reopening of fundamental issues with the Stuarts on either constitutional or religious grounds. William, in the speech from the throne in February, 1701, asserted that it was 'absolutely necessary' to make provision for the settlement, and on March 12 Parliament adopted the resolutions which formed the basis of the important Act of Settlement.[2] Whigs and Tories alike agreed to accept the Electress Sophia of Hanover, the grand-daughter of James I, and the nearest Protestant heir among his descendants, as next in succession to the throne after Anne. By this Act, Parliament not only secured the Protestant succession to the throne, but deliberately reasserted its right to name the ruling house, thereby making it unambiguously clear that British rulers did not hold their office by divine right, but through the express wish and sanction of Parliament.

The first systematic statement of the principles of the revolution of 1688 was made by John Locke. Through his two treatises, *Of Civil Government* (1690), the principles of 1688 emerged from the confines of home politics to take their place in the realm of political philosophy not only in England, which was now occupied with practical problems rather than with political theory, but also in France, where they provided a basis for a philosophy designed to undermine the system upon which absolutism and feudal privilege had rested, and to build up a conception of a political organization more consistent with the ideals and needs of free men.

Locke's purpose was, as he stated in the prefatory address to the reader, a defence of the principles of 1688.

'Thou hast here the beginning and end of a discourse concerning government,' he wrote. 'What fate has otherwise disposed of the papers that should have filled up the middle and were more than all the rest, it is not worth while to tell thee. These, which remain, I hope are sufficient to establish the throne of our great restorer, our present King William, to make good his title in the consent of the people, which, being the only one of all lawful governments, he has more fully and clearly than any prince in Christendom, and to justify to the world the people of England, whose love of their natural rights, with their resolution to preserve them, saved the nation when it was on the very brink of ruin. . . .' [3]

The first treatise was devoted to the annihilation of one of the fashionable arguments in favour of divine right, contained in Sir Robert Filmer's *Patriarcha* (1680). The second contained the political philosophy which recognized the consent of the people as the only lawful basis for government. When ambition, luxury, and flattery taught princes and rulers to have interests distinct and separate from those of the people, it seemed to Locke that it was wise for men to examine more carefully the 'original and rights' of government, to find out ways of restraining the exorbitance of their rulers and of preventing abuses of the power which had been given to them in trust, but which had been used to hurt those it was meant to benefit. Men established political society, Locke believed, for the mutual preservation of their lives, liberties, and estates, which together constituted their 'property'. And if that was the basis of the social contract, it was absurd to imagine that men would subject themselves willingly to an absolute power, over which they had no control, and which would give no guarantee that their rights would be respected. It would be as absurd as 'to think that men are so foolish that they take care to avoid what mischiefs may be done them by polecats or foxes, but are content, nay, think it safety, to be devoured by lions'.[4]

Political society was not founded for the benefit of absolute rulers but for the benefit of free men. It existed to give men a 'standing rule' to live by, a rule that would secure their property and enable them to enjoy the freedom that had been made precarious in the 'state of nature', owing to the fact that all men had not lived in accordance with the law of reason, but had infringed each other's natural rights.

But while freedom was indeed the greatest benefit to be derived from political society, it was not to be understood as Sir Robert Filmer had said, as 'a liberty for every one to do what he lists, to live as he pleases, and not to be tied by any laws'.[5] On the contrary, freedom of men under government was for them to have a standing rule to live by, common to every one of the society to which they belonged, and made by the legislative body erected in it. Law, therefore, was necessary if there was to be liberty for men in society. But to be subject to law was entirely different from being subject to the 'inconstant, uncertain, unknown, arbitrary will'[6] of any other person. It was the essence of a body politic that no one should be subjected to any rule except that of the law which had been enacted by the representatives of the people, and which was acknowledged as the known, standing rule by which the people had agreed to be guided. And no edict issued by anyone else could have the 'force and obligation' of a law, for that alone was law which had the sanction of the legislative power, chosen and appointed by the people.[7]

Furthermore, law was 'not so much the limitation as the direction of a free and intelligent agent to his proper interest'.[8] Its true end was not to abolish or restrain, but to preserve and enlarge freedom. Such a conception of law, inspired by the finest traditions of Roman jurisprudence, was an essential counterpart of the doctrine of government by consent of the governed. Law, guiding men to their proper interests, was also to serve as a hindrance to any hindrances to the enjoyment of those interests. But Locke went further, and he stood firmly on classical ground when he declared that law prescribed 'no farther than is for the general good of those under that law'.⁹ The general good not only limited the sphere of law, but also determined the constitutional principles by which the validity of law could be tested. It was this infusion of classical principles into the idea of law which gradually transformed modern law into a living, progressive force.

It followed from these principles that, while the legislative power was supreme in the state, it was sustained by the consent of the governed. In order to command the full support of the people, Locke stipulated that the legislators must govern by established, standing laws which were promulgated and known to the people, and not by extemporary decrees. And the legislators in their turn must be assisted by impartial and upright judges, whose function was to decide controversies in accordance with the established laws. Furthermore, the force of the community was to be employed at home only in the execution of these laws, or abroad to prevent or redress foreign injuries and to secure the community from invasion. 'And all this', Locke added, 'to be directed to no other end but the peace, safety, and public good of the people.' ¹⁰

The public good, upon which ultimately all legislation had to be based, involved four main points for the guidance of legislators, no matter what their form of government. In the first place, they would have to govern by promulgated, established laws which were not to be varied in particular cases, 'but to have one rule for rich and poor, for the favourite at Court, and the countryman at plough'.¹¹ Secondly, those laws should be designed for no other end ultimately than the good of the people. Thirdly, taxes were not to be raised on the property of the people without the consent of the people, given by themselves or by their deputies. And finally, the legislators 'neither must nor can transfer the power of making laws to anybody else, or place it anywhere but where the people have'.¹²

It was particularly important for the legislature to observe these principles, because the legislative power was supreme in the commonwealth. But it seemed to Locke that it was too great a temptation to human frailty for the same persons who had the power of making the laws to have in their hands also the execution of them. For that reason, it seemed desirable to place the executive in other hands, and liberty in government would be guaranteed through this division of powers. Justice would be further secured by the stipulation that those who framed the laws were not to be absolved from obedience to them.

Although Montesquieu thought he had found the secret of liberty in England in the division of powers,[13] he was mistaken in his judgement because he followed Locke's famous doctrine instead of the actual development of the British constitution· For the trend of constitutional practice led in the direction of an intricate system of checks and balances of power, instead of in the direction of a division of powers such as Locke had anticipated. The King in the past had been the supreme executor of the law, while Parliament, as the legislative body and the guardian of the rights of the people, had held the purse strings of the nation. Constant friction existed between Parliament and the ministers of the Crown, and statesmen of the eighteenth century recognized that it was necessary to resolve the struggle with the Crown for control of the ministers if the work of the nation was to be carried forward.[14] The growing interests and needs of the nation called for carefully thought-out policies, and ultimately the best solution to the problem of effective government was for the King to accept the 'advice' of his ministers, instead of initiating policies himself and informing the ministers what he proposed doing and expected them to do. In this way, policies could be properly organized by responsible parties, and instead of being dominated by the will of the King, they could reflect also the objectives of the responsible representatives of the people.* Thus in practice liberty was found, not

* While the revolution of 1688 transferred power from the Crown to Parliament, it did not transfer it from Parliament to the people. In the eighteenth century, there were 558 seats in the House of Commons. Of these, 234 were under patronage (L. B. Namier: *The Structure of Politics at the Accession of George III*, Vol. I, p. 182), which meant that almost half of the representatives for England did not have to

in the separation of the legislative and executive functions of the government, but in the organization of parties and responsible ministries, particularly in the organization of the Cabinet within Parliament itself, and in the establishment of an harmonious relationship between the Crown and the ministers who, finding it impossible to serve two masters, gave up their attempts to carry out the King's instructions and assumed the leadership of Parliament. Thus the constitutional monarch was divested eventually of practically all his executive power, and the essence of parliamentary diplomacy was to make this as painless a process as possible.

Another point of significance in Locke's doctrine, which quickly became of historical interest only, was his belief that the work of legislation was a relatively simple matter, and did not require the frequent assemblage of the legislature. The executive, on the other hand, had to remain at work constantly because Locke recognized that it was of first importance that the laws should be administered faithfully and justly. Locke's conception of the restricted function of the legislature was coloured partly by public reaction to the encroachments of the Stuarts upon what the people regarded as their own province, and partly by the fact that the England of the pre-industrial era was concerned mainly with agricultural and commercial pursuits and that her needs were relatively stable. The eighteenth century, however, saw England develop into the most important manufacturing and commercial nation in the world, and saw her empire extend to all four quarters of the globe. In order to meet the demands made upon it, legislation had to become a vital force, reflecting the expediency, justice and wisdom that

hink of their constituents, while the others thought of them chiefly at election time. It was only after George III's success in Parliament had opened the eyes of the Whigs to the need for reform, that policies came to be framed with reference to the electors. Indeed, until the closing decades of the century, the doctrine of Whig Trusteeship, enlightened though it was and fundamental in Edmund Burke's political thought (cf. J. MacCunn: *The Political Philosophy of Burke*, pp. 218–272), did not recognize that power should be lodged anywhere except with the representatives of the people in Parliament. Thus responsible government in our sense of the term was not established by the revolution of 1688, since popular self-government involves the responsibility of the members of Parliament to the electors. The eighteenth century, however, saw the transition from the 'principles of 1688' to modern responsible government.

were essential to the welfare of Englishmen both at home and abroad. And failure to meet these requirements was, as in the case of the American colonists, attended with disaster.

After Locke's brilliant vindication of the cause for which Parliament had stood in 1688, further discussion of fundamental principles was felt to be unnecessary. The time had come for the triumphant principles to be given an opportunity to establish themselves in the political life of the nation in order to make a solid foundation for constitutional government. Between the years 1690 and 1760, therefore, questions of fundamental principles receded into the background, while the genius of England was engaged in the slow process of moulding the methods of procedure and the political forms and institutions that would make the British constitution the nation's great repository of free principles. The constitutional problem that confronted the statesmen of the eighteenth century was to find a technique that would enable them to reconcile the monarchy with the supremacy of Parliament, and at the same time to make the executive functions responsible to representative institutions, without sacrificing efficiency. Progress was necessarily slow because they had to proceed cautiously on a basis of trial and error. They were guided by common sense in their efforts to apply Locke's fundamental principle of government by consent of the governed, which became a basic tenet in the eighteenth-century doctrine of Whig trusteeship. Thus they found ultimately not a philosophy of politics, but what has been termed a 'practical way of political life',[15] which was to inspire a tradition for statesmanship of a high order.

The protracted struggle between the Crown and Parliament for control of the ministers, which marked eighteenth-century constitutional history, was a direct outcome of the transference of power to Parliament. It represented an important phase in the evolution of the Cabinet and party system, and its significance lay in the fact that it involved the gathering of the executive power into the hands of ministers whose responsibility was to Parliament. The knell of the personal rule of the monarch was sounded when at length Parliament was able to hold the ministers of the Crown responsible to it alone for the policies they carried out.

William, the first monarch under the new régime, chose his own ministers and, in accordance with the practice of the period, consulted with them or kept his own counsel as he saw fit. He experimented in the selection of his ministers, although his choice usually fell upon those who were willing to provide him with the funds he needed for his wars. The extent of the changes he made was indicated by the ministries in control of the government in the course of the session of Parliament from 1690 to 1694. In 1690, his government was largely Tory in character; in 1692, it was wholly Tory; while two years later, it was Whig. In spite of the fact that his reign was marked by fierce party strife, these changes of Cabinet were not due to pressure from the Commons or from outside, but to 'a nice adjustment of many personal and sectional groups to the royal will'.[16] In 1701, Sunderland suggested that the Cabinet should be a well-defined body and that it should be consulted by the King as a matter of course. But William did not act on this suggestion because he was not willing to allow the Cabinet to become established upon such clear-cut lines. Anne, coming to the throne on the death of William in 1702, was determined not to allow herself to be used as the tool of party leaders. 'All I desire,' she declared, 'is my liberty in encouraging and employing all those that concur faithfully in my service, whether they are called Whigs or Tories.'[17] The word 'Cabinet' was used in an address to the Queen by the Lords in 1711, when it was regarded with disfavour.

With the coming of the Hanoverians in 1714, the situation changed. The prestige of the Crown diminished considerably while that of Parliament reached its zenith,[18] and it was then possible to begin to build upon the revolution settlement. Unlike William and Anne, the first two Hanoverian monarchs could not select their ministers indiscriminately from either party. They had to limit their choice to the Whigs who had supported their right to succession to the throne. George I, in his fifties when he came to the throne, was unable to speak the language of his new subjects. Interested mainly in the affairs of the German electorate he had left, and unacquainted with the traditions or the politics of England, he entrusted the 'management' of the House of Commons to the powerful Whig leaders upon whom he was obliged to rely. He had to permit them to dispense the royal patronage, and they used their power to entrench themselves firmly in office and also to complete the rout of the Tory leaders, who had been discredited at the death of Anne when they were suspected of complicity in a plot to restore the Stuarts. And although the first of the Hanoverian kings was much more than a mere figurehead in the government, he nevertheless weakened yet further the royal prestige by surrendering important privileges, such as attending the debates in the House of Lords and meetings of the Cabinet, because of the difficulty he experienced in understanding proceedings. Thus the way was opened for the Whigs to strengthen, by means of legal checks as well as by unobtrusive and indirect, but none the less effective, forms of procedure, the limitations that had already been placed on the Crown by the Bill of Rights and the Act of Settlement. But also they had the opportunity of building up a constitutional form of government based upon the principles of 1688, in which they firmly believed.

The Crown gradually began to lose its grip upon the Cabinet after George I surrendered his right to attend its meetings and allowed the ministers greater latitude in the formulation of their policies. From that time onward changes, which led to the emergence of responsible party government, began to alter the relationship between the Cabinet and the Crown from what it had been prior to 1714. In spite of these changes, a considerable period had yet to elapse before the idea of personal government was given up and the office of Prime Minister was established, thus making the Cabinet an integral part of the party system. George I kept in close touch with all Cabinet business; George II attended meetings of the Cabinet because he had no difficulty in understanding its proceedings; while George III called meetings of the Cabinet on at least two occasions.[19] During this interval, however, the functions of the Cabinet were becoming more clearly defined; and this development, even more than the failure of the monarch to attend its meetings, was responsible for the change in the relationship between the Cabinet and the Crown.

While these changes played an important part in setting the pattern for constitutional government in England, the political history of the period revealed the vicissitudes of both Cabinet and the party system. Ministers did not hesitate to oppose each other in Parliament,[20] thus showing that the idea of unanimity among Cabinet members was far from being firmly established. Although the period from 1714 to 1760 marked the great era of Whig supremacy, the solidarity that had characterized the Whigs as a party in 1714 had soon vanished. The great 'Revolution' families, the Bedfords, the Newcastles, and the Devonshires, had split into separate factions; and their political fortunes depended upon the strength of their following in the two houses of Parliament as well as upon their ability to gain royal favour. The Tory party was leaderless following the refusal of Oxford to return to public life, and the exile in France of Bolingbroke, and it was completely disorganized. The confusion in the political scene was all the greater because it became almost impossible to draw any practical distinction between Whigs out of office and moderate Tories.[21] Because party allegiance was personal rather than on a basis of principle, the idea of working together as parties in the modern sense had to be built up, and when built up it still took time to gain acceptance.

In its extreme form, Tory doctrine had found expression in Sir Robert Filmer's *Patriarcha*; while the Whigs looked to John Locke's two treatises *Of Civil Government* both for the refutation of the creed of the Tories and for the statement of the principles of constitutional government which were accepted by statesmen until the time of Chatham. When the original distinction between Whigs and Tories broke down, new party lines centred around the interpretation of 'constitutional' government.

Whig doctrine had drawn its strength largely from its faith in the constitution, and from the determination of Whig leaders to make constitutional government the real safeguard for the liberties of the people. The somewhat dull policy of common sense and businesslike methods, even though they were later attended by a considerable amount of corruption, had enabled Walpole, the great leader of the administration between the years 1721 and 1742, to raise England out of the panic of the South Sea bubble and to turn it towards an era of prosperity and quiet expansion. Gifted with a genius for organization, during the long period he was in office Walpole had in a quiet, unspectacular manner laid the foundation for co-ordinated effort in the House on a basis of party. Toryism, in direct opposition to Whig methods, preferred to strengthen the position of the monarch as the chief guardian of the constitution. Tories desired that the King should rule on constitutional lines, and that he should be supported by able ministers who would carry out his policies faithfully. They wanted personal rather than party government. To them, party rule represented government for the benefit of the few, while the ideal to which they subscribed meant government by the King for the benefit of the whole nation. This conflict between Whig and Tory ideas of government played an important part in leading to a clearer understanding of the function of parties in responsible, representative government, and this clearer conception was made by Edmund Burke into one of the fundamental principles of his political philosophy.

The evolution of an organized opposition was an important aspect of the party system, but it was also a slow process. Even in the mid-century, members of Parliament disliked intensely the idea of forming an organized opposition, because they still regarded the King as the head of the government and felt that there was an element of disloyalty in organizing to defeat him.[22] Powerful groups had opposed those in office from time to time, either on principle or for personal reasons, but opposition remained far from systematic. Thus Walpole, before he rose to power in 1720–21, had spent three years opposing ministerial measures indiscriminately. When he came to office himself, he had to face the formidable opposition of Sunderland and his followers in addition to the opposition of groups such as the Tories, the Jacobites and the Hanoverian court circles. With Sunderland's death in 1722, his most dangerous rival was removed; and he had but little to fear from other groups until Bolingbroke returned from exile to organize an opposition that had come into being once more when he aroused the enmity of Pulteney in 1725. After the death of Queen Anne, Bolingbroke lost his power and fled to France. In 1715 he was attainted, but ten years later he was permitted by act of Parliament to own real estate in England, although Walpole succeeded in maintaining his exclusion from the House of Lords. Bolingbroke never forgave Walpole for this, and retaliated by stirring up sustained opposition to him and his policies. Upon his return to England in 1725, Bolingbroke became at once the leading spirit among disgruntled Whigs whom Walpole had alienated and among the men of letters. Unable to take his seat in the upper house, he had to pursue his political activities behind the scenes. With a loudly professed contempt for parties, he shrewdly provided the 'opposition' with ammunition intended to be used against Walpole. Every administration, he asserted en philosophe, was a system of conduct; 'opposition, therefore, should be a system of conduct likewise, an opposite, but not a dependent system'.²³ In other words, the opposition should not confine itself to opposing measures introduced by the ministers, but should build up and follow out its own policy. Bolingbroke did not scruple to use every possible means to wreck the administration that had been in power for so long. He supported his 'opposition' strategy with repeated denunciations of the corruption of the Walpole era in the pages of *The Craftsman*, an important periodical which had been begun in 1726, where he habitually associated 'party' with 'faction'. Bolingbroke discovered incidentally that the channels of regular journalism were most effective for sustained criticism of Walpole's policies, and from his time forward the power of the press became more and more prominent in the political world, until at last it won the right to reflect in its columns every trend of political thought and action.

In order to confound the party system yet further, Bolingbroke evolved his *Idea of a Patriot King* (1749). Whatever there was of sound philosophy hidden beneath the elegance of his style was put to selfish uses. It was the clever work of a broken statesman, who nobly professed to desire the benefit not of a party, but of the whole nation. He declaimed at some

length upon the necessity for a patriot who would restore
liberty to a faction-ridden country. The political corruption
of the Walpole era merely argued stagnation, according to his
version, and where decadence of this kind was present there
could be no true liberty. Corruption and its accompanying
evils, he declared, would pass away only when the people
turned back to the true spirit of patriotism and virtue, but that
day would not come until a patriot king ascended the throne.
A model in every way, this royal paragon would take the
government of the realm into his own hands, and by dispelling
both party and faction, would unite the people once more
and would rule with a single eye to their welfare. He would
think of the state, and not of party ; he would uphold the
constitution in so far as it came up to the high standards
required of it, and he would reward and punish with equity.

While Bolingbroke was advocating a national government
as the solution to England's political problems, the Duke of
Newcastle, one of the ablest and most powerful parliamentarians of the period, was doing much to establish the party
system upon a firm foundation. He became Secretary of State
in 1724, but rose to pre-eminence in national affairs after Walpole's downfall in 1742. Newcastle was fully aware of the
value of systematic party organization, and he believed that
the most efficient administrations were those which were
composed of members of one party only and which acted as a
unity. He thought that ministers should be dependent, not
upon the Crown, but upon their own supporters in Parliament.
At the same time, he was convinced that if ministers did not
rely upon their strength in Parliament, they would have to
submit to the authority of the Crown, an alternative that
seemed to him to be opposed to the revolution settlement.[24]
To him the doctrine of Whig trusteeship meant constitutional
government through the Cabinet and party system. Newcastle's ideas were important both because he remained true to
them throughout his political career and because they inspired
the doctrines of the Rockingham Whig party, to which
Edmund Burke belonged.

The most popular national figure among the statesmen of
the mid-eighteenth century was not Newcastle, but William

Pitt, who had entered Parliament in 1735. He won distinction immediately for the fire of his oratory, and he became conspicuous for the fierceness of his attacks upon Walpole. Pitt's disinterested patriotism won for him the whole-hearted admiration of the nation and set him apart from most of the parliamentarians of his day. It was in striking contrast to Newcastle's acceptance of the corrupt practices of the time to further his own ends. Pitt's conception of constitutional government also contrasted sharply with Newcastle's. By nature incapable of co-operating with others, Pitt had a rooted aversion to the party system. He favoured Bolingbroke's ideas of a national government, much to the confusion of Newcastle and the Rockingham Whigs in the opening years of George III's reign.[25] But it was not so much the ideal of the patriot king that inspired his greatest public service as his vision of England's nobler self. His oratory not only rekindled patriotism, a love of liberty and the ideals for which the constitution stood, but also aroused the nation from cynical indifference to a sense of duty and of enterprise that carried all before it. William Pitt was convinced that England had a great destiny to fulfil, and the people listened to him eagerly. They had grown weary of the continual sacrifice of the enterprising and the spectacular to the monotonous policy of common sense and the balancing of the books of national finance. England was undeniably prosperous, but she was not covering herself with glory and distinction either at home or abroad. Consequently, the important thing at the moment was that the nation was being recalled to life and that it had a leader. With the people behind him, Pitt was able to carry forward a dream of empire that was far beyond the ken of any of his colleagues.

Pitt's great opportunity came with the Seven Years' War (1756–63). The disastrous opening of the war forced the resignation of Newcastle, and as a result of popular demand Pitt became a member of the Cabinet, which was under the leadership of Devonshire. But the new ministry was unable to prevail against a House that was still dominated by Newcastle. Consequently, George II had to allow the formation of an administration in which Newcastle was First Lord of the

Treasury and Pitt, Secretary of State. When it looked as if Bourbon power would triumph over Britain, Pitt played so brilliant a part in the control of the national destinies that he turned defeat into triumph, and in so doing he greatly enhanced his popularity with the people. He was at the height of his power when George III ascended the throne.

In the year 1760, it seemed as if England's fairest dreams might come true. The death of George II placed on the throne a prince who was especially popular because he had been born and reared in England, and who regarded himself as English. His regard for the virtues which Englishmen respected most of all served to increase his popularity yet further. Brought up to respect the revolution settlement, George III proposed to play his part conscientiously as a constitutional monarch. But he believed that it was the function of the King to lead rather than to follow. He had absorbed Bolingbroke's doctrine of the patriot king, and he had no intention of allowing the ministers to retain the power that had wrung from his grandfather, George II, the complaint that 'the ministers were kings in this country'. On the contrary, he proposed regaining much of the executive power that his predecessors had surrendered. In this desire, he could claim the sympathies of many people within his realm, for in 1760 the Cabinet and party system of government was far from popular.[26] Many shared the new King's hatred of the Whig oligarchs, who now found that they had to defend their constitutional ideas.

The coalition ministry of Newcastle and Pitt was in office when George III came to the throne, but it was soon discovered that a new order of things had come into existence. As far back as 1758, there had been discussions as to the ministry that would be formed when the Prince of Wales became King. Lord Bute had the complete confidence of the future King, although he was hated by Pitt and other important leaders, and was destined to become intensely unpopular with the nation as a whole. It was arranged that Bute should become First Lord of the Treasury in the government of the new reign. But this plan was thwarted by Pitt's refusal to serve with him, and by Bute's reluctance to take full responsibility for Newcastle's office at that juncture in foreign affairs. While the Seven Years'

War lasted, Pitt's services were indispensable. Consequently the King made no change in the leadership of the ministry, although he would have been within his rights in making whatever changes he desired. But the policy of the King and Bute was now to bring about peace with France as soon as possible, so that they could undermine the powerful ministers in office. They found that they could use Newcastle to further their ends, both in the matter of the general elections of 1761 and in finding an office for Bute in the Cabinet. Newcastle was satisfied on the whole with the plans for the general elections, but he was reluctant to take any steps that would give offence to Pitt. Through his co-operation, however, Bute became a Secretary of State on March 25, 1761. And Bute's elevation to office was 'the outward and visible sign' that the monarchy had been restored to its rightful prestige.[27]

Peace negotiations were begun almost immediately, and although they were unsuccessful, they were of great importance to the King because they led to the resignation of Pitt in October, 1761. Newcastle had antagonized Pitt by the course he had pursued, but he soon found that he had been duped by the King and Bute and that the Parliament, in which he confidently expected to find himself master, was willing to follow the policies of the Court. His resignation followed in May, 1762, and as a result Bute was left in control of national affairs. Bute's position was far from enviable, as he had to contend with extreme unpopularity. Yet he succeeded in bringing about the conclusion of the war, and did much to consolidate the constitutional position of the monarch. Nevertheless, it was not long before personal dislike for Bute and his Scottish followers resulted in a drive to have them ousted from power. The agitation to have Bute removed from office was supported by clever and informed articles in the *North Briton*, the work of Wilkes and Churchill. While these articles were still appearing, Bute resigned office. The Treaty of Hubertusburg brought the Seven Years' War to a close in February, 1763, and on April 7, Bute withdrew from the ministry.

When George Grenville was named Bute's successor, a new and tragic phase of the King's reign opened. Pitt, whose ideas of constitutional government were not seriously at variance with those of the King, had refused to take office, and he contributed greatly to the confusion of the coming years by his refusal to join with Newcastle and others in organizing a powerful opposition. Indeed, it has been claimed that

'it was his intractable, incalculable nature, his genius tinged with madness, which, at least as much as the immature, unbalanced, passionate obstinacy of George III, produced the chaos of the first ten years of the new reign, and during the next fatal ten years placed the Government in incompetent hands.' [28]

While Grenville was striving to strengthen his position and that of his ministry with the Crown, he stirred up trouble at home that was destined to create political disturbance for years to come by taking steps to punish Wilkes. Before he resigned in 1766, the Stamp Act (1765) had been passed, and the steps had been taken that led to the irretrievable alienation of the American colonists.

It was particularly unfortunate that issues of a fundamental nature should have been resurrected at this juncture. The trend of events seemed to threaten the liberties of the people, both at home and abroad, and this danger became apparent at a time when new forces were stirring in every phase of national life. Reawakening vitality in the life of the nation was clearly indicated by the fact that social, economic, and political questions were absorbing the attention of ordinary thinking people. But the turmoil caused by the King and his ministers introduced an element of bewilderment into their minds, and their immediate reaction was to question the soundness of national ideals. Pitt had commanded their whole-hearted support through his unswerving faith in free institutions and in self-government by a free and self-governing people.[29] But while Pitt had shown that he was a leader who possessed most unusual gifts, his leadership lay in the direction of carrying through spectacular and boldly conceived imperial policies rather than in giving the people a clearer understanding of the course that national destinies were taking.

The unrest that was perceptible in practically every channel of national life, however, made the need for reinterpretation of national ideals urgent. It was obvious that the old ways were inadequate to deal with the new demands. Science, which had opened a vast new world for man's use, and had caused thinkers of the Enlightenment to introduce scientific methods into every field of human endeavour, was slowly but surely revolutionizing life itself. New and more scientific methods of production and new means of transport were changing England into the world's chief manufacturing and commercial centre. The colonies were supplying raw materials that were being manufactured at home as fast as the means for converting them into manufactured goods could be devised. It was not necessary to search for markets for these goods. On the contrary, markets were waiting impatiently for the finished product. Wealth was accumulating while the modern credit system, but imperfectly understood, was emerging from its infancy to wage war with outworn mercantilism, which it sought to oust as unsuitable for the requirements of modern trade. In order to meet the demands of trade, the labouring classes were forsaking the land to become part of the vast industrial system that was slowly coming into being. Their welfare was no longer bound up with agriculture, but with trade. The land was being deserted for the industries of the cities, and the change was giving birth to problems of major dimensions.

This process of change and the discarding of what was outworn in theory and practice involved both unrest and distress; while it was complicated by the emergence of a wealth of new ideas which struggled to replace the old. The Enlightenment had produced much work of a profoundly stimulative nature, and consequently of first importance in the remoulding of national ideals. Locke's immediate influence as a political theorist and economist had run its course as far as England was concerned. His political principles had to be restated in the light of a fuller and deeper understanding of the nature of the state in order to become a vital force once more. But his work had been taken over by French thinkers and had become fundamental in their political philosophy. The most important works of the period, Voltaire's *Lettres Philosophiques* (1734), Montesquieu's *Esprit des Lois* (1748), Helvétius' *de l'Esprit* (1755), and Rousseau's *Contrat Social* (1762), all reflected important aspects of Locke's thought, and all were well known to English readers.

But the influence of French thought had penetrated even deeper than this. Much of it had been absorbed by English men of letters and had appeared in work that was not only characteristically English in form, but was definitely intended to be an attempt in the direction of organizing and reinterpreting English thought. Indeed, it would be difficult to find an important work on political, social, or economic subjects published in England during this period which did not reflect some significant aspect of French thought or which had not benefited by the work of French thinkers. Such a work as Blackstone's *Commentaries* (1755) belonged to the Montesquieu tradition. Behind Bentham's *Fragment on Government* (1776), which heralded an attempt to systematize English law, was a philosophic system which owed not a little to the utilitarianism of Helvétius. Behind Adam Smith's *Wealth of Nations* (1776) was a profound study of the thought of Quesnay and the Physiocratic school, who believed in the operation of natural law in the economic as in the natural world, and encouraged governments to remove hindrances to the natural ebb and flow of trade. But the influence of French thought extended yet further, for it formed part of the intellectual heritage of Edmund Burke who, together with Adam Smith and Bentham, was destined to guide English thought through the difficult period of transition that prepared the way for the work of the nineteenth century. For Burke was the inspired disciple of Montesquieu, whose great work, *de l'Esprit des Lois*, was distinguished by the effective use of the historical method of approach to political thought and by the emphasis he placed upon the empire of circumstance in the development of the different constitutional systems known to history.

Burke's mind was so deeply steeped in the enlightened thought of the age that he had already accepted as settled convictions views which were shaking the intellectual foundations of ordinary men. His entrance into public life in 1766 came, therefore, at an opportune moment for his countrymen. He had accepted as his political creed all that was finest in Whig tradition, and he had brought it to terms with what he regarded as the enduring principles of political philosophy. In the exalted language to which Pitt had accustomed Englishmen,

Burke talked of justice, wisdom and prudence as the everyday stock-in-trade of the statesman. Unlike the Great Commoner, Burke preferred the methods of the party system to the solitary flight of the lone eagle, but his pre-eminence was more than assured through his steadfast adherence to his political ideals and convictions, and through powerful literary gifts which enabled him to give his thoughts lasting form for the benefit of his country. Accustomed to thinking for himself, Burke possessed also the power of stimulating thought in others. Consequently, as he took his modest place in the House of Commons, he was admirably equipped to assume the responsibility of reinterpreting the ideals of his country and of the party to which he offered his allegiance, in the light of the difficulties and growing needs of the times.

One of the most difficult periods in England's history had opened. Yet Parliament seemed pathetically incapable of becoming master of the situation. Signs of gathering storms were in evidence everywhere, but it was not long before Burke thought he had grasped their significance. The first opportunity for discussing them in writing, however, came three years after he had entered public life. In 1768 a pamphlet appeared, entitled *The Present State of the Nation*, believed to have been the work of George Grenville (who was regarded as a leading authority both on finance and on political science), although now attributed to William Knox. In it the administration was charged with responsibility for the ruined fortunes of England. Like many of his contemporaries, the author based his ideas of what the government could do to remedy the situation upon its legal competency. A uniform system of taxation instead of the lax system bequeathed by Walpole, and a direct control of colonial affairs by the home government would, he believed, bring about an immediate improvement. Far from bringing about any such improvement, it seemed to Burke that these proposals would serve only to aggravate the troubles that already beset the government. What was needed, Burke asserted, was not a uniform scheme of taxation, but an understanding on the part of the ministers of the Crown of the principles underlying the art of government. To put forward arguments proving their 'mere right or mere power' to act in the manner proposed was no more than a 'very unpleasant way of misspending time',[30] and Burke made no attempt to conceal his intense dislike for it. Their business was to discover the causes underlying national unrest, and to seek remedies that would remove troubles at their source.

Already Burke demonstrated the method by which he proposed to deal with the troubled conditions of his country. He made effective use of his brilliant literary gifts in order to present a clear analysis of immediate problems. By a critical survey of the various features in the situation, he was in a position to recognize those factors which stood out as most important. And from a better understanding of immediate circumstances, he worked back to underlying causes with a view to obtaining a clue to the right kind of remedy. Thus he introduced the methods of the historical school, and turned aside from the abstract and legalistic methods of his colleagues as unstatesmanlike and unsuitable for practical politics. But over and above immediate and practical considerations, Burke was anxious to teach. He wished to teach the members of Parliament what their duties were in a constitutional scheme of government in which the liberty and welfare of the nation as a whole depended in a large measure upon the integrity and statesmanship of the legislative body. In addition, his thoughts were centred upon making Parliament as efficient a legislative body as possible so that ills resulting from misgovernment could be eliminated first of all from national problems. If government were to become once more an art such as it had been in the golden days of the Greek city-state, it seemed reasonable to believe that it would appeal to men of integrity and of statesmanlike qualities, while the resultant benefits to the nation from such a state of affairs would be incalculably great. But in addition to presenting such an ideal to his fellow members of Parliament, Burke desired to reach a wider circle of readers and to give them an insight into political principles. He looked to those people who, through their public spiritedness and their interest in national affairs, could be relied upon by the government for both co-operation and sympathetic understanding. Burke hoped to lead his readers away from the quicksands of metaphysics so that instead of regarding politics as an abstract science, they would arrive at an understanding of the true nature of political fact. Through the historical method he hoped to resolve the perplexities that disturbed his country.

Continued reflection upon the troubles that were agitating England led Burke to write his *Thoughts on the Causes of the Present Discontents* (1770).

'It will be a matter very proper for the consideration of your lordship and your friends', Burke wrote to his chief, Lord Rockingham, when sending him a considerable section of the manuscript, 'whether a thing of this nature should appear at all. It is, in the first place, a formal attack upon that object which had been nearest and dearest to the court since the beginning of the reign; and of course, if this thing should be supposed to express your sentiments, must put you on terms irreconcilably bad with the court and every one of its adherents. . . .' [31]

It was, in other words, a direct attack upon the theory of the patriot king which had been put in practice by George III for the ten years he had been on the throne. When a whole nation was in disorder, Burke believed the chances were that the root of the evil would be found in misgovernment.

'I am not one of those who think that the people are never in the wrong,' he wrote. 'They have been so, frequently and outrageously, both in other countries and in this. But I do say, that in all disputes between them and their rulers, the presumption is at least upon a par in favour of the people.' [32]

Factions might become discontented either with or without just cause and might inflame sections of the community, but when discontents were widespread and deep-seated, it was time to give serious consideration to the system of government. And in this case it was not particularly difficult to trace the main cause of the trouble. A double cabinet system had been instituted whereby the King had succeeded in imposing his arbitrary will upon the nation.[33] The House of Commons had been alienated from the people. Attacking the theory of the patriot king which he believed was at the seat of the trouble, Burke insisted that the House of Commons was not instituted to be a control upon the people as had been taught 'by a doctrine of the most pernicious tendency'. It was designed as a control for the people. 'Other institutions have been formed

for the purpose of checking popular excesses,' Burke wrote;
'and they are, I apprehend, fully adequate to their object.'[34]
The only way to remedy matters was to return to the true
principles of the constitution, but this could not be done by
the cant of 'not men but measures'. It was in point of fact the
integrity of the men in Parliament that counted most of all, and
their work could be done most effectively through associating
together in parties. A party was anything but a faction. It was
a body of men united for promoting 'by their joint endeavours
the national interest, upon some particular principle in which
they are all agreed'.[35] As the greater part of the measures that
arose in the course of public business was related to, or dependent upon, some great, leading general principles in government, a man must indeed be unfortunate if he could not agree
with those in his company in at least nine times out of ten.

It seemed to Burke that the great principles of government
which had inspired British politics from the time of the 'glorious' revolution of 1688 onwards found their most natural
means of expression in the party system. Indeed, he did not
believe that either principles or policies would be really
effective unless they were transformed into the links that
bound men together in parties. Burke was so profoundly convinced of the truth of this fact that he did not rest until the
Rockingham Whigs, with whom his own political fortunes
were linked, had abandoned their old-fashioned ideas and had
become a group of public-spirited men keenly alive to the need
for statesmanship if the government of the country was to be
true to its trust.[36] In addition, it seemed to Burke that the
strengthening of the bonds of party was the most effective
means that could be adopted in order to check the inroads of
corruption and specious doctrine in the government.

Constitutional troubles at home, however, were augmented,
and indeed were soon overshadowed, by difficulties with the
colonists in America. The King's policies had borne fruit in
increased friction between the home government and the
colonists. As Burke watched bitterness increase on both sides,
he knew that unstatesmanlike methods and a failure to understand human nature were responsible for most of the troubles
the government had brought upon itself, both at home and in

America. He strained every nerve in order to prevent the final disaster, but his task was made unduly difficult because the people, for the most part, were inclined to believe with the King that the colonists were at fault, and that it was time they were taught a lesson. On April 19, 1774, Burke joined in a debate on the question of American taxation with one of the most impressive speeches he had yet made in the House. He pointed out that it was inconsistent for them to enforce taxation, and then to rescind it on all articles save tea, the one item that allowed of an extensive contraband, in order to save their dignity.

'Show the thing you contend for to be reason; show it to be common sense; show it to be the means of attaining some useful ends; and then I am content to allow it what dignity you please. But what dignity is derived from the perseverance in absurdity is more than I ever could discern.' [37]

The members of the House had never, he said, taken a connected view of the matter. Rather they had given an instructive lesson 'upon the mischief of not having large and liberal ideas in the management of great affairs'.[38] It seemed as if they had gone out of their way merely for the sake of insulting the colonies. It was not the tax of threepence on the tea that was too much for the colonists, but rather the 'weight of that preamble, of which you are so fond' that the Americans were unable and unwilling to bear. His advice was for the House to return to its old principles and to follow a consistent policy. Their task was to discover how they could govern a people who thought they ought to be free but thought that they were not. The methods they had tried had not worked.

'Again and again', he appealed, 'revert to your old principles—seek peace and ensue it—leave America, if she has taxable matter in her, to tax herself. I am not here going into the distinctions of rights, nor attempting to mark their boundaries. I do not enter into these metaphysical distinctions; I hate the very sound of them. Leave the Americans as they anciently stood, and these distinctions, born of our unhappy contest, will die along with it. They and we, and their and our ancestors, have been happy under that system.' [39]

If they would only follow that path, Burke was certain that both subordination and liberty could be reconciled, whether sufficiently to serve 'refining speculatists', or a factious demagogue, he did not know; but surely enough for the ease and happiness of man.

Burke's appeal was in vain as far as influencing the policy of the House was concerned, but when the elections were held later in the year, Bristol, which was the second most important city in England, invited him to stand as its candidate. The electors of Bristol had been deeply impressed with the sound common sense and wisdom that Burke had shown in the grave issues that were confronting the nation, while his unusual mastery of the principles of economics and politics also had counted greatly in his favour. When Burke accepted their nomination, he said that his great object in the coming session of Parliament would be to 'reconcile British superiority with American liberty', as he was far from thinking that even then both might not be preserved. In the new year, proposals were brought forward for reconciliation with the colonies. On March 22, 1775, Burke made an eloquent plea to Parliament to do all in its power to regain the loyalty and confidence that had been sacrificed. The first step toward that end was to consider carefully the true nature and circumstances of the Americans.

'Because after all our struggle, whether we will or not,' he asserted, 'we must govern America, according to that nature, and to those circumstances; and not according to our own imaginations; not according to abstract ideas of right; by no means according to mere general theories of government, the resort to which appears to me, in our present situation, no better than arrant trifling.' [40]

He would not enter upon legal arguments as to the rights of taxation or its limits, because he pointed out that the question was rather whether it was not in the interests of Parliament to make the colonists happy. 'It is not what a lawyer tells me I may do; but what humanity, reason, and justice, tell me I ought to do.' The question of legal right ended, he said, in the 'great Serbonian bog, betwixt Damiata and Mount Casius old, where armies whole have sunk'; [41] while the question of the happiness of the colonists led to a solution of the whole difficulty. What they had to do was not to determine a point of law, but to restore tranquillity.

The existing political situation together with its disastrous consequences served to impress upon Burke not merely the fact that the principles of 1688 were the real safeguard for the liberty and unity of the nation, but also that a clear comprehension of the principles of historical development had to replace theories of abstract rights. In his hands, therefore, the principles of 1688 became symbolic of the traditional rights and liberties of the nation as well as of the supremacy of England's free institutions. But in order to re-establish those principles in the life of the nation, he saw that it was necessary to make them the foundation upon which the principles of historical development could be set forth.

At the same time, Burke was profoundly disturbed to observe how deeply theories of abstract rights had entered into the dispute with the colonists. On the one hand, Parliament had insisted upon the assertion of its sovereign rights; while on the other, radicals had joined with the colonists in demanding liberty for America on the grounds of the inalienable right of mankind to life, liberty and happiness. Moreover, he was not unaware of the fact that Paris had an arsenal fully stocked with every kind of argument regarding the rights of man and that her stores were at the disposal of the Americans. While these arguments had been of service to the colonists in a just cause, Burke realized that they were admirably fitted to provide ammunition for future attacks upon established authority, whether in England or France or elsewhere. And he regarded them as an ever-present menace to ordered government because they left out the principle of expediency, of 'compromise and barter', upon which government and all amicable arrangements between peoples and their rulers rested.

But apart altogether from these considerations, Burke was troubled by the complete faith placed in these abstract arguments by the outstanding French writers of the century who had given thought to political and social reform. The author of the *Esprit des Lois*, the only contemporary leader of French thought whom Burke genuinely respected, was apparently the sole exception to the rule. Yet the moderation and statesmanlike methods of Montesquieu had been airily discarded in favour of the more spectacular Utopia-building of Rousseau. Burke felt apprehensive because the brilliant French theorists of the eighteenth century sought to remake society on the basis of their abstract theories instead of by gradual reform which would disturb the social order as little as possible, and because they relied upon logic instead of upon the principle of historical development which required a painstaking study of fact and the empire of circumstance.

CHAPTER III

NEW LAMPS FOR OLD

THREE years before England's 'glorious' revolution took place, Louis XIV had revoked the Edict of Nantes, thereby outlawing the Protestants within his realm.[1] By his act, he triumphantly demonstrated to the world that the sovereignty of the powerful empire of France resided in him, and that it was his will to have a united people. At that moment the power of the Bourbons was at its height. The episode was indeed in striking contrast to the course of events in England,[2] where the rights of the subject were triumphing over the divine right of kings. England had found liberty through constitutional government; France was basking in the power and magnificence of absolute monarchy in the golden age of Louis Quatorze. That which England had gained by constitutional reform, eighteenth-century France had to win by other means. England's traditional resistance to arbitrary power had enabled her to build up institutions that would safeguard her effectively from threats to her liberty. France, on the other hand, had to uproot the *ancien régime* in order to eradicate the evils of the social and political system.

By the revocation of the Edict of Nantes, the one group of dissenters within the realm was given the choice of submitting to the accepted faith of France, or else of suffering the consequences of the loss of civil rights. There was scarcely a murmur of protest to be heard, except from the Protestants themselves. For years they had known the miseries of persecution, which were now intensified for those who were obliged to remain in France. About a million Huguenots fled across the borders of France into Holland, the seventeenth-century 'rampart of liberty in Europe',[3] and into Germany, where they had to re-establish their homes and industries. It was not long before the exiled Huguenots in Holland came into contact with liberal political thought. As a matter of fact, John Locke had been in Amsterdam at the time when they flocked

across the border, and when a few years later they had his
treatises in their hands, they set to work to familiarize Europe
with the principles of constitutional government, based upon
the doctrine of the natural rights of man. Thus they were able
to introduce to France political ideals that had made England a
free country, the adoption of which they hoped would make
France free also.[4]

Of course, the monarch's act had left the way open for
criticism, and it was not long before arguments were heard that
had an increasingly familiar ring later in the eighteenth century.
The Protestant pastor, Jurieu, protested vigorously that kings
were magistrates whose office it was to safeguard the liberties
of the subject. Like the English, he asserted that the people
had a right to depose a monarch who exceeded his authority as
Louis XIV had done. But for the time being, Jurieu's protests
were in vain. Bossuet, who took notice of his attacks, replied
that kings were divinely appointed, and that they were to be
obeyed because in effect divided authority was calamitous.
Bossuet denied the existence of the natural rights that Jurieu
believed kings should safeguard. Like Bentham a century
later, he took the position that rights were the creature of
government. The only rights the Protestants in France could
have, therefore, were those that the King chose to grant them.

In point of fact, the creed of seventeenth-century France left
but little room for the Protestants, although they were among
the most loyal of the King's subjects. The doctrines of the
Roman Catholic Church were accepted implicitly. It was
believed that man was born in sin and that he could find salvation only through the mediation of Holy Church. The King
was divinely appointed, as Bossuet had said, and his power was
absolute. The ranks and privileges of the social order were
likewise part of the appointed and permanent constitution of
things. While the revocation of the Edict of Nantes therefore
appeared to be a perfectly natural course for the King to take,
it nevertheless marked a turning-point in French history.
From that time forward, side by side with political develop-
ments there arose a definite intellectual movement which sought
to provide new lamps of knowledge for old ideas that were
clearly outworn. This new movement was marked by

criticism which, as time went on, was directed towards the evolution of an entirely new social ideal and order. In the old régime, the social order was intimately linked to religious faith, and it was the desire of the King to preserve unity of religious thought and practice that led to the revocation of the Edict of Nantes. But as a matter of fact, age-old disputes within the Church broke out with increased intensity when the King, in his desire for uniformity, followed up the revocation of the Edict of Nantes by taking the part of the unpopular Jesuits in the hope of crushing for ever their Jansenist opponents. In the midst of this renewal of charges of unorthodoxy, which the leaders of the different parties in the Church hurled at each other, the sceptical thinkers gathered strength. They pointed out that if the Church was the fountain-head of truth, it was obvious that it was not agreed as to what that truth was. The men of the Enlightenment therefore set to work with the definite aim of destroying old creeds by the method of subjecting all beliefs to the light of reason, and then, having cleared the ground of superstition and ignorance, they hoped to erect a new social edifice on the basis of reason.

The most powerful stimulus to this movement came from the work of Pierre Bayle of Rotterdam, whose brother had lost his life as a result of the persecution of Protestants following the revocation of the Edict of Nantes. Bayle had been converted to Catholicism and back again to Protestantism, and eventually had become sceptical of all religions. He put his faith in reason rather than in revelation, and he believed that truth could be found by a dispassionate examination of all knowledge. Following the Cartesian method, he believed that all doctrines had to be regarded as doubtful until there was positive proof of their truth. Nothing was too obvious or too sacred to be investigated. Underlying falsehood would quickly reveal itself in absurdity. But fighting errors with blows seemed to Bayle just as absurd as trying to capture a fortress with logical arguments. He carried this rationalistic spirit into every kind of discussion that found a place in his highly influential philosophical *Dictionnaire* (1697),[5] and as a result he made his work a rich store-house of arguments for the use of the eighteenth century. The source of his vitality was to be found in his appeal to the serious reader, in his desire for truth and toleration, in his faith in reason, in his scepticism, in his appeal to common sense as well as in his insistence upon dispassionate discussion. He scandalized orthodox Protestant and Catholic alike, but he gripped the minds of his readers so forcefully that his work could not be neglected by any writer who wished to influence thought.

The first definite indication that the critical movement in France would develop along scientific lines came with the work of Fontenelle, the perpetual secretary of the Royal Academy of Sciences. One of Fontenelle's chief titles to remembrance was the importance he attached to the idea of progress, which later became an important concept in the philosophy of the Encyclopedists. In the famous literary dispute between the ancients and moderns, Fontenelle made a significant contribution to the idea of progress by upholding the cause of the moderns because of the advantage they had in making use of the experience of the ancients. But he also carried this idea into other fields. Whereas Bayle had used the Cartesian method in a deliberate effort to destroy faith and to foster scepticism, Fontenelle saw the constructive uses to which this method could be put. In his *Préface sur l'utilité des mathématiques et de la physique* (1699), he asserted that 'the geometric spirit is not so bound up with geometry that it cannot be disentangled and carried into other fields. A work of morals, of politics, of criticism, perhaps even of eloquence, will be the finer, other things being equal, if it is written by the hand of a geometrician.'[6] The order, precision, conciseness, and exactitude he noticed pervading the good books that had appeared for some time past might well owe their inspiration, he thought, to this geometric turn of thought which he could see growing rapidly in popularity.

At the same time, Fontenelle was chiefly interested in seeing the idea of progress firmly established upon a scientific foundation. Like other Cartesians, he believed that all nature was subject to laws which would be discovered by the sciences. 'Until the present', he wrote at the close of the seventeenth century, 'the Academy of Science has only taken nature in small sections. To-day we ascertain one fact: to-morrow

another, which has no relation to it.'[7] But he believed the time
would come when these separate and apparently unrelated
truths would become unified, and he looked to the mathematical sciences to help in this integration of truth. Nevertheless, the great popularizer of Descartes recognized that it was
also the age of Newton. In his *Éloge de Newton* (1727) he
pointed out that it had been the great honour of the author of
Philosophiae Naturalis Principia Mathematica (1687) to have
unified the discoveries of Kepler and Galileo by means of a
'very profound', indeed 'sublime' geometry.[8] Newton, like
Descartes, was a 'genius of the first order', and, like him also,
had been halted only by the limits of the human mind. Unlike
Descartes, however, Newton had followed the method of careful observation and painstaking effort that Bacon and other
inductive thinkers had advocated. It was obvious that in
Fontenelle's mind Descartes now had a formidable rival.
Newton was being enthroned in his stead. Experience was
winning over rationalism, and it looked as if the future would
work out in favour of the Baconian method.[9]

In his *Éloges*, Fontenelle was careful to point out whenever
possible the orthodoxy of the religious beliefs of the distinguished members of the Royal Academy of Science, whose
memory he honoured. But at the same time the cause of
science and progress that he championed was sharply at
variance with the teachings of the Church, and it could not fail
ultimately to emphasize the gap that existed between orthodoxy
and the new creed that was coming into being. However, as
long as Fontenelle and his followers kept the scientific movement on a basis of abstract speculation and scientific method,
there was relatively little that Church or State officials could
do towards stemming it. Bayle had lived in exile in Rotterdam,
and Fontenelle had been careful to avoid a conflict with the
authorities. But the fact that a movement was growing up in
opposition to authority and to orthodox beliefs meant that it
would link itself to social change at the first possible moment.
Already Fontenelle had suggested that morals and politics
were within the field of its competency.

There were indeed good reasons why men's thoughts should
have turned towards social and political reform. The magni-

ficent reign of Louis XIV had been a period of great expenditure. Added to the wastefulness of the court was the costliness of military enterprises. When Louis died in 1715, there was a staggering burden of national debt to bequeath to his successors, which kept national finances in a chaotic condition and on the verge of bankruptcy for the rest of the century. Luckless attempts at inflation through the introduction of paper money not only ruined countless individuals, but left the finances of the State in a worse position than before. A ruinous policy of borrowing was supplemented by the exhaustion of every possible means of taxation until eventually the middle classes, the working-men and the peasants gave up half their annual earnings in the form of direct taxes alone.[10] But in addition to this, there were indirect and local taxes extorted from the people by collectors. These collectors paid a lump sum to the State and then collected from the people as much over and above this sum as they could. The burden carried by the ordinary peasant became wellnigh intolerable. Half the produce of his land went to the landowner to begin with; he had to pay between thirty and forty per cent more to the government, and then he might or might not be allowed to keep ten to twenty per cent for his own use.[11] A series of better years led to a somewhat improved condition for the peasantry, but the fear of added taxation later in the century, when national finances became desperate, led to the development of a revolutionary spirit. This spirit was imbued with a bitter hatred of the nobility and the Church because both of these estates were in a much better position financially to pay, but through rank and privilege they escaped most of the taxation altogether. And when at length the *noblesse* was called upon to meet a heavier share of the taxation, the landowners extorted as much as they could from the peasants, even reviving dues that had long been in abeyance.

Against such a background, the breaking away from the creed upon which Church and State rested assumed new significance. The infusion of social reform into the intellectual aspirations of the scientific era came with Voltaire and Montesquieu, and through them the new creed received the positive elements that were to be expounded at full length by the

Encyclopedists. Neither Voltaire nor Montesquieu, however, had any thought of radical change in the social or political structure of French society. They believed that it was in the interests of an enlightened monarchy to discover the nature of the abuses that most urgently needed reforming. A great monarch who was true to his high office would foster justice and a love of liberty in his people. He would refuse to countenance intolerance, ignorance, superstition, and all the evils that followed in the train of these vices. Therefore, while they became the powerful critics of the most striking abuses of the age, they also laid at the feet of rulers the most enlightened ideas of philosophy and government that were to be found. Their methods of criticism, their ideals, and their admiration for England as the homeland of both science and liberty, gave the keynote for the great reform movement that the Encyclopedists were destined to carry forward.

Charles Louis de Secondat, Baron de Montesquieu, who belonged to the nobility of the robe, was a thinker who preferred to be known through his writings rather than through his private life and career. His interests included Newtonian science, but he had no aptitude for the metaphysics of the Cartesians. First causes seemed to him to be inaccessible, and consequently he preferred to observe fact and to reflect upon the knowledge he gained thereby. His touch with the intellectual circles was kept through the salons. Until he withdrew from public life to devote his attention to his life's work, the *Esprit des Lois*, he was a familiar figure at the salons of Mme de Tencin, Mme de Lambert, and Mme du Deffand.

In 1721, he made his first thrust in the cause of reform with the publication anonymously in Holland of his *Lettres Persanes*. The literary charm of these letters served to enhance their popularity throughout the century. But the epigram and satire which gave them literary distinction also conveyed a sharp attack upon the weak spots of French society at the close of the age of Louis XIV. Montesquieu meant the people who read the amusing comments of the two Persian travellers to come to the conclusion that perhaps the institutions and customs they admired so much were not altogether commendable to rational people. Usbek, inclined to meditation and to seek for causes, provided the moralizing element; while his friend Rica was gayer, more interested in fashionable manners, and more given to sparkling satire. Their first visit to Paris gave them much to discuss in their letters to friends at home in Ispahan and at Smyrna and Venice.

They found that the King of France was truly a remarkable person. He was the 'most powerful prince in Europe', and although he did not possess gold mines like his cousin, the King of Spain, nevertheless 'he has greater riches, because he extracts them from the vanity of his subjects',[12] a source of wealth that was far less likely to be exhausted than the gold from the King of Spain's mines. He was certainly a great magician, because he even ruled over the minds of his subjects; 'he makes them think whatever he wants.' [13] But there was another person who was equally astonishing as a magician, and he was the Pope. He made people believe that three made only one; that the bread one ate was not bread, and that the wine which one drank was not wine, and a thousand other things like that. . . . He was the chief of the Christians. He was an old idol to whom one customarily offered incense. Formerly he had been somewhat formidable, Usbek discovered, having deposed kings as easily as 'our magnificent sultans depose the kings of Irimetta and Georgia'. However, he was no longer feared. . . . But it touched the hearts of the Persian visitors to think that all these Christians were destined to end their days miserably in hell. They wondered whether there were not moral principles upon which all the world could agree, which would enable every one to be happy. Then they could leave doubtful questions of dogma to the different creeds to settle in their own way.

The future author of the *Esprit des Lois* already had a definite political philosophy. Usbek commenced the remarkable history of the Troglodites [14] in a series of letters to Mirza, in which he threw into relief the idea that the strength of the nation depended upon its virtue, and that the 'common interest' was no mere fiction, but on the contrary it was the very basis upon which the political structure had to be built. The government that was in conformity with reason held a special attraction for Usbek. 'It has seemed to me', he wrote to Rhedi in Venice, 'that the most perfect is that which attains its goal at the least cost; the kind which leads men in the way that is most in conformity with their bent and inclinations is the most perfect.' [15] Justice was always the same, but even when men saw what it was, they were liable to be led away from it because they could always see their interests better. Justice might raise her voice, but she would have trouble in making herself heard in the tumult of men's passions. In a later letter to Rhedi, Usbek made the remarkable observation that in Paris 'liberty and equality' reigned. But his remarks were satirical. 'It is said that the first in Paris is the man who has the best horses in his carriage.' A 'grand seigneur' was a man who saw the King, who talked to his ministers, who had ancestors, debts, and pensions. If he could, with all that, hide his idleness under some guise or other, he might be thought the happiest of men. In Persia, the only great people were those to whom the monarch gave some part in the government. In France, on the contrary, men were great by birth; but they had no credit. Favour was the great divinity of the French. The Minister was the grand-priest, who had plenty of victims to offer to that divinity. . . .

The Persian visitors found it rather ridiculous that every discussion of political principles should be the signal for a careful investigation of the origin of societies. If men had not formed societies, but had kept as far apart as possible, they still believed that people would ask why they did so. 'But they are born with ties that link them to each other; the son is born to take his place beside the father, and he takes it: there is society and the reason for it.' [16] They found that most legislators were narrow-minded. Chance had placed them over other men, but they consulted mainly their own prejudices and fancies. They had failed to recognize the greatness and dignity of their task, and consequently had amused themselves making puerile institutions. They made people think that laws were sacred, because there were so many formalities involved in changing them. Also legislators often made laws too subtle and followed the ideas of logicians rather than natural equity. But whatever the laws might be, they should always be followed, and should be regarded as the public conscience, to which the individual conscience should conform.

Charming and satirical, the *Lettres Persanes* showed the setting for philosophy no less than for pleas for religious toleration that suited fashionable tastes. Montesquieu's attack on the intellectual shortcomings of his age was supported in 1734 by an even more influential although less profound work, Voltaire's *Lettres Philosophiques*. In this, the specific faults of the social system of France were thrown against the background of the new scientific philosophy, which was henceforth fundamental with Voltaire and the *philosophes*. Voltaire, the brilliant satirist, dramatist, historian and *philosophe*, after whom the golden age of literature was named, had a passionate dislike for intolerance and for tyranny in any form. His witty satire made his works exceedingly popular, and consequently enabled him to wield a tremendous influence over the thought of his age. He had been imprisoned in the Bastille for a satire he had written at the expense of Louis XIV, and after a second term of imprisonment for daring to challenge an insulting member of the nobility, he went to England, where he stayed for the better part of three years. While in England, he came into contact with Pope, Congreve, Bolingbroke, and other men of letters; he became acquainted with the philosophical and deistic thought of the period, and above all with the work of Newton and Locke. He came to know something of the parliamentary system, and admired especially the personal freedom enjoyed by Englishmen, which contrasted sharply with the painful memories of his own experiences of the Bastille at home. In England there were no *lettres de cachet*; no need to fear the censor for one's satires, and there was relatively little persecution. Men of science and of letters were respected for their genius, and were not punished for their writings. Incidentally Voltaire enjoyed his own prestige in England as a literary man. Early in 1729, he was back in France; and five years later published his account of the English, the *Lettres Philosophiques*, which was immediately condemned to be torn and burned in the Palace courtyard by the common executioner as being 'scandalous, contrary to religion, good morals, and the respect due to the ruling powers'. [17]

Through Voltaire's work, English ideas and English institutions became well known to French readers. Although so close to France, England had hitherto remained relatively unfamiliar territory for the average Frenchman. But the age of reason brought about a marked change. French thinkers found stimulation in English thought and institutions, while Paris became the literary Mecca for the English as well as for the rest of the 'enlightened' world. It was the distinction of Voltaire's *Lettres Philosophiques* that through them French readers gained their first coherent account of significant phases of English life. But the *Lettres Philosophiques* were even more important for the French. They contained an eloquent plea for liberty and for toleration in France.

'It has not been without considerable cost', Voltaire wrote, 'that liberty has been established in England, and the idol of despotic power has been drowned in seas of blood; but the English do not think for one moment that they have purchased their laws at too high a price. Other nations have not had fewer troubles and have not shed less blood; but the blood they spilled in defence of their liberty has served only to enslave them the more.' [18]

The English were certainly a riddle to Voltaire. He found their mode of living crude, but somehow they enjoyed the substance of blessings that were only a shadow to nations such as his own.

'It took centuries to render justice to humanity,' he said in recounting the fight in England for the Magna Charta, 'to realize how horrible it was that the many should sow while the few reaped; and is it not a source of happiness for the human race, that the authority of those petty brigands has been extinguished in France by the lawful authority of our Sovereign and in England by that of the King and nation together?' [19]

The implications of other observations were equally obvious. In England, Voltaire observed, a peer or a churchman paid his share of the taxes in the same way as the rest of the people. All taxation was regulated by the House of Commons.

'There is no *taille*, no arbitrary poll-tax, but a real tax on lands. They were all evaluated under the famous William III. The tax remains always the same although the value of lands has increased. Thus no one is crushed, and no one has cause for complaint. The feet of the peasant are not tortured with wooden shoes; he eats white bread; he is warmly clad, and he has no need for apprehension on account of increasing the number of his flocks and herds, nor on account of covering the roof of his house with slate for fear his taxes will be increased in the following year. Here there are many peasants who have about two hundred thousand francs in income, and who do not disdain to continue cultivating the ground which has enriched them, and here they are able to enjoy the blessings of liberty.' [20]

Voltaire was an ardent champion of liberty, but in the *Lettres Philosophiques* he was also especially interested in giving an introduction to the philosophy of the Enlightenment as he had come to understand it following his visit to England, for he saw in that philosophy the real hope for the future. The truly enlightened were those whose lives were ordered in accordance with the dictates of reason, the true light of nature. False creeds, false customs, and false traditions were shutting out the light. Already the deist had set to work to discover the tenets of a natural religion, in the belief that reason could establish the fundamental truths of religion without recourse to either revelation or miracles. To Voltaire they were the 'principles of morality common to the human race', [21] for, when stripped of their dogmatic setting, it had been discovered that fundamentally the religious codes were systems of ethics. Because morality laid no claim to supernatural sanction, it could command respect where church dogmas could not. Furthermore, a system of morals was particularly valuable because it has an important function to fulfil in the social order.

Just as the watch argued the existence of the watchmaker, so the existence of the universe proved to the satisfaction of Voltaire and others the existence of a Creator. God, as First Cause, could be accepted as the author of nature; but, having created the universe in accordance with a definite plan He had left it to operate without subsequent interference. It operated in accordance with definite laws, which were both universal and invariable. Although the nature of those laws was only beginning to be discovered, God had endowed man with the gift of reason so that the laws of nature need not remain unknown. It was the work of the *philosophe*, therefore, to understand nature and to define the laws of nature as they applied to man.

There had been translations into French both of Newton's *Principia* (1687), and of Locke's *Essay concerning Human Understanding* (1690). But Voltaire was concerned, not with giving his countrymen an exposition of these works, but with showing their significance for current thought. His *Lettres Philosophiques*, followed by subsequent expositions, such as his *Eléments de la Philosophie de Newton* (1738), were therefore devoted to an understanding of the Newtonian 'philosophy', as he had come to see it in the course of his studies in England. It was no longer necessary to think of nature as an impenetrable and mysterious force, since Newton's patient study had been rewarded by the discovery of some of her profoundest secrets. With instruments such as a prism, he had discovered the nature of light; by understanding why an apple fell to the ground, he was able to formulate the law of gravitation, and to demonstrate its validity as a general law of nature. And it was of first importance to know that results such as these could be obtained, as Newton had said, by searching into things themselves, and then by formulating the 'general laws of nature by which the things themselves are form'd'.[22] Nature was, after all, just the ordinary things that men could observe and handle every day, and natural law was only the uniform way these things behaved.[23]

If, as it appeared, natural law was the harmonious working of the universe, it was only necessary to apply the scientific method to the study of man in order to discover what were the laws by which man himself was governed. In this connection, Locke was able to supplement the work of Newton, for in his *Essay concerning Human Understanding* he demonstrated that the mind could be subjected successfully to scientific investigation. But contrary to orthodox doctrine, he found that the human mind did not begin life in a state of depravity. It did not have innate ideas and dispositions, but was rather a blank sheet upon which every kind of impression could be made by the outside world. Knowledge was conveyed to it through the senses, and reason was employed in organizing and reflecting upon the various kinds of information conveyed in this manner to the mind. If, therefore, society could be brought back into harmony with the law of nature, it would be possible for the mind of man to reflect that harmony and that alone. In the meantime, there were discordant elements which kept man at war with nature. But Locke's great message to the eighteenth century was that it was possible for men, 'barely by the use of their natural faculties', to fashion their lives and their institutions in accordance with the natural order of the universe, and thereby fulfil their nature and attain happiness.

The recognition that there were discordant elements at work in society, however, constituted a serious difficulty. The doctrine that the order of nature bore the stamp of the Creator's plan, and the recognition that God had created man as part of that natural order led logically to an admission that all things must really be in harmony, as Pope had said in the *Essay on Man* (1733–4):

> Cease then, nor order imperfection name:
> Our proper bliss depends on what we blame.
>
> .   .   .   .
>
> All nature is but art, unknown to thee
> All chance, direction, which thou canst not see;
> All discord, harmony not understood;
> All partial evil, universal good:
> And spite of pride, in erring reason's spite,
> One truth is clear, Whatever is, is right.[24]

But scientific philosophy, while interested in proving the harmony of the natural order and in demonstrating how nature worked, was nevertheless not prepared to accept a fatalistic doctrine which would cut the ground from under its own feet. It was anxious to show that the age of reason could bring man back into touch with nature, from which at some time he had strayed. Consequently, while it was desirable to say that universal harmony ought to exist, it was not desirable any more than it was in accordance with common sense to regard it as already in existence. Orthodox theology had explained the existence of evil by the doctrine of original sin. Man was born wicked, and had to be redeemed. The rejection of that doctrine, however, made no difference to the fact of evil as a reality in the world. Evil existed, and therefore called for explanation. If the new philosophy was not prepared to deny its existence on the grounds that all was but part of one stupendous whole, 'whose body Nature is, and God the soul', it was obliged to fall back upon some other mode of argument while at the same time weakening the cause of reason as little as possible. Hume faced this dilemma squarely in his *Dialogues concerning Natural Religion* (written 1751; published 1779).[25] Demea and Cleanthes, representative of two opposing schools of theology, and Philo, the sceptic, followed reason unswervingly only to discover at the end that it was an 'inert principle', incapable of giving any answer to the fundamental questions of God and the meaning of life. His findings were so discouraging to the cause of reason that he locked his manuscript away in a drawer, where it remained until after his death. Instead of proclaiming the defeat of reason in the field of speculative thought, Hume turned quietly to a study of history in order to discover what the records of human experience would reveal. Others also turned to history, the store-house of human experience, to see what lessons were to be learned. There Voltaire found that of all the ages of man, only one had been clouded in darkness, but that was precisely the period during which the Christian Church had dominated the world. This, however, was the very weapon that he and the *philosophes* needed in order to drive home their attacks upon priestcraft and intolerance and to carry forward their gospel of enlightenment.

With the publication of the *Lettres Philosophiques*, the age of reason was inaugurated.[26] That which hitherto had been confined to the few leaders of thought now became the property of the ordinary reader. England had helped Voltaire to grasp the significance of the services that Newton and Locke had rendered to the cause of philosophy, and Voltaire, on his part, was eager to make known the implications of their work so that France also could reap the benefit. He had gathered together the fundamental points of the scientific philosophy, which brilliant young friends were later to use as the basis for their speculative thought.

In the meantime, the interest that Voltaire had aroused in English thought and institutions was further stimulated by Montesquieu. He also had spent several years in England preparatory to writing his *Esprit des Lois*, which was published in 1748. His visit was for the purpose of studying the political system of the only important monarchy under which liberty could really be said to exist. Upon acquaintance, his admiration for the British constitution had increased, and through his *Esprit des Lois* its virtues became a still more important consideration in subsequent political thought in France. The principles of the constitution were already known through Locke's treatises *Of Civil Government*, but Montesquieu gave vitality to them by describing their mode of operation in the life of a nation. The English system, he had found, was perpetuated through the balance of the constitution by means of the 'intermediary bodies' placed between the Crown and the people, which provided a check upon all the powers of the political organization. Honour was still the dominant virtue of the aristocratic part of the government, and it was also to be found firmly embedded in the life of the people. Montesquieu believed that England was the freest country in the world. It was free because the monarch did not have the power to tyrannize. His powers were limited by statute. Similarly the legislature was unable to encroach upon the liberty of the nation. It was 'composed of two parts. The one checks the other by the mutual privilege of veto. They are both limited by the executive power, as is the executive by the legislative body.' [27] Thus liberty was secured through the balance of powers between the King, the House of Lords and the House of Commons. Such a balance between the powers might be expected to result in a state of repose or inaction, but Montesquieu pointed out, 'they are forced to move by the inevitable march of things, but they are forced to move in concert. . . .' [28]

The *Esprit des Lois* was published at a very important moment in the history of the scientific movement, for it appeared almost on the eve of the publication of the preface to the *Encyclopédie*, the monumental work which was to be the contribution of a brilliant group of *philosophes*, led by Diderot and d'Alembert, to the cause of the Enlightenment. The political ideas of the *philosophes* were in the process of formulation. They found much that appealed to them in

Montesquieu's work, although its purport was not readily apparent. With Montesquieu, they wanted a state that would secure liberty for the individual; that was governed by laws which were the 'reasoned application of natural law'; that was tolerant, and at the same time kept guard against all encroachments of the Church in political affairs. But on the other hand, there were disturbing elements in the *Esprit des Lois* which made Helvétius advise Montesquieu in the interests of his reputation not to publish it, and caused Voltaire to criticize it adversely. In important respects it ran counter to their ideas. In the first place, Montesquieu had advocated in it a modification of the individualism of Locke's doctrine. Furthermore, instead of looking for principles which were universally applicable to all states, at all times, he had devoted his attention to the differences that could be observed in the political arrangements of the various countries. From his observations, Montesquieu had come to the conclusion that the constitutions of the different countries were particular applications of natural law, and that those applications were inherent in conditions entirely outside the control of man. In other words, if there was a universal law underlying all political societies, it did not make special prescriptions that were true for all mankind, at all times and in all places. On the whole, the *philosophes* would have preferred it if Montesquieu had not published the *Esprit des Lois*.[29]

The *Discours préliminaire* to the *Encyclopédie* appeared in 1751. It was the work of d'Alembert, and its purpose was to give a survey of the advancement of the arts and sciences since the introduction of printing. D'Alembert classified knowledge as Bacon had done more than a century earlier, and he showed the amazing extent to which the bounds of human knowledge had been extended since that time. While he criticized Descartes as a retarding influence, he observed with satisfaction that during the past thirty years his countrymen had begun to renounce Cartesianism and had turned to the scientific method of Newton. The way of the observer had triumphed over that of the metaphysician, and since that time knowledge of the sciences had progressed rapidly, and man was coming at last to understand nature.

The *Encyclopédie* was designed to meet the current interest in the sciences, which Fontenelle had done much to popularize. There were already compendiums such as Bayle's *Dictionnaire Historique et Critique* and Moreri's *Le Grand Dictionnaire Historique*, which were important in the fields of history and criticism, but there was no work devoted to the most recent scientific discoveries or to philosophical, political, and social questions. Consequently the publication of Chambers' *Cyclopedia* in 1727 aroused considerable interest in France, and André-François le Breton, a bookseller who had set up a printing-press in his home, decided to issue a French translation of Chambers' work.[30] He thereupon engaged an Englishman, John Mills, and a German, Godefroy Sellius, to undertake the translation, but after a time he had to make other arrangements. He then interested a member of the *Académie* in the project, but eventually Diderot was asked to take over the editorial duties. For more than twenty years, Diderot worked faithfully for the *Encyclopédie*, often labouring in the face of hostile criticism and bitter discouragement. D'Alembert assisted him with the editorial work until 1758, when, irritated over the reception of his article on Geneva and annoyed by constant government interference, he relinquished his duties. Despite editorial errors, such as the disproportionate length of some articles, the *Encyclopédie* was a monumental contribution to eighteenth-century letters, and its importance was recognized from the first. The whole work consisted of seventeen volumes, together with four supplementary volumes and twelve volumes of illustrations.

Authority to publish the *Encyclopédie* was given by the Chancellor d'Aguesseau on January 21, 1746. Thereupon Diderot and d'Alembert set to work on the preparation of the first volume of the *Encyclopédie, ou Dictionnaire raisonné des sciences, des arts et des métiers*, which covered the letter A, and was published on July 1, 1751. They took advantage of the golden opportunity that had been given to them to make their work an introduction to the vast field of human knowledge. Through knowledge, man could be moulded after the pattern of nature, for with Locke they believed that man was the product of the impressions implanted upon his mind by the outside world. Implant right impressions, and the goal of the age of reason would be in sight; implant the seeds of useful knowledge in men's minds, and the work of reform would be well on the way towards realization. Thus the *Encyclopédie* was a project with a highly practical purpose. The editors had no difficulty whatever in securing the co-operation of the most eminent writers and thinkers of the day, who between them could speak authoritatively on practically every topic that came under review. The first collaborators were not well-known men, although Rousseau was soon to emerge as one of the most brilliant writers of the period. Rousseau's contributions consisted of articles on music [31] and an important article on *Économie Politique*. But in the course of the next decade, most of the important men of letters wrote articles for the *Encyclopédie*. Quesnay, Turgot, and Necker wrote on political economy; Marmontel, Duclos, and the Abbé Morellet were among those who contributed articles on literary subjects; while there were also contributions from Voltaire and Montesquieu, the two outstanding literary figures of France, whose leadership the Encyclopedists proudly acknowledged. Following Montesquieu's death, an impressive eulogy of him was published in Volume V of the *Encyclopédie*, which appeared in September, 1755.* In Volume VII, published in November, 1757, an article written by Voltaire on the subject of taste appeared. This was followed by Montesquieu's fragmentary article on the same subject, which he had meant for the *Encyclopédie* but which he had not had time to finish. Together with Montesquieu's work appeared an editorial note which stated that

'the glory of M. de Montesquieu, founded on works of genius, does not require the publication of these fragments which he has left us, but they are an enduring proof of the interest which the great men of the nation have taken in this work, and it will be said in the centuries to come: Voltaire and Montesquieu also had a share in the *Encyclopédie*.' [32]

---

* This eulogy of Montesquieu was translated into English, and appeared in condensed form in the *Annual Register* of 1758 under the title of 'Anecdotes of the life of Baron Montesquieu, author of the Spirit of the Laws', from the French of M. d'Alembert. In the same issue of the *Annual Register*, a translation was given of Montesquieu's incomplete essay on *Taste*, which had been published in the *Encyclopédie*, Vol. VII, 1757.

A great enthusiasm inspired the Encyclopedists when they found the ideal channel for giving expression to their views. They saw the ills of their country vanish, once the spirit of enlightenment had had an opportunity to do its work. Unlike Montesquieu and Voltaire, however, they had no faith in attempts to educate princes to the responsibilities of their office. The shortcomings of the old order and the breakdown of old creeds upon which that order had rested encouraged them to expound their own ideas. They believed that they had found a new and positive basis for a new social order in which all men would find freedom and happiness, both of which were conspicuously absent in the existing scheme of things. It seemed to them therefore that they would render the greatest service to their contemporaries by establishing new standards to replace those which had been discredited through the advance of the scientific spirit. Consequently, they turned their attention towards an audience of less exalted rank than that to which Montesquieu and Voltaire had looked in the hope that their ideals would meet with a sympathetic response.

From the outset the Encyclopedists reflected new values, and in so doing, they crossed important bridges leading into the new world. Through the emphasis they placed upon physical science and the practical arts, they infused a sense of dignity and honour into ordinary work and thereby changed social ideals altogether. Hitherto that glory had been reserved for the heroes of the battlefield, and the saints and martyrs of the Church. Now it was to impress upon the minds of ordinary men the fact that there was dignity also in the labour of their hands. Louis Sébastien Mercier, one of the moderates in the National Assembly, and an ardent admirer of Rousseau whose works he helped to edit for the 1788–93 edition, surveyed the glorious opportunities the new régime gave the nobility as well as the ordinary man and asked with pride:

'Where will the nobles find elsewhere more actual advantages? For a miserable coat of arms, the badge of blood and misery, (they were) condemned until now to be the blind instruments of despotism, or else to suffer the most desperate poverty; to-day the vast highways of civic genius, of commerce and of all kinds of work and industry, as well as public office are open to them.' [33]

But with this change of attitude towards work, there was also a significant intellectual change. An interest in things was substituted for an interest in words; positive knowledge engrossed attention rather than verbal disputation.[34] And at last with these changes, the modern world came into existence.

The spirit of the Encyclopedists was that of practical reform through education. Social ideals compatible with an enlightened order had already been inspired by Voltaire, whose ideas were for the most part basic in the philosophy of the Encyclopedists. It had remained for them to emphasize the various aspects of those ideals, to mould them into a philosophy of progress, and to suggest the means for their application. They were accustomed to meet and discuss at length their ideas on these subjects at favourite haunts, such as the cafés or the salons, or for preference at the hospitable home of the Baron d'Holbach. Toleration, humanitarianism, the reign of law and of reason, and liberty were fundamental in their discussions as in their writings. Their attacks upon abuses were pursued with a sincerity and a disinterestedness that won them enduring credit. The evils of slavery, for instance, had been brought to their attention by Montesquieu in the *Esprit des Lois*, where he had given an account of slavery as an institution. Montesquieu's attitude, however, seemed much too aloof and temperate for the Abbé Raynal, the author of the *Histoire des deux Indes* and friend of Helvétius, d'Holbach and Mme Geoffrin. 'Montesquieu', he declared, 'could not make up his mind to treat the question of slavery seriously. In fact, it is a degradation of reason to employ it, I will not say in defending, but even in combating an abuse so contrary to all reason. . . .'[35] The Abbé Raynal's expression of passionate revolt was characteristic of the attitude of the Encyclopedists towards such abuses.

Likewise, the injustices of the social and political order fired them with a zeal for the furtherance of human happiness through every means in their power. While it was 'contrary to all reason' to allow such evils to continue, they had nevertheless to be exceedingly circumspect in the expression of their indignation and in the remedies they proposed, otherwise they could not hope to outwit the ever-vigilant government censor. Figaro's survey of the situation led to an announcement that

'provided I did not write about the authorities, or religious faith, or politics, or morality, or officials, or public bodies which were in favour, or the Opera, or other theatrical performances, or about anyone who had a claim to anything, I was at liberty to print anything—under the inspection of two or three censors.' [36]

As long as enlightened thought was kept strictly in speculative form and had no obvious application to existing conditions, it was reasonably safe. Explaining to Voltaire why there were some inferior articles in the *Encyclopédie*, d'Alembert wrote that

'no doubt we have bad articles on theology and metaphysics, but since we publish under privilege and have theologians for censors, I defy you to make them any better. There are other articles that are less exposed to the daylight, in which all is repaired. Time will enable people to distinguish what we have thought from what we have said. . . .' [37]

Thus while the thought of the Encyclopedists was cast in abstract form, it was only necessary, as d'Alembert had indicated, to read between the lines in order to discover the purport of their work. Abstract terms consequently had special implications which were sufficiently well understood to obviate the necessity for specific definition. The three terms which were central in their philosophy were reason, nature, and humanity.[38] Reason itself was an inclusive term, covering both the rational faculty in man and the judgements of right and truth at which he arrived through the exercise of that faculty. It was the supreme gift of nature to man, and it enabled him not only to master the secrets of the natural world but also to interpret the truths behind nature and humanity. For that reason, it was generally taken to imply an appeal to human as opposed to authoritarian and supernatural sanctions. The Encyclopedists made constant reference to nature as well as to reason. By nature, they meant in general that state of society which was least subject to the evils which marred actual society. For some it meant primitive society, while for others it had the Aristotelian connotation of that state in which men's capacities attained their supreme development. That which was 'natural' was generally regarded as 'right,' as most in accordance with the law of nature. An appeal to nature, therefore, implied an appeal to a standard against which actual conditions could be measured. The Encyclopedists also had much to say about humanity. It was the happiness of humanity that concerned them principally, and for the most part, the appeal to humanity implied an appeal from the established order to those principles which were developed by Helvétius and subsequent utilitarians into the doctrine of the 'greatest happiness of the greatest number'.[39] Governments and laws were judged according to the degree to which they fostered the welfare of mankind. Liberty and equality similarly assumed significance for them in relation to that social order which was based upon scientific principles.

Constant reference to these concepts implied an appeal to natural religion as opposed to orthodox doctrine, and to a social philosophy in which scientific principles and natural law were exalted at the expense of custom and established tradition. The break with the old creed was complete when the *philosophes* found a positive psychology upon which they could formulate a scientific social philosophy. They had already been able to substitute a natural religion for orthodox doctrine, while they became independent of the assumptions upon which the established order was based when Condillac supplied the principles of a materialistic psychology. This psychology gave them reason to believe that it was not only within the power of man himself to recognize and to seek his own happiness, but also that ignorance alone hindered his progress towards perfection.

Condillac's doctrine had its roots in Locke's *Essay concerning Human Understanding*, which he had interpreted first of all in his *Essai sur l'origine des connaissances humaines* (1746), but which he developed yet further in his *Traité sur les Sensations* (1754). With Condillac, all impressions made upon the mind came from the senses only, and he explained away Locke's secondary impressions on the ground that 'judgement, reflection, desires, passions, &c., are only sensation itself, which is transformed in different ways'.[40] He imagined a marble statue endowed with the various senses, the operation of each of which he observed in detail. He pointed out that a sense impression evoked the attention of the statue as soon as it entered the field of consciousness. The attention in turn noticed the kind of feeling response made by the statue. If that feeling was one of pleasure, the statue would wish to have it repeated; if it was painful, the statue would wish to avoid it. Memory played its part in the desire to have pleasant sensations repeated; while judgement compared the pleasant and the painful sensations and selected the pleasant. Ultimately, it was this desire to seek the pleasant and to avoid the painful which determined all human conduct.

Thus knowledge would indicate to man what would bring him happiness and what would terminate in painful experience. Knowledge, therefore, was of first importance since, as far as the Encyclopedists could see, ignorance alone placed a limit upon human felicity. In the pursuit of that knowledge, however, they were convinced that the most fruitful field for their investigation was to be found in following the path of Newtonian enquiry. They assumed that human nature was determined by unchanging and universal laws of nature, and that the greatest measure of happiness for mankind would be found through discovering and following those laws. Reason and the scientific method, which had conquered so many of nature's secrets in the past, they believed would help them yet further so that they could learn a great deal more concerning the laws of nature, both as they applied to the natural universe and to man. And the application of that knowledge would beyond a doubt help the human species on its way towards perfection. The dream which inspired the Encyclopedists as well as those who sympathized with their intellectual ideals was explained by Joseph Priestley, the eminent scientist who discovered oxygen, in his *Essay on the First Principles of Government; and on the Nature of Political, Civil, and Religious Liberty* (1771). Priestley pointed out that it only required a few years for a man to comprehend 'the whole preceding progress' of any one art or science, and the rest of his life, in which his faculties were 'the most perfect', could be devoted to the development of that knowledge. When any art or science grew too large for an easy comprehension, it could be subdivided.

'Thus all knowledge will be subdivided and extended; and *knowledge,* as Lord Bacon observes, being *power,* the human powers will, in fact, be enlarged; nature, including both its materials, and its laws, will be more at our command; men will make their situation in this world abundantly more easy and comfortable; they will probably prolong their existence in it, and will grow daily more happy, each in himself, and more able (and, I believe, more disposed) to communicate happiness to others.   Thus, whatever was the beginning of this world, the end will be glorious and paradisaical, beyond what our imaginations can now conceive.   Extravagant as some may suppose these views to be, I think I could show them to be fairly suggested by the true theory of human nature, and to arise from the natural course of human affairs.' [41]

Helvétius made the first important attempt to apply this dream of perfectibility through knowledge to social and political theory. He had observed the interest Montesquieu had aroused through his study of society and of political institutions, and he was sufficiently astute to realize that the circumstances of the times were such that any contribution to the scientific study of society would undoubtedly command attention. In 1751, therefore, he gave up his office as a *fermier-général* in order to devote his time to the task of writing *de l'Esprit,* which he published in 1758. In his hands, Condillac's hedonism and materialistic psychology became the basis of a doctrine of self-interest, akin to that which Mandeville had expounded in the *Fable of the Bees* (1714), and to which it was in all probability indebted.[42]   Conduct, according to Helvétius, was determined by that which was, or appeared to be, in the interests of the individual, and therefore gave him greatest satisfaction. But it was the function of the state to educate the people so that they would see their greatest good in the good of the whole community. Helvétius scorned the idea that man was born with innate tendencies either towards goodness or badness. He believed, with Locke and still more with Condillac, that sensation was the source of all knowledge. Human beings were all born with the same potentialities, and education made them what they were. He believed that the more knowledge a child had, the more likely he was to be virtuous, for through knowledge he would learn that in the long run honesty was the best policy.[43]

'To be virtuous', Helvétius declared, 'it is necessary to unite nobleness of soul with an enlightened understanding. Whoever unites within himself these gifts of nature, conducts himself by the compass of public utility. This utility is the principle of all human virtues, and the foundation of all legislations. It ought to inspire the legislator, and constrain nations to submit to his laws; because it is to this principle that all sentiments ought to be sacrificed, even the sentiment of humanity itself.' [44]

Furthermore, laws had to be referred to a single principle, he asserted in a passage that made a profound impression upon Bentham,

'such as that of the utility of the public, that is to say, of the greatest number of men submitted to the same form of government; a principle of which no one realizes the whole scope and fertility; a principle that contains all morality and legislation'. [45]

D'Holbach, the most thorough-going materialist and atheist among the Encyclopedists, accepted Helvétius' principle of utility, and joined to it Locke's doctrine that a legitimate government was that which fostered the welfare of the governed. He believed that education, good laws, and good political administration would do much towards making men happy. Nature was the ideal to which he looked optimistically. If men would seek to understand Nature and obey her laws, they would certainly find happiness.

'Nature invites man to love himself, to take care of himself and incessantly to augment the sum of his happiness; religion orders him to love only a formidable God who is worthy of hatred, to detest himself, and to sacrifice to his terrible idol the sweetest and most lawful pleasures of his heart. Nature tells man to consult his reason and to take it for his guide; religion teaches him that this reason is corrupted, that it is only a treacherous guide, given by a deceitful God in order to mislead His creatures. . . .' [46]

While d'Holbach did not believe that men were capable of self-government, he nevertheless pointed out that 'nature says to princes that they are men, and that their fancy cannot adjudicate between the just and unjust', although religion led them to believe that they were gods and that nothing in the world had the right to resist them.[47]

While Helvétius, d'Holbach, and other Encyclopedists were planning the foundations of the scientific political society that would lead men towards happiness, confident that education was the magic key that would unlock the gates to human felicity here on earth, the economists were actively engaged in attacking the basis upon which privilege in French society rested, so that they also could do their part towards ushering in the reign of science and of human happiness. They accepted Locke's doctrine that nature had scattered her riches lavishly for the benefit of all her children, and that a man had a natural right only to that amount of property which he could use himself. They wished to see taxation placed upon land, which was the primary source of wealth, and they wished to see the barriers removed from trade, so that the laws governing commerce could operate without undue hindrance. Above all, they wished to establish economic principles upon a basis of natural law, and to remove them altogether from the realm of arbitrary opinion. To this end they sought to establish a 'tableau économique' which would reduce economics to a simple matter of mathematical calculation. Thus it seemed that economics, no less than the principles of government, could be brought within the domain of science, where truth and impartial reason were competent to guide man infallibly to his proper interest and to his true happiness.

The Physiocrats and their successors in economic thought were no less optimistic regarding the future than the other Encyclopedists. No matter how fiercely storms raged about them for the boldness of their speculations and the fearlessness of their attacks upon the forces of intellectual darkness, they kept their eyes fixed upon the distant horizon, where the glowing colours of the new dawn already seemed to be visible. But the severest blow to their dreams came not from officialdom, but from within their own ranks. The cultivated Parisian society, which the Encyclopedists admired so profoundly, with its luxury and its sparkling wit, its godlessness and its wickedness, contrasted so vividly and so painfully with the simple austerity and goodness of his native Geneva, that Jean Jacques Rousseau could not forbear tearing to shreds the ideals of his friends, insisting that there could be no hope of progress towards perfection until man had been regenerated, morally and spiritually. The objectives of the Enlightenment could not be reached by the ways they advocated. Rousseau was convinced that they had placed a wrong estimate upon the competency of reason and knowledge to bring about the perfection of the human race. But he was particularly troubled because they lacked a deep and true understanding of human nature and of the springs of human action.

Although Rousseau scandalized the Encyclopedists completely by his rejection of their creed, he was just as intensely interested as they were in the reconstruction of the social and political order. And like them he believed that the problems involved in the reconstruction of society had to be met in a strictly scientific spirit. Adequate solutions to those problems called for quiet reflection and clarity of thought as well as insight. Consequently, when he came to formulate his political principles, he chose the Cartesian method which had still retained its popularity as the best method for the presentation of speculative thought. He did not overlook the newer historical method which Montesquieu had introduced. Indeed, he perhaps alone of all the Encyclopedist group had recognized the importance of Montesquieu's method, but he turned aside from it because the purpose of his *Contrat Social* was entirely different from Montesquieu's in the *Esprit des Lois*. He was in search of principles which ought to exist in a society, taking men as they were and laws as they ought to be, whereas Montesquieu had observed that which already existed, hoping to discover from a study of facts the underlying 'spirit' or principles of political institutions. And while the historical method could show the nature of political 'facts', it could not help in establishing philosophical principles of what ought to be. The Cartesian method, therefore, suited his purpose, while the historical method did not. And in the faith that right was a universal principle which bent neither to man nor to circumstances, he wrote his *Contrat Social*, just as before him his great master, Plato, had written the *Republic* in the belief that there was only one kind of justice.

Anticipating possible criticism for the rigour of his logic, Rousseau suggested in the *Émile* that people might say that he had built his edifice with wood instead of with human beings, every piece fitted so exactly into place according to rule and line. That was indeed the case, he acknowledged, but he would have his critics remember that 'right does not bend to human passions', and that it was necessary to establish 'first of all' the true principles of political right.[48] For whoever would 'pass judgement on actual governments ... must know what ought to be if he would judge what is'.[49] Until Rousseau was sure that his principles of political right were sound, he did not wish to examine what men had built upon them. But the development of those principles called for all the logical discipline and scientific method that had been the pride of the age of reason.

CHAPTER IV
ROUSSEAU, MAN AND THINKER

THAT Edmund Burke could have regarded the *Contrat Social* as of 'little or no merit', and thought of its author as an 'insane Socrates', can be explained only on the ground that the temperament, outlook, experience, and mode of thinking of the two men were so radically different that he could not see the true value of Rousseau's work. Because he admired so greatly the ranks and orders of England's social structure and the love of tradition which characterized English thought, he was quick to resent Rousseau's challenge to the class state. He unhesitatingly rejected Rousseau's title to serious consideration as a political philosopher, because he found no reason to believe that his thought was anything more than the hollow logic of a *philosophe*. Fundamentally, he could not find evidence of intellectual integrity either in what he knew of Rousseau, or in what he had read of his life in the *Confessions*. It seemed as if Rousseau's whole life was at variance with his claims to serious consideration as a moralist and a political philosopher. He believed that Rousseau was the dupe of his fantastic imagination, and that his life could be explained only on the assumption that he was 'deranged in his intellects', an hypothesis that he felt to be confirmed by the *Confessions*. The real significance of the *Confessions* escaped him entirely. Yet, rightly understood, it provided the key to the interpretation of Rousseau's thought.

The fact that Rousseau had felt the need for publishing an *apologia pro vita sua* was in itself significant. It was, in point of fact, something other than the painful 'confession general of his sins', which Burke had found so repulsive. It was Rousseau's attempt to bridge the gap between himself and his contemporaries; the attempt of the prophet to make his fellow-men understand that no matter what his shortcomings might have been, at least he had been desperately in earnest, and that he had striven to show them the light as he himself had seen it. Like his contemporaries, Rousseau had also desired to understand nature and to find the way of life that was most in accordance with its laws. But he had turned in revolt against their materialistic theories, their ideas of progress through scientific knowledge, and their calculating hedonism. Essentially a moralist and a religious thinker, Rousseau could find no system of morality in Diderot's worship of nature; no thought of a living God in their metaphysical First Cause, which d'Holbach had cast aside summarily as non-essential; and no beauty in the coldly scientific reign of law that the age of reason looked for as the hope of the future. Furthermore, he believed that it was fundamentally false to base their theories on the infinite perfectibility of mankind through reason.[1] Rousseau had no doubt that man was capable of improvement, but he was convinced that if theories were to be of any practical value, they would have to be based on an understanding of men as they were, and as they would continue to be.[2] For all these reasons, he found himself out of sympathy with his friends, and unable to accept their ideals. The inevitable outcome had been the loss of friendships that he had valued, in consequence of which he had had to follow his own path in loneliness.

Apart from the solitude that had been forced upon Rousseau by the great divergence between his views and those of his friends in the Encyclopedist group, he was by nature a 'solitaire', and his unusual upbringing had increased rather than diminished his tendency to loneliness. His mother had died when he was born in Geneva on June 28, 1712, and the delicate infant was left to the care of his temperamental father and of an aunt. Until the age of ten, he lacked almost entirely the companionship of children of his own age, and in his isolation the lonely Jean Jacques built for himself an imaginary world far from reality.

In this world he found a retreat when the harsh contacts with society vexed his sensitive spirit beyond endurance. He had never been schooled to face difficulties and master them. Instead he found it easier to run away, as he did from his apprenticeship because, as he put it, his master had cast 'a shadow over my radiant childhood'. He was an undisciplined spirit, unsuited to the monotony of routine, restless and longing for change, and dreaming of some ideal good while rebelling against the real and imaginary wrongs of the existing situation.

In conformity with the loneliness and sensitiveness of his nature, his interests and occupations were those of the recluse. Books and music had an irresistible attraction for him, and they carried him into the pure air of art where he felt that he could breathe freely. At the home of Mme de Warens, he had ample opportunity to develop his intellectual pursuits. Mme de Warens was an admirer of Pierre Bayle, and through her interest in him, Rousseau early became acquainted with the highly influential *Dictionnaire* of the great free-thinker. When at length he settled down to study seriously, he devoted his attention to mathematics, history, science and politics. He came into close touch with the philosophy of the Enlightenment through M. de Conzié, one of his music pupils who had become interested in him. The music lessons were usually spent in discussing literature and philosophy. It was M. de Conzié who placed in his hands Voltaire's *Lettres Philosophiques*, thereby bringing him into contact with the intellectual horizons of his contemporaries. Together they read everything they could find of Voltaire's. 'The taste which I formed for this kind of reading', Rousseau wrote, 'filled me with a desire to write with elegance, and I tried to imitate the beautiful word-painting of this author with whom I was so charmed.' [3] For many years he looked to Voltaire with the profoundest respect, not only on account of his literary style, but also because Voltaire reflected the scientific and philosophical aspirations of the Enlightenment.

But in religion, Rousseau and the *philosophes* trod divergent paths. At times his earlier Calvinistic training showed itself in a deep concern for the eternal salvation of his soul. But these were only passing moods. It was in communion with nature that his soul found God. The beauty of nature touched him profoundly, and gave him a deep sense of reverence for God, a reverence that his contemporaries had transferred from the Deity to science. He liked to rise before dawn and go out onto a beautiful road that skirted the woods near by. Here, as he walked in the beauty of the dawn, he would pray, and then his prayers were no mere repetition of words without vital meaning. They were the sincere aspirations of his heart towards the Author of the nature which stretched before his eyes in all its magnificence. For he loved to contemplate God in the majesty of His works.[4]

Rousseau had been helped to organize his ideas regarding religion and life by the Abbé Gaime, the prototype of the *vicaire savoyard*, whom he met while serving for a time as lackey in the home of Mme de Vercellis in Turin. The Abbé was a cultured man, and he recognized that the youthful Rousseau possessed unusual talents. But he quickly discovered also that he was living in an unreal world and had no sense of the real values in life. He therefore tried to turn Rousseau's altogether exaggerated admiration for worldly things into a saner view of life. But he accomplished even more, for he succeeded in arousing the young man's self-critical faculties, which was more effective than anything else in giving him a truer sense of values. In succeeding years Rousseau's deep consciousness of his own shortcomings, of what he called his *grand penchant à dégénérer*, haunted him and caused him to turn with great seriousness to the fundamental questions of religion and philosophy in the hope of finding that which would give him peace of mind.

His urgent desire to penetrate through the mysteries of the universe to the eternal truth relating to God and man impelled him to undertake an ambitious programme of studies. But in addition, he believed that intense study would be the best way of equipping himself for a vocation so that he could take his rightful place as a useful member of society. In reality, he went far beyond the bounds of study that would be required for a vocation and equipped himself for the important work he was to undertake later in life. He roamed through French and Latin literature, and studied rationalistic philosophy from Descartes onward in the hope of finding argument that would fortify his belief in God and in the goodness of natural forces. The dreamer responded eagerly to all idealistic thought and was at his happiest in the search for first principles.

One of his favourite authors was the Jansenist disciple of Malebranche, Father Bernard Lamy. Rousseau found great pleasure in reading and re-reading Lamy's *Entretiens sur les Sciences* (1742). Lamy believed strongly in the natural goodness of man. 'We are the work of God,' he wrote in the discourse entitled *Idée de la logique.* 'Therefore we have no ground for believing that our nature is bad.' [5] But having been made for God 'we should not occupy our minds with anything less than God. The first truth ought to be the object of all our thoughts, and the sovereign good that of the impulses of our hearts.' [6] He asserted also that 'heaven and earth instruct us better than books, and without a profound knowledge of theology we can love God more than the most learned can'. [7] This was exactly what Rousseau wanted to believe. From the Abbé Prévost's *Cleveland* (1732) he learned in addition that nature was always pure. 'I was convinced', Prévost wrote, 'that the simple promptings of nature, when not corrupted by evil habits, are never opposed to innocence. They do not require repression, but simply to be directed by reason.' [8]

Gradually the central thoughts of his own doctrine became firmly implanted in his mind. Many of the works which had impressed him most of all reflected the thought of Plato. Fénelon's *Les Aventures de Télémaque* (1699) had presented a utopian society that had much in common with Plato's *Republic.* Father Lamy had also seriously recommended a study of Plato's works, though with the warning that they should not be read too early.

'We see things in Plato which are very similar to our own religion,' he had written. 'He devoted himself to abstract sciences such as geometry, which take him away from material things and make him better fitted to consider spiritual things. Also he has spoken most worthily of God, of the immortality of the soul and of its spiritual nature. His ethics is very elevated and detached from material things; besides which he speaks divinely, and by the force of his words as well as by that of his reasonings, he inspires a love of truth. . . .' [9]

Not satisfied to know the 'divine Plato' through the authors who admired him so profoundly, Rousseau had to know the wisdom of Socrates and of Plato at first hand. And henceforth, the 'divine Plato' was his guide.

In the spring of 1740, Rousseau went to Lyons to become tutor to the two sons of M. de Mably. One of the first things he did was to draw up a *Projet pour l'éducation de M. de Sainte-Marie*, in which he outlined his ideas for the education of the de Mably boys. This *Projet* reflected much that his own experience had taught him, and much that he had gathered from authors he had been studying, notably Montaigne. It was also strongly reminiscent of the doctrine of education he had found in Plato's *Laws*. True to his views as a moralist, Rousseau believed that the first function of education was the development of character. After giving details of his proposed programme and method, he concluded by announcing that if he kept his position long enough, he would venture to instruct his pupils in ethics and the laws of nature, using Grotius and Pufendorff as his authorities, 'because it is fitting that a good and intelligent man should know the principles of good and evil, and the foundations upon which society rests'.[10] The introduction of Grotius and Pufendorff into his *Projet* was no less significant than the influence of Platonic doctrine. It pointed to the fact that his studies in political philosophy had been extensive, and that already he was profoundly interested in authors from whom he learned much that was to become fundamental in his own doctrine of political obligation. Hugo Grotius, the author of the highly influential *De Jure Belli et Pacis* (1625), whom Rousseau later criticized severely for his error in inferring 'the right from the fact',[11] had favoured the doctrine of popular sovereignty, although he placed the supreme power in the hands of a prince who was expected to recognize a moral obligation towards the people. Through Barbeyrac's French edition of *Les devoirs de l'homme et du citoyen tels qu'ils sont préscrits par la loi naturelle*, which had been among the books he had found in his room at Mme de Warens' home, Rousseau had come to know the thought of the important German thinker, Samuel Pufendorff. In this work, Pufendorff carried the doctrine of popular sovereignty further than Grotius, because he desired to place limitations upon the powers exercised by the prince in the state. He developed the idea of the general will as the true essence of sovereignty, and consequently his ideas assumed particular significance for Rousseau.[12]

With the passing of the years Rousseau's interests turned

more and more definitely to the problems of political philosophy. He had found intellectual stimulus in the authors he studied, but in addition he had come into immediate contact with the oppression suffered by the peasants of France. On one occasion, while on the way towards Lyons, he stopped at a peasant's hut and asked for food. He was told that skim-milk and coarse barley bread were all that the peasant had to offer. As he was famished, he was glad even of that. But after a while, the peasant became more communicative and offered his guest more tempting fare. When Rousseau offered to pay, the peasant's distress became apparent immediately. He explained that he had to hide his good food and wine from the tax-collectors, otherwise he would be taxed until he was really as poor as he seemed to be. Rousseau was deeply impressed by the episode.

'It became the germ of an unquenchable hatred in my heart for the torments which this unhappy people had to endure and for their oppressors. . . . I left his house full of pity and indignation, deeply deploring that this beautiful country upon which nature had lavished her gifts was the prey of barbarous toll-collectors.' [13]

No such thing existed in Geneva, and consequently the grim realities attached to the system struck him all the more forcibly when he actually saw what was happening in France.

In Lyons he had made friends with M. Bordes, a member of the Academy of Lyons and with a surgeon, M. Parisot. After leaving, he wrote them both letters in verse. To M. Bordes, he spoke with evident satisfaction of the fact that he was a 'proud republican'; that he despised the rich to whom one had to cringe in return for patronage, and that his praises were reserved for those who lived simple lives and were discriminating in the customs they adopted. Many pompous discourses had appeared on the happiness of poverty, which seemed to him to have been brought forth from the bosom of abundance. There could be no wisdom where misery reigned, and under the weight of hunger, crushed merit would allow virtue to perish. To M. Parisot, he told how he had been asked to fulfil his duty as a citizen of Geneva ; to honour the great, the magistrates and kings, without undue humility; to cherish his fellow-men, and to obey the laws.

'I was taught that I had a right to participate in the supreme power; although an insignificant citizen, I was nevertheless a member of the sovereignty; that it was my duty to uphold this noble right with a courageous heart and a wise spirit; and that liberty, the precious gift of Heaven, was only a fatal scourge for the wicked.' [14]

Although the Swiss lived in humble obscurity, freedom reigned within their walls.

'We have no knowledge of proud insolence, no glittering titles, no unjust power; wise representatives, chosen by our own direct vote, judge of our controversies, watch over our laws. Diplomacy is not the pillar of our republic; justice is our only policy; all classes, differing without being unequal, retain severally the rank that has been accorded them. Our chiefs, our magistrates, simple in dress, without luxury or gilding, are not lost to view in the crowd, but distinguish themselves by their virtue. ., .' [15]

The political order of Geneva began to appeal to him with a new force. He liked to think that in the little republic there was a reign of law to safeguard the rights and privileges of the citizens and that in a real sense there was freedom for the Genevans. He also liked to think that Geneva expected its citizens to live virtuous lives and that it was glad to reward meritorious service.

By 1742, Rousseau had settled in Paris. He had failed miserably as a tutor, yet his experience had been invaluable. He had made friends not only with MM. Bordes and Parisot, but also with members of the de Mably family and with the young Condillac, who was to become the leading exponent of Locke's psychological principles, and life had been pleasant when he enjoyed their friendship. He had come to Paris in the hope of persuading the Academy to accept his scheme for musical notation. Fontenelle had received him graciously, and Rousseau had been permitted to present his scheme before a meeting of the members of the Academy. He had also made the acquaintance of Diderot, whose interest in music and literature was later to establish a firm basis for friendship between the two men.

His hopes for a brilliant career suddenly brightened in 1743. He was appointed secretary to M. Montaigu, the ambassador to Venice, and he set out to undertake his duties with the highest hopes. He had an excellent opportunity of seeing the inside workings of diplomacy, and he realized perhaps for the first time the importance of politics in human affairs. Until his visit to Venice, his thoughts had been concerned very largely with the attainment of the good life. He had paid some attention to the function of education in the fostering of virtue, and through virtue, of happiness. But the Socratic dialogues had impressed upon his mind the fact that true virtue was to be learned through the discipline of society. And as he reflected upon the thoughts that were uppermost in his mind, he came to the conclusion that ultimately everything depended upon the political organization. It seemed to him therefore that his logical starting-point as a moralist and educationalist would be with the principles of political philosophy. Given the right kind of state, man's natural goodness could be trained to develop into virtue.

'I had seen', he wrote in the *Confessions*, 'that fundamentally everything depended upon the political order, and that however one might look at it, no people would ever be anything else but what the nature of their government made them. Thus that great question of the best possible government appeared to me to reduce itself to the following: What is the nature of a government fitted to form the people which is most virtuous, most enlightened, wisest and best, taking this last term in its widest sense? I believe that question itself was closely bound up with this other question, although it was somewhat different: What is the government which, by its nature, is always nearest the law? Thence what is law, and a series of problems of similar importance.' [16]

He planned a work that would cover the vast range of problems that these thoughts opened up. It was to be his *Institutions Politiques*.

He had not done much more than think out the scope of his work when troubles with M. Montaigu led to his return to Paris towards the close of 1744. Bitter indignation at the injustice of his treatment caused him to seek redress, which was not forthcoming from officialdom. Neither could he find cordiality from the lady who had been mainly instrumental in obtaining his appointment for him. Deeply offended, he had written to her,

'I thought you were just; you belong to the nobility and I should have remembered that. I should have understood that it is unbecoming of me, a foreigner and a plebeian, to make complaints against a nobleman. Have I ancestors or titles? Is justice without a title of nobility justice at all? . . . And these ancestors of whom people boast so loudly, who were they? They were men without position, without fortune, my equals; they had ability and made names for themselves; but nature, which fills life with the good and the bad, has also given them worthless descendants, whose fatuity goes so far that they cannot appreciate those who are the equals of their forefathers. . . .' [17]

The futility of his 'just' complaints kindled in Rousseau's soul 'a feeling of indignation against our foolish social order', [18] which sacrificed the true welfare of the state as well as justice to a so-called system. With thoughts such as these smouldering in his mind, and with the infinitely attractive picture of the more just political order of Geneva heightening the contrast with present injustices, Rousseau set to work to pick up the threads of his life in Paris once more. He began revising his opera, *Les Muses Galantes*, and soon undertook other work as well in order to make sufficient money to pay his debts and also to meet obligations that he was soon to assume. For he had not been long at his lodgings in the Quartier Latin before he met Thérèse le Vasseur, the humble girl from Orleans, whom he shielded from the merciless teasing of others at the dinner-table. Thus Thérèse entered his life, to give him much-needed comfort and solace, but also to add to his perplexities. And despite the fact that he longed passionately for freedom, Rousseau undertook the duties of secretary to Mme Dupin and her stepson, M. Francueil, in order to meet his new obligations.

At the same time, he began to show his interest in the literary world. He re-established friendship with Diderot, and before long they had made a standing engagement to meet once a week for dinner, when they could devote themselves to the congenial occupation of discussing subjects of mutual interest. Diderot at the time was interested in the neo-Platonism and the doctrine of moral sense to be found in Shaftesbury's *Characteristics* (1708), and he was engaged in writing his *Pensées Philosophiques* (1746), in which he gave expression to religious scepticism that was fast approaching atheism. But he was soon to turn from these interests to devote his attention to the great *Encyclopédie*, of which he was to become editor.

Condillac, who had been invited to join them for dinner, had just prepared to publish his *Essai sur l'origine des connaissances humaines*, and he, like Diderot, found scepticism in harmony with the materialistic psychology which he had accepted from Locke's *Essay*. Beyond some work on music, Rousseau was not preparing anything of consequence for immediate publication. He kept prominently before his thoughts, however, his ambitious plan for the *Institutions Politiques*, although he was careful to preserve the strictest silence on the subject. Nevertheless, his friends recognized him as an authority on political philosophy, and in that direction as well as in music, he was to contribute his share to the vast project that was already being planned. While Rousseau found the conversation of his radical friends stimulating, and while he joined with them at the home of Baron d'Holbach, where every imaginable subject was discussed *en philosophe*, he was fully aware of the fact that he could never accept their sceptical outlook. Indeed, their arguments merely served to intensify religious convictions that were already assuming fundamental importance in all his reflections. 'That moral justice which seems to the philosophers a presumption against Providence', he wrote later in the *Émile*, 'is to me a proof of its existence.' [19]

Rousseau clung desperately to his religious faith. His moral nature weakened when faced with the dilemma in which he found himself when Thérèse gave birth to a child. It was the ordinary practice of the day to send unwanted children to foundling homes, and Rousseau had listened to men telling of how these homes had solved their problems for them. Unable to cope with circumstances that seemed unpropitious for rearing children, Rousseau resolved to abandon his child also at the *Enfants Trouvés*. But in spite of all his sophistry, and in spite of the fact that his other children were subsequently consigned to the same fate, his conscience troubled him to such a degree that he could not escape from its harsh judgements. In genuine need, therefore, and in the depths of his distress, he turned to religion for help. He reflected upon the teachings of Father Lamy, and convinced himself with all the sincerity of his nature, that man's nature was good, and that conscience was its natural guide. If man would obey his conscience, he would be both good and free. And from Lamy his thoughts turned back to Plato, whom in his sophistry he cited as the authority for the abandonment of his children to the state,[20] but from whom he had also learned profound truths. While soul-struggles had not disturbed the speculative thought of his friends, Rousseau was impelled to seek for the deeper realities of life in order to find that which alone could give him peace of mind. Thus out of the problems of his own life a profounder understanding of life itself began to emerge, which gradually coloured the philosophical thought that was slowly becoming organized in his mind. The questions that had suggested themselves to him while in Venice were never far from the surface of his thoughts. He was preoccupied with finding a solution to the problem how political institutions could be readjusted so that they would further, instead of retard, the good life. In terms of political philosophy, this involved the statement of political principles that would foster institutions which were in harmony with man's nature. Plato had impressed upon him not only the fact that life in society was man's natural medium, but also that the attainment of true virtue depended largely upon the discipline of society. But as things actually existed, Rousseau knew that the forces of society were tending to distort rather than to perfect man's nature. Unless there could be impartial justice, there could be neither happiness or contentment, because the citizens would have to suffer the sting of cruel injustices, even as he himself had done. Furthermore, unless there could be some readjustment of the social order, there was grave danger that the misery induced by poverty and the grind of oppression would crush all love of virtue out of the hearts and minds of the citizens. He knew from experience that virtue had fled from the highly artificial society of Paris, where vice and luxury now flourished. But he also knew that the ordinary people he had met on his travels through the country were simple and good. Nevertheless, he had seen forces at work which were liable to crush them in misery, and consequently would kill their love of virtue. And to crush all impulse towards virtue out of them was as far as tyranny could carry its iniquitous work.

In the face of these problems, the theories of the Encyclopedists seemed hopelessly inadequate. Fundamentally they were unable to help because they had not learned to know human nature as it actually was. It seemed to Rousseau that their ideas were not only based on a superficial view of human nature, but that they were also purely theoretical. The *philosophes* had complete faith in the ideals of the Enlightenment, and they believed that man would choose virtue because it was in his interests to do so. They also believed that enlightened governments would seek the happiness of the governed because it was also in their interests to do so. But at the same time, none of them was concerned primarily with the formulation of a systematic political philosophy. For the most part, they were content to make incidental applications of their principles to political thought.

In 1748, however, Montesquieu's *Esprit des Lois* was published, and in it Rousseau found an important contribution to political philosophy. He was brought face to face with the doctrine of Locke, and with the author's great admiration for the British constitution. But he found, in addition, a significant corrective to his own political philosophy. For Montesquieu showed him the world of political 'fact', the world that was less familiar to him since he had devoted his attention mainly to the subjective aspects of political philosophy. Moreover, except for the very brief glimpse he had had of political life while in Venice, the political world in which the legislator worked was inaccessible to him. Through his studies in classical philosophy he had learned to regard the state as an organic whole, and consequently had invested it with a degree of significance that had been notably lacking in individualistic theories. But while he was beginning to define more clearly the functions of the state in the furtherance of the welfare of the individual, he did not yet attach sufficient significance to the elements of which the life of the state was composed. He came to see customs, manners and traditions in a new light. He saw them through Montesquieu's work, not as the hampering survival of outworn beliefs, as the Encyclopedists were accustomed to regard them, but as the natural expression of community life, and he saw in the legislative systems of the different countries the expression of the varying ideals and aspirations of the different peoples. He learned to recognize that all these factors were themselves conditioned by physical conditions over which the political philosopher had no control. The empire of climate, in the language of Montesquieu, was the most important of all empires. The locality in which a community was settled determined the nature of its daily pursuits, and therefore its interests and its customs. The physical constitution of the individuals who composed the different communities was in its turn determined by the warmth or rigour of the climate. All these factors could be found reflected in the spirit of the laws which the different communities had adopted. The empire of climate was so important that the political philosopher would ignore it at his peril.

But of equally great importance to Rousseau was the stress that Montesquieu had placed upon the relative nature of political principles. According to Montesquieu, political principles were not absolute and universal, true for all peoples, at all times, and in all places. They were relative to circumstances. Consequently, the liberty that Rousseau believed was the birthright of every one, he now found was 'not the fruit of all climates'.[21] Rousseau had therefore either to abandon his search for absolute and universal principles, or else to carry them as far as he could, and he realized clearly that if they were to be of significance in actual societies, they would have to bend at all times to that 'empire of climate' that Montesquieu had called the greatest of all empires.

But in spite of the fact that Montesquieu's contribution to political thought came at so opportune a moment for Rousseau, and that its importance for him could not be overestimated, it seemed to Rousseau that Montesquieu had not dealt with the problem that was ultimately of fundamental importance to political philosophy. He had confined himself to an observation of that which already existed, hoping to discover from a study of facts the underlying 'spirit' or principles of political institutions. But while the historical method could show the nature of political 'facts', it could not help in establishing philosophical principles of what ought to be, in which Rousseau was primarily interested. The *a priori* method was more suited to the purely speculative thought. Yet at the same time

Rousseau recognized that the principles he was thinking out would have to be revised in the light of Montesquieu's teaching. All of a sudden, Rousseau saw the significance of his thoughts, and awoke to a realization of the great destiny that lay before him. Diderot was in prison in Vincennes, and on a hot October day in 1749, Rousseau set out to visit him. On the way he began reading the *Mercure de France*, and saw the announcement of a prize to be offered by the Academy of Dijon for a discourse on the subject: 'Whether the progress of the sciences and the arts has helped to corrupt or to elevate morals.' From his youth onwards, Rousseau had often wondered why all men were not good, honest, and happy, as it seemed to him they were intended to be by nature. While he admired the progress of human intelligence, he was puzzled to observe the 'increase' of social miseries. It seemed to him that there must be a hidden opposition between the constitution of man and the order of society. The thought was an intuition rather than a clear and logical judgement.[22] Now that intuitive thought suddenly illuminated his mind; he saw in all the vividness of sharp contradiction the two sides of truth. He saw on the one hand, mankind making itself miserable through the abuse of its inventive capacities and of its culture, and on the other hand he saw the inexorable forces of society at work that could either crush man or else become his ally. The discourse would give him an opportunity to denounce the culture his friends thought so admirable, but which he knew to be full of evil also because it reflected false values. Nature, which reflected true values for mankind, was the ideal he would set up in antithesis to civilization.

Rousseau's discourse was awarded the prize, and he became famous for the brilliance of his paradoxes and the beauty of his style. His friends were pleased, but a little startled when they realized that he had been intensely serious in his attack on civilization and modern culture. An attack on modern civilization was indeed amusing and *piquant*, but a little naïve if coming seriously from the pen of a *philosophe*. What the *philosophes* did not realize was that it was the prophet of nature making war upon them, and that if hitherto his voice had been unknown, it would not be an unfamiliar sound in their ears for the future. Although the central theme of the discourse was relevant to the main trend of Rousseau's thought, it was not the most important aspect of his ideas. It was a necessary step towards the breaking down of values which he conceived to be wrong, despite the fact that they counted for much with his Encyclopedist friends.

Having taken the initial step, Rousseau had now to begin to achieve his life's work. Some of his friends were brilliant thinkers and writers, but they cultivated an air of scientific detachment. There was no room for detachment in Rousseau's mind; he showed that he was completely in earnest. His brilliance as a writer at once brought him the fame for which his soul had always longed. But suddenly it became meaningless. The work he had to do was of far greater importance. And although he stained his character at this time through deeds that humanity has found it hardest of all to understand or condone, nevertheless his constant awareness of his great *penchant à dégénérer* was leading him steadily toward a more profound understanding of the forces that were at work in the human mind and soul, and his knowledge made him grasp out toward the good. For he had discovered that the forces of regeneration were at work in the good and the right. His worship of the God of nature had brought to him not only a sense of peace, but a deep love for the beauty and simplicity that characterized all nature. And his work was fundamentally to see whether the pursuit of the good and the right would not bring back beauty and simplicity, and with them happiness, into the lives of human beings.

The success of his discourse kept Rousseau busy not only answering questions raised by his critics, but also in modifying and clarifying his thought. He tried to make it clear that he had not intended to condemn the advancement of the arts and sciences. His message as a moralist was that man's character had suffered through getting away from the state of nature. A second discourse carried forward the destruction of false ideas, in order to prepare the way for the constructive thought that was to follow. In the *Discours sur l'inégalité parmi les hommes* (1755), Rousseau showed that if, in the golden ages of the past, there had been a 'natural' man, he was a simple individual who had lived in the woods, and who was well able to provide for his few wants through his own exertions. He was both happy and carefree, and wasted no thought on the morrow. The 'noble' savage breathed only repose and liberty; he wished only to live and to stay idle. Man in society, on the other hand,

'is always active, always sweats, hurries, torments himself incessantly to seek still more laborious occupations; he works himself to death. . . . He pays court to the great whom he hates and the rich whom he scorns; he spares nothing to obtain the honour of serving them; he boasts proudly of his own baseness and of their protection; and proud of his slavery, he speaks with disdain of those who have not the honour of sharing it. . . .' [23]

There was in man an impulse toward perfectibility, which made impossible any 'return' to the state of the 'natural' man. In his delusion, man had thought he was improving his condition by developing the arts and sciences, but he had merely forged chains for himself. And the man who first thought of enclosing a plot of land, and of saying that it was his, was the true founder of society, the real 'enemy' of mankind. The accumulation of wealth had followed, and in the mad pursuit of his false gods, man had paved the way for the injustices beneath which he now found himself crushed. Rousseau's pessimistic thoughts concluded with the observation that it was 'manifestly contrary to the law of nature, however defined, that a child should command an old man, that a fool should lead a wise man, and that a privileged few should gorge themselves while the starving multitude is in want of the necessities of life'. [24]

With the publication of the *Discours sur l'inégalité*, Rousseau's literary reputation was established beyond all dispute. Voltaire mockingly thanked him for his 'new book against the human race', [25] while he was praised and ridiculed in turn by his critics.

The dedication of the *Discours* was to the Republic of Geneva. Rousseau paid graceful tribute to his native land by describing the characteristics of the country in which he could wish to have been born.

'I should have wished to be born in a country in which the interest of the Sovereign and that of the people must be single and identical; to the end that all the movements of the machine might tend always to the general happiness. . . . I should have wished to live and die free: that is, so far subject to the laws that neither I, nor anybody else, should be able to cast off their honourable yoke. . . .'[26]

He counselled his fellow-countrymen to allow 'equity, moderation and firmness of resolution to continue to regulate all your proceedings, and to exhibit you to the whole universe as an example of a valiant and modest people, jealous of their honour and of their liberty. . . .'[27]

Geneva was much in Rousseau's thoughts in 1754, when he wrote the dedication to the *Discours sur l'inégalité*. He had praised it so consistently to Diderot and Grimm that they were coming to take an interest in it as a shining example of constitutional government, fit to be set beside England, which represented the ideal government for all who loved liberty. Geneva had become the model for the *Contrat Social*, the first draft of which was already being written out, and it had not been far from his thoughts when he wrote his article on *Économie politique* for the *Encyclopédie*. Furthermore, during the year 1754, Rousseau had planned to visit his native city once more. While there, he had not only familiarized himself with the details of the constitution and government of Geneva, but he had also formally renounced the Roman Catholic Church, and had been received back into the communion of the Church he had forsaken in his youth. When he returned to Paris, he was entitled to call himself once more a *citoyen de Genève*, a title of which he was exceedingly proud, and which he renounced only when his country had joined in persecuting him following the publication of his *Émile* and *Contrat Social*.

For a long time Rousseau had longed for the peacefulness of the country, where he felt that he could carry through the ambitious projects that he had planned. His life had become exceedingly busy, and he was beginning to feel the strain. Moreover, the great divergence between his ideas and the ideals of his friends had aroused jealousies which were beginning to be reflected in painful episodes. But away from it all in the solitude of the country, he believed that he could think quietly, and could expand freely in sympathy with the beauty and serenity of nature. In the faith that

Nature never did betray
The heart that loved her, [28]

Rousseau believed that he could regain his personal integrity and could cast off the evil that had come into his life in Paris and had brought him much intense suffering. Mme d'Epinay, a friend of M. Francueil, had offered him a quiet retreat a few miles from Paris. It had the advantage of being away from the city, and yet was not far enough away to cut him off from the copying upon which he relied for a livelihood, nor yet from those friends whom he cared to see. In April, 1756, therefore, he moved with Thérèse to 'The Hermitage', near Montmorency, and began to readjust his life once more.

There was much work at hand to claim his immediate attention. Saint-Lambert had written asking him how far he had progressed with his work on Saint-Pierre. Two years earlier, Rousseau had been urged by Mme Dupin and M. de Mably to undertake a critical revision of the voluminous works of the Abbé de Saint-Pierre, the great believer in perfectibility and one of the earlier utilitarians. Rousseau had undertaken the work because he was deeply interested in the subjects with which Saint-Pierre had dealt. A project for perpetual peace in Europe gave him an opportunity to express his hatred of war and the miseries it entailed, a theme that Kant followed up in his even more famous *Zum ewigen Frieden* (1795). Furthermore, Saint-Pierre had advocated federations of small states, rather than powerful empires, and had also condemned the folly of monarchs, sentiments with which Rousseau had profound sympathy. But while Rousseau enlarged upon the advantages that were to be gained through the development of a public opinion that would grow from the interest of the citizens in the affairs of their state, he had also learned enough from the practical viewpoint of Locke and Montesquieu to realize that Saint-Pierre's idea of splitting up great nations into small republics was impossible,[29] and he criticized him accordingly.

In a few weeks, Rousseau had completed all that he was ever to write on the subject of Saint-Pierre's projects. Then he began to wait impatiently for visits from Diderot and other friends in Paris, visits that Diderot delayed so long that Rousseau's suspicions were thoroughly aroused. He feared that

Grimm was trying to replace him in Diderot's confidence, as he had done with Mme d'Épinay. The pleasant visits of the young Deleyre, who came to 'The Hermitage' frequently in order to seek Rousseau's advice and help, and who brought news of Rousseau's friends, were not sufficient to give him back peace of mind. Also Rousseau took alarm when Deleyre expressed concern for him and suggested coming with Diderot to take him back to Paris. He feared that there was some plan afoot to interfere with his affairs, which he was quick to resent. And instead of making progress with the important work he had thought of undertaking, he spent his time dreaming of imaginary people who would not betray friendships, and of lovers who would not become jealous. He began a series of letters from St. Preux to the Julie of his imagination, in which he poured out his surcharged emotions and built around these characters a story that fitted into his own conception of human loyalties. Incidentally he gave expression to his intense dislike for the city, and protested vigorously against the levity with which the duties of marriage were regarded by contemporary French society. Mme d'Épinay claimed some of his time, and distracted him from his unhappiness that had been caused by misunderstandings, distance from his friends, and suspected interference in his personal affairs. At times she was accompanied by her sister-in-law, Mme d'Houdetot, with whom Rousseau promptly fell deeply, passionately in love. But he had to follow the difficult path of renunciation, for Mme d'Houdetot grieved for the absent Saint-Lambert, the lover to whom she remained loyal. Under the circumstances, there was nothing for Rousseau to do but to respect that loyalty. As they wandered together in the woods of Montmorency, he listened to her as she poured out her love for Saint-Lambert, and echoes of the story of his own unrequited love for the lady in whom he saw his Julie reverberated through the closing part of his *Nouvelle Héloïse*.[30] The completed work was thus a mixture of reality and of the sentimental creations of his own imagination.

Out of what seemed a painful and unhappy digression that culminated in a stormy break with his Encyclopedist friends, however, Rousseau had gained a truer insight into those forces which made for nobility of mind and soul. He had learned that his respect for Mme d'Houdetot had imposed restraints upon him and that in accepting those restraints, he had been able to rise above his weaker nature to self-mastery. This fact had a profound significance for him. He realized at last that in the autonomy of the human will was to be found true liberty. And if complete obedience to the rules which the will imposed was the fundamental condition for individual liberty, it seemed to him that complete obedience to the general will, or to the rules of civil association, was the secret of political liberty for mankind. And the ideal body politic was the one which embodied those rules most completely in its fundamental law. For such a body politic would be free in the truest sense of the term; it would have no master, and would be governed only by the conditions of civil association. When he discovered the full significance of that final truth, he was ready to continue his life's work. The *Émile* and the *Contrat Social* unfolded themselves readily into the pattern of his thought.

The final step forward in his political thought was accompanied by an increasing interest in the application of his theory to actual political conditions. He could see no hope for freedom so long as the 'tyrannical' political régime under which he lived retained its stranglehold on France. But once there was a possibility of reorganizing the political structure, he believed that the doctrine of the autonomy of the will would resolve the major problems that confronted the modern state.

When his doctrines were challenged, Rousseau turned aside from the analytical method of the *Contrat Social* to the method of Montesquieu and the historical school, in order to show the way in which his political principles applied to the constitutional history of his own country. Thus in the *Lettres de la Montagne* (1764), he entered the field of practical politics and showed by his clear grasp not only of principle but also of the exceedingly intricate detail of political fact that he was completely master of the situation. And this, as Vaughan pointed out, was the kind of political writing in which Edmund Burke also was supreme. But beside the *Lettres de la Montagne*, Burke's *Thoughts on the Present Discontents*, published in 1770, became 'dull and laboured', whereas Rousseau's work was 'aflame with passion'. The difference was due

'not merely to the magic of his style; but also, and yet more, to his firmer grasp of principles, his gift for presenting a long train of detail as a living whole, his genius for making us see the effects in their causes, the causes through their effects.' [31]

It was therefore not lack of knowledge of the historical method that had caused Rousseau to use the Cartesian method for his *Contrat Social*. He had used the method of the older school deliberately because it suited his purpose.

CHAPTER V

THE DISCIPLE OF MONTESQUIEU

WITH the career of Edmund Burke, the methods of political thinking represented by the Montesquieu school became more firmly established in England. Abstraction found itself confronted with concrete fact; the non-historical with history and experience. In the sweep of Burke's vivid historical imagination, the complex and varied phenomena of national life were transformed into the living effects of causes that had their roots deep in the history of the nation's past. History itself came to be interpreted in a different light. It was no longer philosophy teaching by example, but rather the story of the life of nations—a story of the past that made it possible to understand more clearly the present with its manifold problems. With the idea that there was a thread of continuity in national life, and with a new understanding of political 'fact', the legislator found at his command the method of approach to political thought that the nineteenth century adopted as its own.

Born in Dublin on January 1, 1729 (O.S.), Edmund Burke was the second son of a lawyer who practised in the Superior Courts. His early years were supremely happy and were spent in surroundings filled with historic memories. He grew up in circumstances that could scarcely have failed to create in him a genuine toleration for religious belief, and a deep sympathy for those who were obliged to suffer on account of their faith. He was brought up in the Protestant faith of his father, but his deep love for his mother quickly taught him to regard with sympathy the persecuted Roman Catholic Church to which she belonged. When he was twelve years of age, he was sent to school at Ballitore. Here he found that many of his school-mates were boys of Huguenot descent.[1] Their families had fled from France at the time of the revocation of the Edict of Nantes, and thus it was brought home to Burke that if his mother's faith was persecuted in Ireland, his father's was subjected to even harsher persecution in France. He had much reason to wonder why people with such fine qualities as his mother and these Huguenot friends possessed should be subjected to persecution for beliefs that obviously did not detract from their character or their loyalty to their country.

Among his school-mates Edmund was distinguished for his aptitude for learning. His brother Richard wondered how it was that 'Ned had contrived to monopolize all the talents of the family; but then, again, I remember when we were at play he was always at work'.[2] He read extensively on his own account, turning for preference to the old romances. All that was beautiful and majestic appealed irresistibly to his vivid imagination. He devoted much time to history and poetry, and turned study of the classics from a duty into a genuine diversion. Although his studious nature made him enjoy being left alone, he was naturally affectionate and made friendships with boys which lasted through life. One of his chief friends was Richard Shackleton, son of his Quaker school master. Not only was Burke an affectionate friend, but even in his school days, it was possible to arouse his sympathies quickly on behalf of those whom he saw suffering from injustice.

In 1744, Burke entered Trinity College, Dublin, where he found time not only for his set studies but also for developing his special interests as well. The regular university course included special studies in 'abstract' Christianity, mathematics, natural, moral, and political philosophy, and classics. Scholastic logic, which Burke contemptuously termed a 'hoard of exploded nonsense',[3] was brought up to date through the inclusion of Locke's Essay on the Human Understanding. Burlamaqui and Locke were the chief authorities in political philosophy. Less attention was devoted to composition in Greek and Latin than in the English universities; while more time was spent in becoming better acquainted with the sentiments and 'beauties' of the classical authors studied. Classics, history, philosophy, metaphysics, and general literature were among his favourite studies. His interest in metaphysics was quite marked for a time, but it was largely determined by its usefulness in 'clearing the judgement and strengthening the understanding'.[4] It was later relinquished altogether, because Burke was convinced that it was of 'doubtful utility' and that it tended neither to make men better nor happier, but rather the reverse.

He turned with greatest pleasure to those authors who were able to give him the most profound insight into human nature, into the springs of human motives and actions, and into manners. Through literature he could see human nature in its many and varied aspects, as interpreted by the great masters. Among his favourite Greek authors were Homer, Demosthenes, Plutarch, Euripides, and particularly the historians; while among the Latin writers, his preferences were for Horace, Lucretius, and Virgil. He studied Bacon's *Essays* attentively, and found the works of Addison, Le Sage, Fielding, and Smollett particularly congenial. Significantly enough, Burke did not care greatly for Richardson, whose sentimental novel *Pamela* was the English precursor of Rousseau's *Nouvelle Héloïse*. From references to Mirza and Usbek in his correspondence with Richard Shackleton, it was apparent that Burke was interested in Montesquieu's *Lettres Persanes*. Thus his attention was already attracted by the great French writer in whom he later found a kindred spirit.

On April 23, 1747, 'Edmundus Burke, filius secundus Ricardi Burke de civitate Dublin', was admitted as a future student at the Middle Temple, London. In deference to his father's wishes, Burke consented to study law after he had completed his work for his degree in Dublin. He had no predilection for legal studies and had no desire to enter the legal profession. He disliked and feared its narrowing influence upon the intellect. Although law was 'one of the first and noblest sciences', he did not believe that it was apt, 'except in persons very happily born', to open and liberalize the mind. But until it was necessary for him to consider the uncongenial subject further, he thrust it into the background and continued his studies at college as well as the collegiate activities in which he had taken an interest. Chief among his interests at this time was the establishment of the college Historical Club, which was duly constituted four days after his name had been entered on the rolls of the Middle Temple. He became first president of this club, which subsequently became the famous College Historical Society, and he was one of its most energetic members. After a time it was decided, although Burke was opposed to the proposal, 'that no questions relating to the government of our country, which may possibly affect our loyalty', were to be discussed. He feared that this might take away their spirit, but his fears were soon dispelled. Burke was usually on the side of authority, and already he showed his desire to uphold the traditions of enlightened government. He made an excellent president of the club, although his vehemence usually told against him in debate. He was constitutionally incapable of moderation in his attitude towards subjects that interested him. He either advocated them with his whole heart, or else opposed them with the same degree of vehemence.

Another indication of traits that were later to become characteristic of him was to be found in the readiness with which he took up his pen for causes that enlisted his sympathy. Towards the close of 1748, Irish politics claimed his attention. Several candidates had offered themselves for election on the issue of rescuing Irish trade from the control of the English parliament. In November, 1748, the first of a series of pamphlets entitled, *A Free Briton's Advice to the Free Citizens of Dublin*, appeared. These pamphlets were written by Burke with a view to persuading the voters of Dublin to elect men

'of pure, unvaried principles, with extensive abilities, clear conceptions and sound judgement, who can so far penetrate into the interest of the various parts of the community, that the good of your city might be connected with the general good of the Nation, who are intrepid in the cause of freedom, and who scorn to gloss over truth to Power'.[5]

He believed that such men, and such men only, could carry forward the cause of Irish freedom.

Burke's pamphlets were the work of the student interested in public affairs and steeped in the course of Roman history and the principles of Roman institutions, rather than the work of the mature thinker. Yet they showed that he had already formed clear ideas of the qualities most essential for true public service. He had accepted Locke's political philosophy wholeheartedly, and he began his pamphlets with the statement that the true end of all society was certainly the 'happiness of the associated'. It was

'hardly possible to conceive that any set of men would agree to form themselves into a particular government, and confer such and such powers on one or more men, without consulting the happiness and welfare of themselves, who are the constituents and givers of those powers'.[6]

Furthermore, the greatest security of the people against the encroachments and usurpations of their superiors was to 'keep the Spirit of Liberty constantly awake',[7] a task that would be made less difficult if they elected men with statesmanlike qualities. For Burke these were no platitudes, but sober truths upon which he built his political principles.

In 1750, he left for London in order to commence his course at the Middle Temple. But once in London, he found many attractions beside studies at the Middle Temple. Westminster Abbey filled him with a sense of awe. Carried away by the beauty and charm of the old church buildings of England, he could well imagine that *Il Penseroso*, which to him then was the 'finest poem in the English language', had been composed in the 'long resounding aisle of a mouldering cloister or ivy'd abbey'. For the next five years or more, his restless mind was kept busy weighing the obvious attractions that literature held for him as a profession against the calling his father had desired for him. His heart had not been in the legal profession at any time, and as he continued his studies, his dislike for it increased. Unfortunately for him, his father began to grow suspicious. Edmund had not only failed to make a start towards establishing himself, but had even entertained some project of going to America. This idea was given up only when his father protested vigorously, but Edmund's affairs remained in so unsatisfactory a state that his father finally decided to precipitate a crisis by cutting short his allowance. What readjustments Burke had to make when thrown upon his own resources remain a matter of some conjecture. Naturally reticent concerning his affairs, he was even more reticent at this time. Fellow-students were well on their way towards distinction in their chosen professions. He did not yet know what he was going to do. However, he had manuscripts that needed little more than final revision in order to be ready for the press and, among other things, he devoted his attention to them. His health, which was not at any time particularly robust, soon began to show the effects of the strain to which he subjected himself. He went to Bath to recuperate, and while there he met the daughter of his physician, Dr. Nugent, and in 1756, married her. But even his marriage did not help him to settle down immediately, for when he wrote to Richard Shackleton in August, 1757, offering apologies for his long silence, his plans were still somewhat indefinite.

The year of his marriage saw the publication of two of his literary efforts. One of these, the *Philosophical Inquiry into the Origin of our Ideas of the Sublime and the Beautiful*, had been written about nine years previously, and was apparently the outcome of his studies of Locke and Addison on the subject of aesthetic theory. It impressed the polite world of letters, and consequently gave Burke a reputation as an author. The second essay was in reality a *jeu d'esprit*, and Burke did not acknowledge authorship of it at the time. It appeared as *A Vindication of Natural Society*; or, a View of the Miseries and Evils arising to Mankind from every Species of Artificial Society, by a late Noble Lord. The unsuspecting world immediately accepted it as the work of Lord Bolingbroke. It deceived such literary critics as Chesterfield and Warburton, although Mallet, who had edited Bolingbroke's works, protested that it was an imposture. Bolingbroke's graceful style was usually regarded as inimitable, but it was a different story when the imitator was Burke, whose literary touch was 'sometimes almost divine', and whose gifts were such that Matthew Arnold believed he was unquestionably the greatest master of English prose. Unfortunately for Burke, the irony of the essay was missed. The *Vindication of Natural Society* was regarded as a brilliant contribution to the 'noble savage' literature which advocated a return to the state of nature, and was not recognized as an eloquent argument against it, as its author had intended. With the publication of Rousseau's *Discours sur l'inégalité* in the previous year, the cult of the noble savage had become exceedingly popular, and little as he intended to do so, Burke now enhanced its popularity. But he made certain, when he brought out a second edition of the *Vindication of Natural Society*, that future readers would know that it had been written in ironical vein, and had most certainly never been intended to increase the influence of Rousseau's writings in England. In a special preface, he said that it was the outcome of bitter disappointment at the work of Bolingbroke. Those who, like himself, had looked forward to a real contribution to philosophy in Bolingbroke's works had been recompensed by finding every mode of religion attacked in a lively manner, and the foundation of every virtue and of all government sapped with great art and much ingenuity. What delight, he asked, could a man find in employing a capacity which might have been usefully exerted for the noblest purposes, in a sort of 'sullen labour', which could only do untold harm to mankind if by any chance it should succeed in its purpose? Such had been his thoughts when he set about showing that 'without the exertion of any considerable forces', the same engines which were employed for the destruction of religion 'might be employed with equal success for the subversion of government; and that specious arguments which might be used against those things which they, who doubt of everything else, will never permit to be questioned'.[8] What would become of the world if the practice of all moral duties, and the foundations of society, rested upon having their reasons made 'clear and demonstrative' to every individual? Already Burke had come to the conclusion that where matters of faith and obligation were concerned, the authority of an enlightened tradition was to be preferred to the speculative search for an authority acceptable to reason. He believed that the sense of security which came with the acceptance of custom and tradition was a valuable stabilizing factor in society, and that the loss of that sense of security was only one of the harmful effects that ensued when the foundations of faith were disturbed. Unlike the author of *Areopagitica*, whom he admired so much, Burke did not believe that full and free discussion was a salutary thing for a nation. He would curb it the moment it threatened to undermine the props upon which national stability rested.

But Burke's essay was more than a thrust at the speculating propensities of the times, which he definitely regarded as among the most perniciou stendencies of his age. It was also an implicit attack upon a widely-accepted interpretation of history. More than ever before, people had become historically minded. Not only were important literary men devoting attention to it, but the ordinary man was also reading it with considerable interest. From the point of view of the Enlightenment, history was but little more than the record of the crimes and miseries of mankind. If that were so, then, in ironical mood, Burke discovered that it was nothing but the ghoulish story of bloody warfare. The more civilized men became, in fact, the more competent they became in the sanguinary art. Political society was therefore 'justly chargeable' with much the greatest part of the destruction of the species through war.

'From the earliest dawnings of policy to this day', he declared, 'the invention of men has been sharpening and improving the mystery of murder, from the first rude essays of clubs and stones, to the present perfection of gunnery, cannoneering, bombarding, mining, and all these species of artificial, learned, and refined cruelty, in which we are now so expert, and which make a principal part of what politicians have taught us to believe is our principal glory. . . .' [9]

Following the publication of the *Vindication of Natural Society*, Burke devoted his attention seriously to history. The 'furor historicus' of his college days had been replaced by a deep appreciation of the significant role that historical process had played in the moulding of national customs, ideals, and institutions. But it was even more than this. It was the unfolding of the Divine purpose in the universe. Burke's deeply religious nature recoiled in horror at the interpretation of history given by some of the leaders of the Enlightenment, at which he had already made a preliminary thrust. They had no thought that the history of civilization might be the 'known march of the ordinary providence' of God. To such a man as Voltaire, for instance, history was only a pack of tricks we played on the dead; or, in less flippant terms, he announced that the history of great events in the world was scarcely more than a record of the crimes of humanity. To Hume, history had nothing 'new or strange' to relate regarding mankind, which was 'so much the same, in all times and places'. Its chief use was 'only to discover the constant and universal principles of human nature. . . .' [10] From a contempt for the past which had prompted such interpretations of history,[11] Mostesquieu had pointed the way toward a truer understanding of its meaning and purpose.

Burke had studied Montesquieu's works attentively ever since his attention had been drawn to the *Lettres Persanes* in his early college days. In the *Considérations sur les Causes de la Grandeur des Romains et de leur Décadence* (1734), he recognized a philosophical interpretation of history far more profound and far more satisfying than any other writer of the period had offered. Montesquieu had turned aside from abstract theorizing regarding the past in an attempt to understand history through a study of 'fact'. He had sought to explain the facts of history by a careful examination of them, and to see them not as fortuitous accidents, but as the necessary consequences of anterior facts. Above all, he had sought to find underlying relationships between events, and to present history, not as an unrelated succession of happenings, but as a related series of effects produced by definite and traceable causes.

'Chance does not rule the world,' he explained. 'There are general causes, either moral or physical, which operate in every monarchy; which contribute to its rise, its continuance, or else cause its fall; and if the hazard of a battle, that is, a particular cause, has ruined a state, there was a general cause operating so that a state could not but perish through a single battle; in a word, the main current of events bears along with it all the particular accidents.' [12]

When Burke had grasped the full significance of Montesquieu's doctrine, he turned aside impatiently not only from generally accepted interpretations of history, but also from the non-historical approach to political philosophy.

Montesquieu had developed his philosophy of history yet further in the *Esprit des Lois*, which had been published not long before Burke came to England. More than ever, Burke was impressed by the fact that Montesquieu was an historian with a clear grasp of facts and with a sincere reverence for the past. But his work was particularly valuable because it reflected the attitude of the statesman towards the problems of political philosophy. There was a conservative strain in Montesquieu that called forth Burke's approbation; a desire to understand the meaning of institutions and to preserve them. Although he presented a method of approach to history and political philosophy that was in revolt against accepted ideas, Burke knew that his method was both sound and practical. Because it was so firmly rooted in fact, it seemed to Burke that it was far preferable to the abstract method of the speculative school of thought. In Montesquieu's hands, history was being transformed into a study of laws, manners, customs and traditions, as they varied in different localities, in order to illustrate the relativity of natural law. Through his attempt to trace the relationship between the various factors in the life of a nation, Montesquieu saw clearly that in any given period there was a fundamental unity in that life. But although he was on the verge of the dynamic view of history, he did not grasp firmly the principle that history was the story of the evolution of societies, and it remained for Burke to see that there was a thread of continuity running through the different periods of history also.

Having grasped that principle of continuity, Burke began a short account of the beginnings of England's history in order to apply the new method to the study of history. He referred to Montesquieu as 'the greatest genius, which has enlightened this age',[13] and indeed the whole work bore tribute to the author from whom he had learned so much. He thought that his method of approach would 'clear up the darkness, and supply the defects' in the information left by earlier historians. But he thought that it would also 'lay open a noble field of speculation for those who study the changes which have happened in the manners, opinions and sciences of men, and who think them as worthy of regard as the fortunes of wars, and the revolutions of kingdoms'.[14] The student of Montesquieu would not confine his attention to the 'crimes' of mankind, but would study social history with the closest attention. And his reward would be in the discovery that behind the complexity of the events he was describing, there had been a steadfast love of liberty in the nation, which had been a unifying force, moulding in its own fashion not only incidental events, but also the character and institutions of the nation. In a concluding fragment to his history, Burke gave an account of the legal history of the later period which culminated in the signing of the Magna Charta. He found it most instructive to 'observe the first principles of RIGHT springing up, involved in superstition and polluted with violence', but finally 'by length of time and favourable circumstances, it has worked itself into clearness'. [15]

Unlike Montesquieu, Burke was an incurable romanticist. He transformed scorn for England's past into admiration, even into a longing for the return of the romance and colour of former times. In his *Essay Towards the Abridgement of English History*, he not only reconstructed a living past out of the bare facts preserved by chroniclers, but showed a genuine love for the 'dark ages', which were scorned as Gothic and barbaric by the enlightened sons of the pre-romantic era. To Burke, they were the glorious days of medieval lore, when crusades called brave knights to the defence of the Holy Land against the infidel, and when 'our ancestors' struggled to regain the liberty that had been their ancient heritage, and they contrasted strikingly with the stagnation and 'effeminacy' of the present, which Brown satirized in his *Estimate of the Manners and Principles of the Times* (1757), a work which Burke had been reading. Burke had no love for some of the manners and principles that characterized the period in which he lived. His imagination found an escape in another world, where he revelled in the majestic 'Gothicism' of the new spirit of romanticism. As he followed the story of English history from the days of the invasions of Julius Caesar to the fights of King John with the barons, he paused by the way to tell of such things as Druid lore and the manner in which knight-errantry arose, and he concluded by showing that the 'grand article' of the Magna Charta, and that which 'cemented all the parts of the fabric of liberty' was 'that no freeman shall be taken or imprisoned, or disseized, or outlawed, or banished, or in any wise destroyed, but by judgment of his peers'. [16]

Burke's love of history led him to attempt a literary project that was designed to be a faithful representation of current events. While he could cast all the glamour of romanticism over England's past, he was equally interested in the history of the present, and with the Seven Years' War in progress, history was unquestionably in the making in Europe no less than in the new world. The war was not only of vital concern to England, but it had also aroused considerable interest throughout the nation. Pitt's stirring appeal to the patriotism of his countrymen and his spectacular success in the conduct of the war caused the average Englishman to express a desire to understand more clearly the significance of events as far as they concerned England's imperial affairs. It seemed an opportune moment to begin a periodical that would convey accurate information in the fields of current politics, history, and literature. On April 24, 1758, Edmund Burke signed an agreement with Robert and James Dodsley 'to write, collect and compile from such materials as may arise a work entitled the Annual Register, or Retrospections on men and things for the year 1758'. [17] The first volume was to be ready for publication by Lady Day of 1759, and Burke was to receive a salary of one hundred pounds for his work for it. This was the beginning of the *Annual Register*, and with its publication, Burke became associated with a second project that was destined to come down through the years to the present time. Like the Historical Club at Trinity College, Dublin, the *Annual Register* has been kept up without intermission. Burke was connected with it probably until 1789, and possibly even later, [18] and in the earlier years of its existence he wrote a great deal for it. The opening volumes provided a valuable chronicle of the Seven Years' War which concluded in 1763, while the political history of England was faithfully recorded. Reviews of outstanding current literature were given prominence, and in the first volume a translation of the incomplete essay on taste that Montesquieu had written for the *Encyclopédie* was published. 'It is saying enough in its praise', the reviewer commented, 'to say it is written by Mons. de Montesquieu, who so happily employed philosophy to illustrate and improve the laws of all the nations of the world.' [19]

In the second volume of the *Annual Register*, for the year 1759, Rousseau's *Lettre à d'Alembert* came under review. The critic, most probably Burke himself, showed on the one hand a readiness to acknowledge Rousseau's intellectual gifts, but on the other, gave expression to a feeling of perplexity regarding him and a sense of the futility of his work.

'None of the present writers have a greater share of talents and learning than Rousseau,' he asserted; 'yet it has been his misfortune and that of the world, that those of his works which have made the greatest noise, and acquired to their author the highest reputation have been of little real use or emolument to mankind. A tendency to paradox, which is always the bane of solid learning, and threatens now to destroy it, a splenetic disposition carried to misanthropy, and an austere virtue pursued to an unsociable fierceness, have prevented a great deal of the good effects which might be expected from such a genius.'

He closed with the warning that 'a satire upon civilized society, a satire upon learning may be a sport, but if carried further could only unsettle notions of right and wrong and lead to scepticism'.[20]

Three years later the *Émile* was reviewed, and the critic announced that it was 'easy to discern' how it had happened that the work was censured so severely in Paris and Geneva.

'To know what the received notions are upon any subject, is to know with certainty what those of Rousseau are not,' he wrote. 'In his treatise on the inequality amongst mankind, he has shown his man in a natural state; in his *Emilius* he undertakes to educate him. . . . He forms him to morals, to science, to knowledge of men, and to manual labour, and at length gives him a wife, whom he has previously educated for him according to ideals little different from that model which he had formed in his *Eloisa*.'

The criticism was not entirely hostile, however, for in spite of the 'whimsies' into which Rousseau's 'paradoxical genius' continually hurried him, it was acknowledged that there were a thousand noble hints relative to his subject, 'grounded upon a profound knowledge of the human mind, and the order of its operations'. Moreover, every now and then the reader came across 'strokes of the most solid sense', and 'instructions of the most useful nature'.[21]

While Burke was gaining invaluable knowledge of current affairs and literature in the course of his work for the *Annual Register*, he was also making slow progress towards establishing himself as a literary man. He was becoming better acquainted with men who were taking part in public affairs.

His growing reputation as a writer had attracted the attention of his fellow-countryman, Lord Charlemont, and through him Burke met William Gerard Hamilton, who had entered Parliament in 1755, and was subsequently known to fame as 'Single-Speech' Hamilton. Burke's literary abilities were already known to Hamilton, and ultimately personal acquaintance led him to offer Burke an appointment as his secretary. He did not interrupt the work for the *Annual Register*, but required Burke to devote the rest of his time to his service. In March, 1761, the Earl of Halifax was made Lord Lieutenant of Ireland, and Hamilton, as Chief Secretary, accompanied him to Dublin. Burke, of course, went with Hamilton, and his services were so completely satisfactory that two years later, Hamilton obtained for him a pension of three hundred pounds a year from the Irish Treasury. In acknowledging it, Burke made the stipulation that he should be allowed some liberty to continue his own literary pursuits, as it was highly desirable for him to maintain the reputation he had already made. In the autumn of 1763, following a visit to London, Hamilton offered Burke a definite income from his personal fortune if he would become legally bound to devote himself exclusively to his service. Burke refused to consider such a proposition, and Hamilton immediately charged him with base ingratitude. Charlemont tried to restore cordial relations between the two men, though with indifferent success. For two years more Burke remained with Hamilton; then in April, 1765, he resigned and returned to London. The prospect of security was most enticing, but it would have had to be purchased at so great a cost that Burke preferred to make his way as best he could rather than allow himself to be fettered in the way Hamilton proposed.

Back again in London, with no definite prospects for the future but hopeful that he would find success in the profession of letters, Burke began to pick up the threads of his earlier life once more. He hastened to renew friendships that he valued, and the most important of these was the acquaintance with Dr. Johnson, which had begun on Christmas Day, 1758, when they had both been guests of David Garrick. The acquaintance of such long standing developed quickly into a settled friendship because Burke shared many interests and intellectual tastes in common with the great moralist. Through the Literary Club, of which they were both foundation members, they had ample opportunities of getting to know each other better. Johnson, of course, was the leading spirit of the Club, and Burke was the only member who was a match for him, either in breadth of knowledge or in argumentative powers. The story of the affection of these two high-minded men for each other was unquestionably one of the most attractive that the eighteenth century has to offer. It was particularly attractive on account of the fact that it was based on a mutual regard for each other's sterling qualities. 'Yes; Burke is an extraordinary man,' Johnson said with conviction when Boswell had mentioned his name to see how far Johnson would retract a sweeping statement he had just made to the effect that no credence should be given to extraordinary characters certain people were supposed to have, because they were certain to be exaggerations. With Burke it was different. 'His stream of mind is perpetual.' And Boswell added that it gave him pleasure to record

'that Johnson's high estimation of the talents of this gentleman were uniform from their early acquaintance. Sir Joshua Reynolds informs me, that when Mr. Burke was first elected a member of Parliament, and Sir John Hawkins expressed a wonder at his attaining a seat, Johnson said, "Now we who know Mr. Burke, know that he will be one of the first men in this country." ' [22]

At last, toward the close of 1765, Burke saw whither the way was leading him. Lord Rockingham, deeply impressed by his wellnigh encyclopedic knowledge of men and affairs and greatly attracted by his unassuming personality and his charm, had chosen him as his secretary, and soon afterwards he was elected to Parliament as member for Wendover. His long period of apprenticeship was over at last, and he looked forward to the future with a heart full of hope. The great lessons he had learned from Montesquieu and had applied with conspicuous success not only to the history of the past, but also to the present, he could now transfer to politics itself, to the field of thought and action where history was made. His maiden speech was in favour of the repeal of the Stamp Act. No less a person than William Pitt, who had fought to the utmost to prevent a crisis between England and the Americans and was now anxiously watching the preliminary debates leading up to a decision on the part of the House, expressed his delight at the support the new member had given to the cause of peace by his first speeches. Burke had proved himself a 'very able advocate' and Pitt congratulated him on his success, and his friends on the acquisition they had made to their ranks. Horace Walpole, who knew Burke slightly, having met him at dinner at Hamilton's residence in London years before, also referred to the speech which had aroused Pitt's admiration. 'There appeared in this debate a new speaker, whose fame for eloquence soon rose high above the ordinary pitch,' Walpole reported in his *Memoirs of the Reign of George III*. 'His name was Edmund Burke . . . an Irishman, of a Roman Catholic family, and actually married to one of that persuasion.' [23] Although some of his information was incorrect, Walpole was reliable enough in giving the general impression Burke had made. Burke's oratory was impassioned and left no doubt of the deep sincerity of his convictions. 'Everything seemed a kind of new political philosophy,' [24] Dr. Marriott remarked significantly as he told Burke of the impression his speeches had made.

Burke had scarcely entered upon his new sphere of activity when Rousseau arrived in London as the guest of Hume, a fugitive from the constant persecutions he had endured ever since the publication of the *Contrat Social* and the *Émile* in 1762. His arrival caused a stir of excitement in the literary world, for Rousseau was one of the most striking literary figures of the period and most people were intensely interested in him. Important men hastened to greet the illustrious visitor, and Boswell was proud of being allowed to escort Thérèse to England. But Burke and Johnson stood aloof. The mere mention of Rousseau's name or of his *Discourse on Inequality* was sufficient to make Johnson furiously angry. Johnson gloried in his prejudices, and Rousseau was one of them. Burke, more open-minded than Johnson, had been profoundly disturbed by stories that were being constantly circulated about the man who seemed to be the stormy petrel of Parisian literary circles; who seemed to quarrel in a most ungracious manner with friends and benefactors who deserved to fare better at his hands, and whose life of vagabondage was unconventional in the extreme. In the malicious *Le Sentiment des Citoyens*, published anonymously by Voltaire in 1765, the story of Rousseau's 'crimes' had been unfolded. Among other things, it contained the story of his abandonment of his children, later confirmed by Rousseau himself in his *Confessions*. The spiteful gossip of the Encyclopedists as well as printed calumnies followed their victim across the Channel. As Burke thought with pride and affection of his own home and his son, he found it impossible to think dispassionately of a man who could show such complete depravity and inhumanity as Rousseau had done. The crime that stained Rousseau's reputation so deeply seemed all the worse to Burke, owing to the fact that Rousseau had assumed the role of moralist in all his writings, and in the *Émile* had seemed to show a genuine understanding of children and affection for them, only to belie that sympathy in his treatment of his own children.

Boswell wondered whether the two men he admired so much above all others might not be brought to unbend a little if they were to come into actual personal contact with Rousseau. He was not ashamed of his own hero-worshipping, and he treasured the memories of visits to Rousseau in his 'wild retreat' in 1765,[25] but he was not able to bring about a meeting between his friends and Rousseau. Johnson flatly refused to have anything to do with Rousseau; while Burke remained steadfastly aloof. The unfortunate outcome of Rousseau's visit to England, moreover, alienated completely the last vestiges of Burke's desire to understand him. Like most Englishmen, Burke looked on with amazement as the hurricane suddenly swept up and over, leaving in its course sensational accounts of a bitter quarrel between Hume and his 'guest'. Charges that Rousseau had shown 'monstrous ingratitude, ferocity, and frenzy', quickly followed. Before the storm had passed over, Rousseau had fled back to Paris, while the astonished world had time to marvel at the information contained in *A concise and genuine account of the dispute between Mr. Hume and Mr. Rousseau, with the letters that passed between them during their controversy*, which Hume had published.

Six years later Burke visited Paris, where Rousseau was spending the last days of his storm-tossed life in seclusion, but he made no attempt to see him in spite of the fact that he was most interested in meeting the literary men of Paris. The golden days of the Encyclopedists were almost over. The giants had scattered; some of them were no longer alive. The great Montesquieu had died as far back as 1755, while Voltaire had forsaken both Paris and the court of Frederick the Great for his home near Geneva. Nevertheless Burke did meet some of the *philosophes*, including the ageing Diderot, at the famous salons he visited.

The brief days spent in France left a deep impression upon Burke, but what burned itself into his memory was the contact, such as it was, with the intellectual life of the *philosophes*. This struck more deeply than anything else and troubled him most profoundly, because he was well aware that the influence of their works extended far beyond the borders of France. Witty, irreligious, and materialistic, they were like a menacing thunder-cloud in the fair blue sky, which suddenly assumed threatening proportions when he came into their midst and saw their attitude towards life. Voltaire, Rousseau, Helvétius, Condorcet, Diderot, one and all, assumed satanic qualities when Burke reflected upon the misuse they had made of their great intellectual talents. This 'literary cabal' had formed something like a regular plan for the destruction of Christianity, Burke believed, and they had pursued their object with marked zeal.

'They contrived to possess themselves, with great method and perseverance, of all the avenues to literary fame,' he wrote in his *Reflections on the French Revolution* when events seemed to confirm his judgement of the Encyclopedists. 'Many of them stood high in the ranks of literature and science. The world had done them justice; and in favour of general talents forgave the evil tendencies of their peculiar principles.' [26]

But they had returned this liberality by

'endeavouring to confine the reputation of sense, learning, and taste to themselves or their followers. I will venture to say that this narrow, exclusive spirit has not been less prejudicial to literature and to taste, than to morals and true philosophy. These atheistical fathers have a bigotry of their own. . . . To those who have observed the spirit of their conduct, it has long been clear that nothing was wanted but the power of carrying the intolerance of the tongue and of the pen into a persecution which would strike at property, liberty, and life. . . . A spirit of cabal, intrigue, and proselytism, pervaded all their thoughts, words, and actions.' [27]

Furthermore, it was a matter of indifference to them whether the changes they desired to see were 'to be accomplished by the thunderbolt of despotism, or by the earthquake of popular commotion'.[28] Like the propagators of all novelties, these writers had 'pretended to a great zeal for the poor, and the lower orders, whilst in their satires they rendered hateful, by every exaggeration, the faults of courts, of nobility, and of priesthood'.[29]

On his return to England, Burke determined to sound as impressive a warning as he could against the Encyclopedists and their writings. He grasped an opportunity to do this in the course of a debate in the House of Commons on the subject of relief for Protestant dissenters. With the fire of the prophet who believed that the welfare of his country was at stake, he begged the House to give the dissenters the liberty for which they asked. It was not the dissenters that would do harm to their country, but rather it was the atheists they had to fear.

'The most horrid and cruel blow, that can be offered to civil society, is through atheism,' he declared with conviction. 'Do not promote diversity; when you have it, bear it; have as many sorts of religion as you find in your country; there is a reasonable worship in them all,' he argued in desperation. 'The others, the infidels, are outlaws of the constitution; not of this country, but of the human race. They are never, never to be supported, never to be tolerated. Under the systematic attacks of these people, I see some of the props of good government already begin to fall; I see propagated principles which will not leave to religion even a toleration. I see myself sinking every day under the attacks of these wretched people—How shall I arm myself against them? by uniting all those in affection, who are united in the belief of the great principles of the Godhead that made and sustains the world. . . .' [30]

Burke's speech was a curious mixture of vision and lack of statesmanship. He arrived at a solution to the issue in the white heat of his fear, so that his speech lost not a little in effectiveness by his inability to look at the situation calmly and to exercise cool judgement.

Burke's outburst was no surprise to his listeners. It was characteristic of him, and it revealed at once his strength and his weakness as a statesman. His mastery of the significance of intellectual movements and his ability to see them in their relationship to both circumstances and political principles placed him in the forefront of the public men of his age. But his attitude toward those movements revealed a headstrong temperament that was totally unfitted for keeping the ship of state upon a steady course; while it also indicated Burke's intellectual limitations. His sensitivèness to disruptive forces disclosed the essentially conservative bias of his mind, and the intensity of his emotional reaction to such forces caused him to lose all sense of perspective. The brief visit to France had been sufficient to impress upon his mind very clearly the fact that the writers of the Age of Reason had sown seeds of social upheaval. He took alarm immediately, and came to the conclusion that no time should be lost in taking measures to protect England against the time when the whirlwind should be reaped. He regarded the frankly irreligious spirit that had constituted no inconsiderable part of the charm of the Parisian intellectual circles for Hume, Gibbon and others, as one of the important danger-signals. His certainty that the so-called 'atheists' were the outlaws of the human race was characteristic of his exaggeration and of the form his thought took when he felt strongly upon an issue. It was this over-emphasis upon future dangers together with his lack of sound practical judgement of men and affairs that detracted from the value of his forceful warnings as far as his fellow-members of Parliament were concerned.

Unlike many of his colleagues with intellectual gifts far inferior to his own, Burke was frequently not wise in the course he pursued, so that ultimately he had to be counted a political failure. In the three big issues that confronted him in the course of his long political career, he was on the right side only in the struggle with the colonists in America. His judgement was at fault in the impeachment of Warren Hastings; while his historical imagination failed him in the issues of the French revolution, thus causing him to fight on the wrong side. His inability to lead men was shown by the tactics he adopted in Parliament. All too frequently he allowed asperity to enter into his debates, and while he asked no quarter from his opponents, he would give none in return. The profound understanding of human nature that characterized his writings did not help him to judge men aright; neither did it help him in his dealings with them. Consequently it was no wonder that he had moments of bitterness when he reflected upon his failure to obtain the high office to which his high sense of duty and his talents entitled him. Goldsmith summed up the curious antithesis in his friend's nature when he wrote in *Retaliation*:

> Though equal to all things, for all things unfit,
> Too nice for a statesman, too proud for a wit:
> For a patriot, too cool; for a drudge, disobedient;
> And too fond of the *right* to pursue the *expedient*.[31]

Yet in spite of his shortcomings as a politician, Burke's mind was cast in a statesmanlike mould. His writings showed that he constantly referred his thought and judgement to the fundamental principles upon which the art of the statesman was based. From the outset of his career he rejected the 'great Serbonian bog' of the appeal to abstract and legal rights, 'where armies whole have sunk', and unhesitatingly demanded that the statesman should follow the dictates of 'humanity, reason, and justice'. He insisted that political questions had to be dealt with on a basis of expediency, but he also demanded that the statesman must have a high sense of his responsibilities, a clear conception of political principles, and that he must have vision. He must see present problems in the light of the circumstances that gave them birth, and he must arrive at a solution of them in the light of the welfare and happiness of the people who had placed him in a position of authority. Also he must act at all times upon the sovereign principle of prudence, 'the first in rank of the virtues political and moral', and upon a sound knowledge of human nature. And because Burke insisted in all his speeches and writings that these were the basic principles of good statesmanship, he exerted a strong influence for good and won for himself an important place in the history of political thought.

CHAPTER VI

THE FOUNDATIONS OF THE MODERN STATE

FROM the time of Aristotle onwards, it became customary in treatises on political philosophy to classify the different kinds of polities that could be regarded as 'legitimate', and to offer criticisms of the various forms of government as each in turn came under review. In classical political thought a kingdom was defined as a state governed by one person for the common good; an aristocracy was one in which the few governed, while a democracy was a state in which the citizens at large governed for the public good. All of these forms were recognized as legitimate so long as the power which was necessarily placed in the hands of the one, the few, or the many, was exercised for the common good. Rousseau gave the name 'republic' to every state that was governed by laws, no matter what the form of its administration might be, 'for only in such a case does the public interest govern, and the *res publica* rank as a reality. Every legitimate government is republican. . . .'[1] Burke usually preferred to use the term 'commonwealth',[2] rather than 'republic', but otherwise he was in accord with Rousseau regarding the fundamental characteristic of the 'legitimate' state.

In selecting the kind of state that most nearly approached his political ideal, Rousseau turned aside regretfully from democracy in the classical sense of the term. 'Were there a people of gods,' he wrote in the *Contrat Social*, 'their government would be democratic. So perfect a government is not for men. . . .'[3] He then considered aristocracy, which could assume any of three forms: natural, elective, or hereditary. 'The first is only for simple peoples,' he explained, and 'the third is the worst of all governments; the second is the best, and is aristocracy properly so called.'[4] Elective aristocracy, to which he gave his preference, became the 'democracy' of modern political philosophy. Rousseau preferred it because it was the 'best and most natural arrangement' that the wisest should govern the many. In revolt against the privilege of the feudal state, he looked to a new order of society in which men would be free and equal before the law, and in conformity with these ideas, he preferred a republican form for his ideal state to a monarchy. Burke, on the other hand, looked upon the constitutional monarchy of his country as the 'best of all governments'.[5] It was a class state, but he pointed out that it was 'perfectly susceptible' of reform as well as of a balance of power, and when it was both 'reformed and balanced', it was the best form of government for a great country. Outwardly, Rousseau's ideal state would resemble the Republic of Geneva, compact, austere and free; while Burke's ideal would be like the British monarchy, powerful, majestic, enlightened, and the cradle of free government.

Beneath the surface, however, divergences between their views diminished to a marked degree, and there was much agreement in their conceptions of the fundamental principles upon which the modern state rested. In the first place, both Rousseau and Burke stood upon common ground in their demand for liberty for the citizen and in their resolute opposition to tyranny in any form. The only kind of state that appealed to Rousseau as worthy of free men was that which was built upon the principles of freedom and justice; the only kind of statesman that appealed to Burke was the champion of liberty.

'You pay me the compliment to suppose me a foe to tyranny and oppression,' Burke wrote to Captain Mercer in 1790. 'I *am* that determined foe to tyranny, or I greatly deceive myself in my character.'[6] Again, 'My endeavours in the Irish business, in which I was, indeed, very active and very earnest, both in public and in private, were wholly guided by an uniform principle, which is interwoven in my nature, and which has hitherto regulated, and I hope will continue to regulate, my conduct,—I mean an utter abhorrence of all kinds of public injustice and oppression; the worst species of which are those which being converted into maxims of state, and blending themselves with law and jurisprudence, corrupt the very fountains of all equity, and subvert all the purposes of government. . . .'[7]

Rousseau likewise made liberty the basis of his political principles. More than once he stressed the sharpness of the antithesis between his system as given in the *Contrat Social*, and the absolutism of a Leviathan state. In a letter to Mirabeau, he remarked that he could see 'no tenable middle course between the most austere democracy and the most perfect Hobbism'.[8] The body politic could guarantee liberty only if all men breathed the invigorating air of freedom, and if they were steadfastly true to the principles of right that were at the foundation of their political organization. Otherwise they would have to renounce their freedom in the interests of a strong government such as Hobbes had advocated. To follow the principles of the *Contrat Social* meant following the high standards dictated by moral freedom, and respecting the freedom of one's fellow-citizens as well as one's own. It also meant recognizing that the body politic was an organic whole, and that the ties which bound the citizens to each other and to the state were of an organic nature, and had to be regarded as such. The problem which the *Contrat Social* attempted to resolve was, in Rousseau's phraseology, to find that 'form of association which will defend and protect with the whole common force the person and goods of each associate, and in which each, while uniting himself with all, may still obey himself alone, and remain as free as before'.[9]

For Burke as for Rousseau, freedom was to be regarded in the light of the means whereby the state could achieve its end. Indispensable as it was, liberty was not in itself the end of the state. Rousseau, the moralist and the disciple of Plato, was concerned chiefly with the state as the means for the achievement of the good life.[10] In its obvious aspect, the function of the state was to provide security for life and property. But it did not seem to Rousseau that there was any permanent basis of union for society to be found in provision for man's material needs alone. On the contrary, he was prepared to agree with Hobbes that the fundamental material needs of mankind could be satisfied readily, and that they tended to make for the disruption of society rather than for peace and unity. 'Man is by nature sociable,' he wrote in the *Émile*, '. . . for if only physical well-being were considered, men would certainly be scattered instead of brought together.'[11] But on the other hand, man had spiritual aspirations and needs over and above his material wants, and it was only in and through society that they could possibly find satisfaction. It was in man's spiritual nature, therefore, that the real and enduring basis for society and the state was to be found. Consequently, in Rousseau's political philosophy, the fulfilment of man's spiritual nature became the supreme end of the state. Furthermore, as he recognized in the desires of the individual an ineradicable impulse towards the achievement of his own good, so also he found in the life of society a similar impulse toward the good of mankind. Through the discipline of society the good life could be fostered, and it was therefore the object of the state to provide the means for the attainment of that life.

In so far as happiness was an accompaniment of the exercise of man's moral, mental, and physical gifts, it was included in Rousseau's conception of the end of the state. The rhetorical emphasis on the misery of man's lot in society that characterized the *Discourses* and found occasional expression in his later works, gave way before the serious recognition in the *Émile* and the *Contrat Social*, that man was by nature a social animal, and that he found his happiness in the welfare of his kind.[12] The state of nature, which had been the ideal of the *Discourses*, had been drawn in sharp contrast to the evils of the life of society. In his more mature thought the antithesis vanished with the recognition that man himself was responsible for much of his own misery. Instead of following nature, he had followed false gods, and had created thereby his own unhappiness. When giving an account of 'The Happiness of a life led according to Nature', in *Rasselas*, Dr. Samuel Johnson phrased Rousseau's meaning perfectly. But Johnson did not subscribe unwittingly to the doctrine of the man he hated above all others, the mere mention of whose name was sufficient to make him fly into a towering passion. His chapter was a summary of one of the current philosophies that he regarded as sheer nonsense. Rasselas solemnly promised to devote 'the closest attention' to the discourse of the philosopher when he said that

'the way to be happy is to live according to nature, in obedience to that universal and unalterable law with which every heart is originally impressed; which is not written on it by precept, but engraven by destiny, not instilled by education, but infused at our nativity. He that lives according to nature will suffer nothing from the delusions of hope, or importunities of desire; he will receive and reject with equability of temper and act or suffer as the reason of things shall alternately prescribe. Other men may amuse themselves with subtle definitions or intricate ratiocinations. Let him learn to be wise by easier means: let him observe the hind of the forest, and the linnet of the grove; let him consider the life of animals whose motions are regulated by instinct; they obey their guide and are happy. Let us therefore at length cease to dispute, and learn to live; throw away the encumbrance of precepts . . . and carry with us this simple and intelligible maxim, that deviation from nature is deviation from happiness.' [13]

For the happiness to which Rousseau looked was that which accompanied the fulfilment of man's nature. With Bacon, he recognized that complete obedience to nature was mastery of it,[14] and that therefore the happiest man was the one who subjected himself most completely to the laws governing his physical, moral, and spiritual nature.

As he had learned from Father Lamy as well as from other favourite authors, it was not necessary to become erudite in order to find the way of life that was in accordance with nature, and which alone could bring true happiness. But natural goodness could only rise to virtue when there was a moral sphere for man such as the legitimate state afforded. For that reason, the state was 'natural' to man, and in the pursuit of virtue he would find his highest happiness. Thus man could still be in a 'state of nature' when achieving his highest destiny as a member of the state as when he was the true 'child of nature' wandering carefree in the woods or in the islands of the southern seas. Not only so, but with his acceptance of his rights and duties as a member of the state, man assumed his moral nature and found the path that led to moral freedom, which alone could make him truly master of himself, and consequently could bring the happiness of which he was in search. For the conception of human progress through reason and knowledge, which was the ideal of the Encyclopedists, Rousseau substituted a perfection that was to be found through the development of man's moral and spiritual nature as well.

Ultimately, Burke's conception of the end of the state differed but little from Rousseau's. As a statesman, his thoughts moved readily in a practical groove, and his views expressed the judgement of the man of affairs. The happiness and the welfare of the people were not only the statesman's supreme charge, but constituted the obvious duty of the state. In a speech in the House of Commons on May 11, 1792, he stated explicitly that

'the object of the state is (as far as may be) the happiness of the whole. Whatever makes multitudes of men utterly miserable can never answer that object; indeed it contradicts it wholly and entirely; and the happiness or misery of mankind, estimated by their feelings and sentiments, and not by any theories of their rights is, and ought to be, the standard for the conduct of legislators towards the people. . . .' [15]

His opinions on the subject had not varied throughout his political career. 'Reflect', he had challenged his fellow-members of Parliament during the crisis with the American colonies, 'how you are to govern a people, who think they ought to be free, and think they are not.' [16] Or again, when in 1780, he informed the electors of Bristol that 'no man carries further than I do the policy of making government pleasing to the people. . . . I would not only consult the interest of the people, but I would cheerfully gratify their humours. We are all a sort of children that must be soothed and managed'. But there was one thing that Burke would never do. 'I will never act the tyrant for their amusement. If they will mix malice in their sports, I shall never consent to throw them any living, sentient creature whatsoever, no not so much as a kitling to torment.' [17]

Like the utilitarians who had formulated their famous doctrine of the 'greatest happiness of the greatest number', an adaptation of the hedonistic formula that played a prominent part not only in late eighteenth-century, but also in early nineteenth-century political thought, Burke fully recognized the importance of happiness to the welfare of the nation. But he was critical of their conception of happiness, and had no particular sympathy either with the mathematical or with the markedly individualistic aspects of utilitarianism.[18] As opposed to the utilitarian idea that society was an aggregate of individuals, each of whom was to 'count for one', Burke thought of society as an organic whole. In that organic whole, the people fitted naturally into their different ranks and orders, and their happiness was to be found, not in the principle of levelling class distinctions which utilitarians accepted, but in the continuance of the class state. Levelling seemed to Burke to lead directly to social chaos and consequently to misery; whereas the happiness of the people was to be found through the preservation of the established order of society. And the legislator would fulfil his trust, Burke believed, if he were guided by the degree of contentment or of discontent that was to be observed in the nation, rather than by a mathematical computation of the number of individuals who found the sum of their pleasures greater than the sum of their pains, or vice versa. In so far as Burke proclaimed the organic unity of society and demanded the orderly functioning of the whole as a pre-requisite for happiness, he was on sounder philosophical ground than the utilitarians.

Similarly, Burke had no hesitation in criticizing the views of those who claimed that happiness was one of the natural and inalienable rights of mankind. He contended that the true estimate of a people's condition was to be gained, not by paying attention to their theories of natural rights, but rather by giving heed to their reactions to actual conditions. Their feelings and sentiments were a truer guide for the statesman than their theories could ever be. But while discounting the significance of theories, Burke overlooked the fact that the tendency of people to adopt theories was in itself symptomatic and should therefore be regarded as one important form of 'reaction' to actual conditions. He· regarded the theorizing propensities of his time with suspicion and thought of them as the work of people who deliberately wished to upset the smooth functioning of the state rather than as a symptom that something was amiss in the social order. He said that as a practical statesman he listened for the cry of distress as the signal for action, but he did not make it clear what form the cry to which he responded took. Instead of striving to increase the sum of human happiness by some process of reform involving extensive political reorganization, he thought it was better to remove hardships. If radical or extensive change, such as the theorists proposed, were introduced, it would be hard to say whither it would lead. For that reason he preferred to deal with the problem of reform by making certain first of all that the administration was functioning effectively. He felt that there were more certain ways of securing the happiness of the people than by extensive political reorganization and that fundamentally their happiness was determined by good government. It would be time enough to consider the question of radical reform when actual conditions demanded it: until such time came, Burke preferred not to speculate on the subject.

Like Rousseau, Burke was not prepared to accept the view that the ultimate end of the state was fulfilled by securing the happiness of the people. Owing to his profound aversion to the speculative approach to political thought, Burke had refused to develop a systematic philosophy of the state. Nevertheless he had devoted considerable thought to the purpose of the state in the life of mankind. While he accepted as sound, both in theory and practice, the idea that the happiness and welfare of the people should be among the first and most obvious of its charges, he saw that beneath the surface, the life of the state assumed a more profound meaning for man. His mind fitted philosophical thought into a conception of the state as an historical growth. With its institutions and its traditions, the state was the living form that had been moulded through the ages in order to help man to fulfil his destiny here on earth. More than that, in its proximate efficient cause, it was the product of the human mind. It was the creation of man himself, whose supreme distinction it was to have to a considerable extent the shaping of his own destiny in his own hands. The state was therefore the sacred heritage that the past had bequeathed to the present, a mystical gift infinitely enriched by the collective wisdom of the ages, and intended to help the generation of the living to play more adequately its part in the great drama of history.

Convinced that the state was so important and so sacred a heritage for mankind, and faced with the tragedy of the French revolution, Burke stressed the profound significance of the state, not only for Frenchmen and Englishmen, but for all mankind. Without the state, he solemnly asserted that 'man could not by any possibility arrive at the perfection of which his nature is capable, nor even make a remote and faint approach to it'.[19] Without the state, it would be impossible for human nature to develop and expand as the Author and Founder of human society had obviously intended that it should. And in reply to those who looked to the 'state of nature' as the ideal, and who believed that happiness and the good life were to be found through it rather than through civil society, Burke added that

'the state of civil society . . . is a state of nature; and much more truly so than a savage and incoherent mode of life. For man is by nature reasonable; and he is never perfectly in his natural state, but when he is placed where reason may be best cultivated, and most predominates. Art is man's nature. We are as much, at least, in a state of nature in formed manhood, as in immature and helpless infancy.' [20]

Burke was convinced that man's destiny was to be achieved in and through the institutions that he himself had built, and that the state was as necessary to civilized man as the cradle to the infant, or the South Sea strands to the noble savage.

But if the state was to fulfil so vital a role in the life of mankind; if it was to be looked upon as the means ordained by nature for the attainment of the good life; and if this life was to be achieved through the medium of freedom and happiness, then it was obvious that it could play its part only upon certain very definite conditions. And in their conception of the nature of those fundamental conditions, Rousseau and Burke again stood on common ground, although the viewpoints from which they deduced them remained far apart. For Rousseau, they were the conditions that followed logically from the purpose of the state. Not only were they implicit in the social contract itself, but without them it would be impossible to build up a coherent philosophy of the state. For Burke, they were important principles that had to be accepted unconditionally if the state was to function properly. They were the intellectual assumptions that were based upon the observation of forces actually in operation in society, the significance of which had to be impressed upon the minds of men who had not thought or reflected as profoundly upon the problems of the state as Burke had done.

The first and most important condition involved the supremacy of the state. In point of fact, the question of the limits of its competency had become confused primarily owing to the arguments of the adherents of the doctrine of the rights of man who maintained that man was the possessor of certain definite inalienable natural rights. These rights belonged to man *qua* man. The state had been instituted in order to guarantee the enjoyment of those rights, and if any were alienated to the state, they could be resumed immediately if it were discovered that the state had exceeded its powers. The sphere of the state's competency had been interpreted in so many different ways that confusion of thought had followed almost inevitably. Rousseau, when faced with this confusion of thought, had believed as Hobbes had done before him that there could not be any qualifications placed upon the supreme authority in the state. To limit it, he argued, was to destroy it. Therefore he had to determine where the supreme power in a body politic ought to reside, and to shape his theory accordingly. If his ideal state was to be for free men, then it seemed to him that those who assumed the responsibilities of citizenship were those in whom the supreme power of the state should be vested. Thus his doctrine of the sovereignty of the people was evolved in the interests of a sound theory of the state. The people needed liberty in order to pursue their interests, but they also needed a strong state with unquestioned authority if their liberty was to be safeguarded. For that reason, it was clearly understood that those who either tacitly or explicitly accepted the terms of the social contract alienated without reserve those rights and liberties which had belonged to them as independent individuals in the hypothetical state of nature. The clauses of the social contract, as a matter of fact, could be reduced to one—'the total alienation of each associate, together with all his rights, to the whole community, for . . . as each gives himself absolutely, the conditions are the same for all. . . .' [21] But if, on the other hand, individuals retained certain rights, 'there would be no common superior to decide between them and the public', and consequently each, 'being on one point his own judge, would ask to be so on all; the state of nature would thus continue, and the association would necessarily become inoperative or tyrannical'. [22] On the violation of the social compact, however, Rousseau explained that each individual would regain his 'original rights', and would resume his 'natural liberty'. But he would lose the 'conventional' or civil liberty and the advantages of civil society, in favour of which he had originally renounced the state of nature. Here Rousseau was not so much presenting an alternative for the citizens, as stressing the fact that if they were to enjoy the advantages of society, there could be no question of the limits of the competency of the body politic. It was particularly important for him to state his position thus clearly, because the 'state of nature' was a purely speculative concept. Whether it implied the golden age of the past before the dawn of civilization, or whether it implied the goal towards which men and indeed civilization itself were striving—the kind of state fit for a Socrates, or worthy of the services of great lawgivers such as Moses or Lycurgus had been—it was definitely not a practical alternative for actual men. The state of civil society was the only possible state for them. But there was no reason why civil society should not strive towards a higher and finer standard, so that it could reflect more adequately the ideal of the 'state of nature'. As Rousseau surveyed the miseries and the evils attendant upon the operation of false principles in society round about him, he believed that the first step towards reform was to evolve a system of political philosophy based upon his knowledge of men as they actually were, and of laws as they ought to be. And the first point in his political philosophy was to establish the unlimited authority of the state on a legitimate basis.

Nevertheless, the 'total' alienation that the state of the *Contrat Social* demanded of the citizen called only for 'such part of his powers, goods and liberty as it is important for the community to control',[23] and did not imply the renunciation of private interests. Many of the private concerns of the individual citizens would be of no importance to the state and would, therefore, not fall within its jurisdiction. On the other hand, Rousseau insisted that the sovereign would be the sole judge of what was of interest to the state and what was not. In other words, if at some time any of the private concerns of the citizens impinged upon the interests of the community, it would be for the state to say that those impinging interests fell within its jurisdiction, and not for the citizens to say so.[24] If the citizen required further assurance that his 'total alienation' to the state would not involve any undue encroachment on the part of the state on his private affairs, he would find it in Rousseau's interpretation of the scope of the law. Very briefly, according to Rousseau, law was not concerned with the particular interests of individual citizens, but solely with those affairs that were of common concern to the citizens as a whole.

The publication of the *Contrat Social*, with its justification of the 'total alienation' of the citizen together with his goods and liberty to the state in the interests of the common good of all, did not close the subject. The rights-of-man theorists persisted in their individualistic doctrine that they had inherited from Locke, and they still emphasized in varying degrees the limitations upon the competency of the jurisdiction of the state. Indeed, they read Rousseau's doctrine itself in the light of extreme individualism, although it was clearly intended to present the attributes of the state that would be essential to a balanced political philosophy.

Faced with the triumphant individualism of the French revolutionists, Burke recognized no less clearly than Rousseau had done before him that it was essential to assert the supremacy of the state.* But whereas Rousseau had attempted to present the corrective to political thought and thus to cut off fallacy at its source, Burke had to try to make the thinking and reading public understand the nature of the errors of the individualistic doctrine underlying the French revolution in order to make them see the seriousness of attempting to engraft that doctrine on the British scheme of government. He had to show them the weaknesses both in theory and in practice of doctrines that overemphasized the rights of the individual and underestimated the importance as well as the fundamental nature of the state. He criticized in particular the doctrine of the sovereignty of the people with its implication that the people were the masters of the state and could do as they pleased. This

---

* Here Burke is attacking not the economic, but the extreme political individualism of the French revolutionists. Like Rousseau, Burke saw the inadequacies of the Locke school of political thought and he looked to a philosophy of the state which took into account the organic nature of society. But at the same time he was not an anti-individualist pure and simple. Burke recognized with the individualists that the sphere of government should be severely restricted, especially where certain private interests were concerned.

doctrine, which had been drawn avowedly from the *Contrat Social*, seemed to Burke to be at the source of all the other fallacies connected with the doctrines of the French revolution. The author of it had, Burke believed, done a grave disservice to political thought. In his stand on this point, Burke took issue not only with Rousseau, but with the Whigs led by Fox who were willing to step from the doctrine of trusteeship to the more modern conception of government by the people and for the people. It seemed to Burke that in acting upon the Rousseau-inspired doctrine of the sovereignty of the people, the leaders of the revolutionary movement had destroyed the ancient French state altogether in their attempts to refashion it upon principles that recognized the inalienable rights of man. He was convinced that they had not produced a better state than the one they had destroyed. Indeed, ironically enough, he believed that the distempers of the new order indicated that the arch-individualists in France had not been able to enjoy the 'natural' rights they had claimed as inherently and inalienably theirs. In addition, the confusion and hardships that they had brought upon themselves were due to the fact that they had denied to the state its proper attributes.

'Man cannot enjoy the rights of an uncivil and of a civil state together,' he criticized. 'That he may obtain some justice, he gives up his right to determining what it is in points the most essential to him. That he may secure some liberty, he makes a surrender in trust of the whole of it.' [25]

If there was to be any such thing as a political organization, the rights and liberties of the people would have to be left without reservation in the keeping of the state.

Conversely, also, it was possible for the state to encroach too much upon individual affairs. When the doctrine of the sovereignty of the people was interpreted to mean that 'the people *is* sovereign', the state became all in all. There was neither individuality nor liberty left for the people who collectively composed the state. The extreme of collectivism was as abhorrent to Burke as the extreme of individualism. He believed that the true relationship between the people and the state was to be found by avoiding both extremes. An understanding of the nature of the state, on the one hand, and of the moral ties which bound the people to it, on the other, would save mankind much unnecessary suffering.

From his experience, Burke came to the conclusion that in principle the sovereignty of the state should be unlimited. His convictions on the subject rested ultimately upon the interpretation of the state that he had evolved under the inspiration of his vivid historical imagination. The state, it seemed to him, was the supreme form in which the life of the nation found expression, and in that fact he found definite reasons why the supreme authority of the nation could be vested in it with confidence. In the first place, the state with its institutions, its traditions and its customs had remained while many generations of citizens had come and gone. It was enduring, while in contrast the life of the individual citizen was fleeting. For the idea of the state was not an idea only of 'extant, and individual momentary aggregation,' but it was also an idea of 'continuity, which extends in time as well as in numbers and in space'.[26] It had grown, developed and had also been modified, as in the course of the ages succeeding generations had left their mark upon it. That which had been of value in their political experience had enriched the state, while that which had been foreign or inimical to the welfare and genius of the nation had fallen by the wayside. It was therefore peculiarly fitted by nature to be the ultimate court of appeal for the citizens and also the institution to which they could 'alienate' their rights, liberties and property, and yet remain secure in the knowledge that their trust would not be misplaced.

Philosophical doctrine no less than history lent support to his contention that the state so far transcended the individual as to be the logical repository of the ultimate authority of the nation. At the same time, it demonstrated clearly to Burke that the citizens were 'life-renters' in the state, rather than masters of it and at liberty to change it at will. According to contemporary philosophical doctrine, the state was a contract, a concept that had been bequeathed to the modern world by the ancient Sophists. Although he had no profound regard for that doctrine, he used it for the purpose of reinterpretation. If the state was a contract, he contended that it was no mere legal contract that could be broken at will. It had to be regarded with other reverence. In terms of his famous definition, the state was 'a partnership in all science; a partnership in all art; a partnership in every virtue, and in all perfection'.[27] And as the ends of such a partnership could not be obtained in many generations, it became a partnership not only between the living, but between those who were living, those who were dead, and those who were yet to be born. And when thus viewed in the broad sweep of history, through an imagination tinctured with mysticism, it would be found that 'each contract of each particular state is but a clause in the great primeval contract of eternal society'.[28] It was but a link between the 'lower and the higher natures', connecting the visible with the invisible world. Furthermore, it was in accordance with a 'fixed compact sanctioned by the inviolable oath which holds all physical and all moral natures, each in their appointed place'.[29] With his attention upon the deeper poetic truths of the universe that were to be seen with the prophetic eye as well as upon the practical significance of the reality of those truths, Burke contemplated an appointed order in which the various individual states had each its own assigned place and its appointed work to do. It was a moral order, preordained by the Creator.[30] Even more, it was an order that transcended the ordinary processes of nature. In the mystic-romantic world of historical imagination that order took definite shape and form, and Burke's complete faith in its existence led him to adopt a dogmatic attitude on the subject. 'I know there is an order that keeps things fast in their place,' he asserted confidently. 'It is made to us, and we are made to it.' [31] To act in defiance of that order was to wage war with nature.

The fundamental characteristics of that moral order were justice and virtue. Together they fitted into the vast framework of the moral dispensation of the universe.

'The diversified but connected fabric of universal justice, is well cramped and bolted together in all its parts,' Burke declared with conviction; 'and depend upon it, I never have employed, and I never shall employ, any engine of power which may come into my hands, to wrench it asunder. All shall stand, if I can help it, and all shall stand connected.' [32]

In the 'final proportions' of that eternal justice, the inevitable inequalities of rank and fortune here on earth at last would find compensation. But for the legislator, the principle of justice had a more immediate significance. For justice was ultimately the principle that held communities together. It was the bond that linked man to man in civil society. Common interests were the foundation upon which civil society itself had been built, and indeed, there could only be peace and security for the individual in the common interest of all.[33] But that security in its turn, depended upon the operation of the principle of justice in society. In the days of the American revolution, Burke stressed over and over again the fact that justice alone could establish bonds of unsuspecting confidence, the 'true centre of gravity amongst mankind about which all the parts are at rest'.[34] In that unsuspecting confidence all difficulties could be removed, and the reconciliation effected of all the contradictions which occurred in the complexity of all political establishments of long standing. It was vital, therefore, to the welfare of the state and of all the citizens who composed the body politic that the legislator should keep justice intact and secure. His first duty was consequently to control the forces of oppression and injustice that presented an active hindrance to the operation of the principle of justice in society. But in order to enforce the principle of justice, the legislator himself had to follow the path of virtue. It was necessary for him to be both upright and just.

'Constitute government how you please,' Burke challenged impressively; 'infinitely the greater part of it must depend upon the exercise of the powers which are left at large to the prudence and uprightness of the ministers of state. Even all the use and potency of the laws depends upon them. Without them, your commonwealth is no better than a scheme upon paper; and not a living, active, effective constitution.' [35]

Life itself fled from the state if there was no integrity in high places, for lack of integrity in high places argued lack of virtue in the nation itself.[36]

Burke did not expect to find perfection in man. But he did expect, and in point of fact acknowledged that he had found, much human virtue. While he knew that in society, some men were good and others were bad, he believed that the human race instinctively patterned itself upon virtue, just as the state was modelled upon justice.

'Man is a most unwise and a most wise being,' he wrote in giving his own version of Rousseau's doctrine of the natural goodness of man. 'The individual is foolish. The multitude, for the moment, is foolish when they act without deliberation; but the species is wise, and when time is given to it, as a species, it almost always acts right.' [37]

In the long run, the human race would find virtue, and would find in the state the necessary means to the achievement of it.

The operation of justice and virtue in the life of men and of nations was constantly in the background of Burke's thought, and he made frequent reference to it in order to stress the 'moral essence' of the state and the fundamental connexion between the state and that order. He hoped thereby to impress upon men who had been deluded by the doctrine that they were the masters of the state the fact that the body politic was to be regarded as the sphere of their duties, of their service and of their loyalty and affection. Under no circumstances whatever was it to be thought of as the creature of their will, to be remade whenever the fancy took them. It was as necessary for men to realize that a moral relationship subsisted between them and the state as it was for them to acknowledge the unlimited sovereignty of the body politic, to which they alienated in trust their natural rights, their liberties and their property.

Once again, it seemed to Burke that this would be a case of elaborating the obvious, were it not for the fact that political theorists had interpreted the state as a contract, as the creature of human will. And while not prepared to deny that in a sense and from a philosophical point of view there was truth in their doctrine, it seemed to him that the adoption of the historical, rather than the speculative, viewpoint would have obviated much fallacy. From the historical viewpoint, it was amply evident that the state had emerged as the medium through which the vast complexity of human needs, physical as well as spiritual, could find the greatest possible degree of satisfaction. But in order to function adequately, the relationship of the citizen to the state must necessarily be that of duty. Thus Burke brought forward the argument upon which aristocratic privilege rested in order to strengthen the defences of the established order against the dangers that threatened it from speculative thought.

Territorial extent, while it was the most obvious attribute of the state, was also the most superficial. Because it was the most superficial, it was also the most fertile source of error regarding the true relationship of the citizen to the state. Burke found a glaring example of the dangers to the body politic resulting from this kind of error in the geometric scheme for the division of France which the French 'political architects' had devised. 'They divide the area of their country into eighty-three pieces, regularly square, of eighteen leagues by eighteen,' he explained, in describing what seemed to him one of the most outrageous projects that the French had yet undertaken.

'These large divisions are called *Departments*. These they portion, proceeding by square measurement, into seventeen hundred and twenty districts, called *Communes*. These again they subdivide, still proceeding by square measurement into smaller districts called *Cantons*, making in all 6,400.' [38]

From the point of view of mathematics, the territory of a nation lent itself admirably to such schemes of subdivision. But from the point of view of the state, such a scheme was suicidal because it tended to the destruction of the less obvious, but more important attributes of the state.

'Mere locality', Burke stressed, 'does not constitute a body politic. . . . The body politic of France existed in the majesty of its throne; in the dignity of its nobility; in the honour of its gentry; in the sanctity of its clergy; in the reverence of its magistracy; in the weight and consideration due to its landed property in the several bailliages; in the respect due to its movable substance represented by the corporations of the kingdom. All these particular *moleculae* united, form the great mass of what is truly the body politic in all countries. They form so many deposits and receptacles of justice; because they can only exist by justice. Nation is a moral essence, not a geographical arrangement, or a denomination of the nomenclator.' [39]

In simpler language, 'Our country is not a thing of mere physical locality,' Burke wrote as if unable to stress sufficiently the truth of his assertion. 'It consists, in a great measure, in the ancient order into which we are born. . . . The place that determines our duty to our country is a social, civil relation. . . .' and furthermore, 'the place of every man determines his duty. . . .' [40] Even more explicitly, Burke had stressed the fact that 'the sphere of my duties is my true country'.[41]

When it encountered this rock of duty, Burke saw the current conception of 'will' dashed to pieces. And with the destruction of that concept, Burke felt that the overthrow of the doctrine that the state was subject to the will of the people would be assured. At least, he hoped that the harmful consequences of regarding the state as a contract, made and sanctioned by the will of the people, would be considerably lessened. 'I cannot too often recommend it to the serious consideration of all who think civil society to be within the province of moral jurisdiction,' he wrote impressively, 'that if we owe it any duty, it is not subject to our will.'[42] Duty and will were even contradictory terms. Even if, as the social contract theorists had insisted, civil society had been at first a voluntary act, and Burke was prepared to concede that it may have been so in many cases, nevertheless its continuance depended upon a 'permanent, standing covenant', which bound every individual without any formal act of his own. The basis for such an assertion was to be found in the general practice, arising out of the 'general sense of mankind'. It was simply the way in which society had invariably operated. The citizens were born into a social order, and unquestioningly they took their places in it.

'Men without their choice derive benefits from that association,' Burke pointed out, 'without their choice they are subjected to duties in consequence of these benefits; and without their choice they enter into a virtual obligation as binding as any that is actual. Look through the whole system of duties. Much the strongest moral obligations are such as were never the result of our option.' [43]

As far as the state and the social order were concerned, 'will' and 'duty' found reconciliation not in the variable wills of individual citizens, but in that 'sovereign reason' which belonged to the moral order of the universe, and which Burke recognized as paramount. A wide gulf separated the will of the ordinary man from that sovereign reason. That gulf could only be crossed and harmony established with sovereign reason itself when the individual will had divested itself completely of all selfish motives, when it had transcended fleeting and contradictory aims and interests, and when it was prepared to concentrate upon those which were enduring and non-contradictory. On that exalted level were to be found justice and virtue, and all full recognition of the equity of the duties and obligations that followed in the train of man's relationship to man in the life of the state.

Burke's thought had led him far into the realm of political philosophy—further perhaps than he would have been willing to go, had it not been for the challenge that the French revolution presented to the established order in England. That he used his insight into the fundamental nature of the state and of man's relationship to the body politic in order to reinforce the political and social institutions of England was due in large measure to the fact that he believed more firmly than ever before that the only safe changes that could be made in a state were those that were brought about by historical processes themselves in the 'silent lapse' of the ages. The deliberate changes wrought by any individual or group of individuals might prove harmful to the delicate, living fabric of the state and were therefore to be condemned. In order to make people think carefully before they attempted any such dangerous project as introducing radical change into the social and political order, he presented his conception of duty to the state.

What, then, was the sanction for the state? Where could Burke look for a power sufficiently strong to transform his doctrine of duty into reality? Was there anything more enduring or of greater strength than ties of interest or affection to which the state could look for the ultimate basis of its authority? 'I allow,' he admitted, 'that if no supreme ruler exists, wise to form, and potent to enforce, the moral law, there is no sanction to any contract, virtual or even actual, against the will of prevalent power.' 44

In religion, therefore, he found the sanction for the state. It satisfied him absolutely and completely. It coloured and gave meaning to all life. Religion was so powerful a force in society that it was able to reinforce the sanction of moral law, and to command the respect of the greater part of mankind. A conscientious believer in the faith of the established Church of England, Burke was convinced that all would be well ultimately because there was a Supreme Ruler of the universe.

Although his optimism was overclouded frequently owing to the fact that he was acutely aware of a growing, hostile spirit of unbelief that had followed in the train of deism and of the 'Parisian philosophy', he nevertheless had no hesitation in reasserting his faith in God as the moral ruler of the universe. But he admitted that if the atheistically inclined refused to acknowledge the existence of God, then might was right and there was no sanction for the moral order of the state. The circumstances of the French revolution called forth the fundamentals of the faith Burke had always held, but 'it was no service to our understanding when Burke enveloped once more in mystic obscurity the office of government and in the sphere of politics appealed once more against reason to tradition and religion'.[45]

Burke found inspiration in his creed. It illuminated his whole conception of the moral order of the universe, and gave it a sure foundation. 'We know, and, what is better, we feel inwardly', he asserted, 'that religion is the basis of civil society, and the source of all good, and of all comfort.'[46] Furthermore, 'we know, and it is our pride to know, that man is by his constitution a religious animal; that atheism is against, not only our reason, but our instincts; and that it cannot prevail long. . . .'[47] The religion to which he looked was far removed from 'uncouth, pernicious and degrading superstition'. The Christian faith that had ennobled the race and had been a powerful civilizing influence was the basis of the religious establishment of the nation. And taking ground on that religious system,

of which we are now in possession, we continue to act on the early received, and uniformly continued sense of mankind. That sense not only, like a wise architect, hath built up the august fabric of states, but like a provident proprietor, to preserve the structure from profanation and ruin . . . hath solemnly and for ever consecrated the commonwealth, and all that officiate in it.'[48]

The consecration of the state was made so that

'all who administer in the government of men . . . should have high and worthy notions of their function and destination; that their hope should be full of immortality; that they should not look to the paltry pelf of the moment, nor to the temporary and transient praise of the vulgar, but a solid, permanent existence, in the permanent part of their nature, and to a permanent fame and glory, in the example they leave as a rich inheritance to the world.' [49]

The consecration of the state was of profound significance to citizens who desired to be free. In order to secure their freedom, they had to enjoy some determinate portion of power.

'To them therefore a religion connected with the state, and with their duty towards it, becomes even more necessary than in such societies, where the people by the terms of their subjection are confined to private sentiments, and the management of their own family concerns. All persons possessing any portion of power ought to be strongly and awfully impressed with an idea that they act in trust; and that they are to account for their conduct in that trust to the one great master, author, and founder of society.' [50]

Where there was a collective sovereignty, Burke regarded it as of first importance that this principle should be impressed upon the minds of those who were called upon to exercise authority in the state. For the people should learn that their will, no more than that of kings, was the standard of right and wrong. Indeed, one of the fundamental reasons why the commonwealth and the laws were consecrated was 'lest the temporary possessors and life-renters in it, unmindful of what they have received from their ancestors, or of what is due to their posterity, should act as if they were the entire masters'.[51] They were not at liberty to 'destroy at their pleasure the whole original fabric of their society'.[52] If they left desolation in their wake, and taught their successors to respect the state as little as they themselves had done, then it would not be long until the ruin of the state would be complete.

'By this unprincipled facility of changing the state as often, and as much, and in as many ways, as there are floating fancies or fashions, the whole chain and continuity of the commonwealth would be broken. No one generation could link with the other,'

Burke declared as he gave expression to a thought which struck to the root of his objections to individualistic doctrine no matter what form it assumed. Unless due recognition were given to the fact that the life of the state constituted the element of permanence in the midst of change and that men could destroy that permanent element only at their peril, the thread of continuity would be broken and 'men would become little better than the flies of a summer'.[53]

But those who had given time to reflecting upon the consecration of the state knew that it was right that they should individually, and in their corporate capacity as citizens, offer homage to the 'institutor, and author and protector of civil society'. For they believed that 'He who gave our nature to be perfected by our virtue, willed also the necessary means of its perfection—He willed therefore the state—He willed its connection with the source and original archetype of all perfection.'[54]

That God willed the State as the only means whereby man could achieve virtue and thereby fulfil his nature was the fundamental conclusion upon which Rousseau also had based his political philosophy. In last analysis the belief that Burke and Rousseau shared in common was based upon intuition, upon that gift of seeing into the 'life of things' which both possessed. But whereas Rousseau had endeavoured to show that his fundamental tenet was in accordance with reason, Burke made no attempt to prove the truth of his convictions, and indeed would have scorned to do so. Such things could be relegated to the 'schools'. As far as he was concerned, he had merely given expression to an assumption that any rational man could accept as unquestioningly as he could the soundness of the principles of the British constitution. Rousseau, however, neither shared the sturdy British contempt for logic, nor could he afford to discard it as a test for the validity of his ideas, because his interest in political thought was primarily from the philosophical angle and not from the pragmatic point of view which Burke found so congenial. Moreover, Burke's view of the state was essentially traditional; whereas Rousseau was less concerned with studying the state as an historical growth than he was with analysing the principles which would order the life of the state if justice and right were the recognized ideals.

Rousseau's outlook on life, like Burke's, was essentially religious, but he looked to religion to fortify rather than to provide the sanction for the state. He had added the chapter on civil religion to the *Contrat Social* because he was fully aware that 'no State has ever been founded without a religious basis',[55] and that his political system would be incomplete if he failed to show the relationship of religious belief to his political principles. The essential points of faith of importance to the state would be limited to the acknowledgement of the existence of a powerful, intelligent, and beneficent God, who was also foreknowing and providential; a belief in the life to come; the happiness of the just; the punishment of the wicked; the sanctity of the social contract and of the laws. The only other essential point was tolerance, but the contemplation of the abuses to which religion was subject at the hands of the unscrupulous transformed the tolerant Rousseau into an advocate of intolerance. The state had no power over men's beliefs, he acknowledged, but it could banish those who refused to subscribe to the simple articles of faith he set forth, not as unbelievers but as anti-social individuals, while he would inflict punishment of death upon those who were treacherous enough to subscribe to those articles while in their hearts they mocked them. From the *Profession de foi du vicaire savoyard* in the *Émile*, however, it was apparent that his remarks were directed primarily against the 'philosophers', the torch-bearers of enlightenment who delighted in scepticism, and who sowed 'destructive doctrines' in men's minds. With a vehemence as intense as Burke's when he dealt with the subject in later years, Rousseau denounced sceptics because

'overthrowing, destroying, and trampling under foot all that men venerate, they rob the afflicted of their last consolation in their misery and take from the rich and powerful the sole bridle to their passions; they tear from the depths of men's hearts all remorse for crime and all hope of virtue; and they boast, in addition, that they are the benefactors of the human race'.[56]

Irreligion and the 'argumentative philosophic spirit in general' were to be viewed seriously because they sapped 'silently the true foundations of all society'.[57] But in addition, the neglect of all religion which scepticism engendered soon led to the neglect of a man's duties. Therefore, as long as there was any true faith left, Rousseau, no less than Burke, would do all in his power to save it from destruction. 'But when once everything is shaken', he wrote, 'the trunk must be preserved at the cost of the branches.' [58] He would strengthen men's conscience so that their feet could be set again upon the sure foundation of eternal truth.

If there were no God, then Rousseau acknowledged that the wicked were right, and the good man nothing but a fool.[59] But such an assumption was contrary to all that he had observed of the moral order of the universe, the reality of which was as obvious to him as it was to Burke. And satisfied that God not only existed, but was the moral ruler of the universe, Rousseau reasoned that man was free because God willed his freedom. The free man, moreover, was not left to grope blindly. In addition to his reason, he had the guidance of his conscience, which was to the soul 'what instinct is to the body', and if he allowed his conscience to direct his reason, he would not only 'follow nature', but he would not go astray. Furthermore, if moral goodness was in accordance with man's nature, then Rousseau was led to the thought that man could be healthy in mind and body only when he was good. If it were not so,

'if man is by nature evil, he cannot cease to be evil without corrupting his nature, and goodness in him is a crime against nature. Made to do harm to his fellow-creatures as the wolf is made to devour his prey, a humane man would be as depraved a creature as a pitiful wolf; and virtue alone would cause us remorse.' [60]

But men delighted in injustice only when it was to their advantage; when they looked on as disinterested spectators, they were stirred to the depths by an 'instinctive anger and wrath'. But Rousseau was even more profoundly impressed by the universality of the ideas of justice and right. They linked man directly to the moral order of the universe.

'Cast your eyes over every nation of the world,' he commented, 'look through every volume of its history . . . among this extraordinary variety of customs and of types of people, you will everywhere find the same ideas of right and justice; everywhere the same principles of morality, the same ideas of good and evil.' [61]

In the universality of the principles of justice and right, as reflected on the one hand in the conscience of man, and as embodied on the other in the moral order of the universe,

Rousseau found a stable foundation upon which the body politic could be established.

If justice and right were the principles to which the political philosopher could look to bring law and order out of the warring elements in society and to turn aimless strife into purposive activity, then that which made those principles effective would constitute the sanction for the state. Rousseau looked to the reality of the moral person which was born of the social contract to provide his sanction. He hoped to invest it with attributes that would make it the bulwark of freedom that the citizens desired, but at the same time to make it sufficiently strong to defend them against foes from within as well as from without. If he could prove that the body politic brought into existence by his social contract was not an *ens rationis*, an abstraction pure and simple, but that it was in fact a reality with power at its command to enforce the 'act of association', he believed he would be in a position to demonstrate the validity of his sanction. His first step therefore was to show that the state was not an amorphous aggregate of individual wills of the citizens, but that on the contrary it was a *persona* in its own right. Created by the corporate will of the people, it was an organic unity and was endowed with a life and will of its own. And when created, the state assumed its own personality and its own functions, the chief of which was the direction of the social forces of justice and right, and of enforcing their operation even against the desire of the citizen, if necessary.[62]

Rousseau was less interested in the idea of the social contract as a speculative study in historical origins than he was in it as the means for the transference of his conception of the autonomy of the will to the sphere of the state. He looked to the self-governing state as the only kind of body politic worthy of the name, and the only kind that would appeal to citizens who had learned to love liberty. Through the idea of the social contract, he threw into relief the fact that while the state had emerged as a separate entity and with attributes of its own, it was nevertheless created by man as the means whereby he could foster his material and spiritual welfare and for no other reason. In other words, from Rousseau's point of view, the state gave man a moral sphere of action. The 'passage' from the state of nature to the civil state, he pointed out, produced a very remarkable 'change' in man. Justice was substituted for instinct in his conduct; while his actions assumed moral qualities that had been lacking previously. It was only then, when the voice of duty took the place of impulse, and right took that of appetite, that man who had 'previously' thought only of himself, 'now' found himself obliged to act upon different principles and to consult his reason before listening to his inclinations. And although in the civil state he 'deprived' himself of some advantages he had received from nature, yet he gained others so great,

'his faculties were so stimulated and developed, his ideas so extended, his feelings so ennobled, and his whole soul uplifted to such a degree that if the abuses of this new condition did not often degrade him below that which he left, he could not fail to bless incessantly the happy moment that snatched him from it for ever, and which made an intelligent being and a man out of a stupid and limited creature'.[63]

By ascribing such a 'change' in man to the state, Rousseau not only acknowledged fully the part the body politic played in helping man's nature on its way towards perfection, but he also showed that he was not the arch-advocate of individualism that Burke proclaimed him to be.[64] The individualist would not be prepared to accept the doctrine that man owed his moral attributes to the state, whereas Rousseau not only laid stress upon the fact that in himself man was hopelessly limited, but that in the state he found the necessary means for the fulfilment of his nature and could rise to both virtue and perfection. In other words, when Rousseau got away from the position of the *Discours sur l'inégalité* and presented his mature thought, he recognized that man himself was an integral part of the social organism, and that to cut himself off from the life of society where he belonged would be about as fatal to his welfare as cutting off his supply of air would be to his life. On the other hand, neither was Rousseau the arch-advocate of collectivism as Burke would also have us believe, nor could his thought be justly regarded as 'one of the most potent implements of tyranny that maniac ever forged'.[65] His thought was directed constantly toward the ideal of liberty for the individual; to the stabilizing of conditions which made that liberty possible, and to making the individual worthy of what was, after all, his natural right. The stabilizing of man's social conditions, however, involved the important question of dependency. Nature, according to Rousseau, had made men dependent upon things only, and, since things were non-moral, they had no power to harm him or his liberty. But there was another kind of dependence which was the work of society, and that was dependence on men. And in opening the way for tyranny and every kind of vice, it seemed to Rousseau that the dependence on men could not be denounced loudly enough. He recoiled in horror at the thought of man's inhumanity to man, but at the same time he thought that even this grave weakness could be overcome.

'If there is any way of remedying this social evil', he wrote in the *Émile*, 'it is to be found by substituting law for the individual; by arming the general will with a real strength superior to the power of any individual will. If the law of nations, like the law of nature, were so inflexible that no human power could conquer it, dependence on men would become dependence on things; all the advantages of a state of nature would be united with all the advantages of social life in the republic.'

Then the liberty 'which preserves a man from vice would be united with the morality which raises him to virtue'.[66] From the rebellion against society which found eloquent expression in his early writings, Rousseau found a bridge that enabled him to regard society as man's rightful sphere, and that made it possible for man to live in society and at the same time to enjoy the freedom from injustice that had characterized life in the 'state of nature'.

If the social contract could establish the rule of law so firmly that any attempt to overthrow it would meet with the resistance of the whole body politic, then Rousseau would have no fears for the welfare of the citizens. Only under such conditions could the state dedicated to freedom, 'the masterpiece of political art', be saved from the 'most frightful abuses', for only under such conditions would the moral person which constituted the state be able to function effectively.

But Rousseau looked to the social contract not only to

secure the rule of law, but to impress upon the citizens the meaning of the sovereignty of the people. The decision or even the desire of an organized body of people to become self-governing entailed, individually as well as collectively, a deep sense of responsibility and a high ethical standard. Their duties had to be carried through conscientiously because the freedom and hence the welfare of all depended upon the acceptance of obligations as well as privileges by all alike. Furthermore, a people could assume control of its destiny only if it was prepared to accept the greater demands which the state would necessarily impose upon it. And if the 'supreme direction of the general will' was to be anything more than an empty formula, the state would have to look to its citizens not only for a full measure of active co-operation in public affairs, but for that creative spirit which alone made a sovereign people worthy of the name.

CHAPTER VII
THE GENERAL WILL

ROUSSEAU brought the State directly under the rule of moral law when he ascribed a moral personality to it. With the contract the moral person emerged, to be known henceforth as the Sovereign when active, and the State when passive. Its will was the general will. In his contract formula, the citizen placed his person and all his power under the 'supreme direction of the general will', and gradually the idea of contract faded into the background while Rousseau devoted his attention to the presentation of his idea of the general will. The doctrine of the general will was essentially an attempt to apply his conception of human freedom to political institutions.[1] It was the superstructure that unified and gave meaning to the kind of state that came into being with his contract. The general will was the constitution of the state; the living body of constitutional law, embodying the eternal principles of justice and right, which assumed reality as a people, conscious of its unity and destiny and desirous of liberty, struggled towards the realization of its highest good, and gave expression to that good in its legislation.

The doctrine of the general will was not only Rousseau's most original, but it was also his most important, contribution to political philosophy. Ideas leading toward the formulation of the doctrine had been gathered from such sources as Grotius, Pufendorff, Gravina, Hobbes, Locke, Montesquieu, and probably also from animated discussions on the subject with Diderot.[2] In the *Contrat Social* they were transformed into a synthesizing principle in which the apparently contradictory claims of individual rights and obligations, of liberty and law, were brought to terms with each other. Rousseau had, in short, examined critically and carefully the most significant contributions that had been made in the course of the previous hundred years or more toward an understanding of the problem of political obligation. Viewed in the light of his own

clearer insight, together with his appreciation of the principles
of Greek political philosophy, he saw that the individualistic
doctrine of contract, whatever its virtues, was fundamentally
inadequate. So in place of the doctrine of contract, he presented the theory of the general will.

He fully realized that to be significant for political philosophy, his theory had to be firmly rooted in the eternal
constitution of things. In this, the general will had the advantage over earlier theory owing to the fact that it belonged
essentially to the objective moral order of the universe. As
he explained in the *Profession de foi du vicaire Savoyard*,
through the 'right use' of his reason, he had analysed the
experience of the individual as well as of the human race,
and had become aware thereby of certain fundamental truths.
He had gained an intuitive perception of the operation of
universal principles in society. Together these principles
constituted a constructive, organizing force, and in the form
of justice and right, they permeated the whole of human
society. In the operation of this force, Rousseau recognized
the activity of the general will. Furthermore, the fact that
society was constantly striving with more or less success to
bring order out of disorder, and that redemptive forces were
everywhere at work, indicated to him the existence of a will-
power guiding and directing the destinies of mankind. And
just as in the experience of the individual, it was rational to
affirm the existence of a will, so also in the organic life of
society it was rational to postulate the existence of a corporate
or general will.

In a perfect society, the general will would be an infallible
guide, leading a people directly towards the common good of
all. In such a society, it would be possible to see so clearly
what was just that it would be done forthwith. In other
words, there would be no hindrance to the free play of social
forces. Anti-social influences would not intrude, and consequently selfish interests would not obscure the clear perception of that which was just and right. Neither would such
influences lead men to act unjustly. Such were the characteristics of the ideal state.

But Rousseau was only interested in utopia-building in so

far as it enabled him to present a rational ideal toward which actual states could strive. It seemed to him that social theory could lead society onwards toward progress and perfection only if it grasped principles that actually existed. Then instead of taking those principles out of their natural setting, Rousseau would probe their fundamental characteristics and would point to those elements in society which prevented them from operating as they should. Because his thought was so firmly rooted in reality, he looked askance at the ideals of the Encyclopedists, who represented the enlightened spirit of the age. They looked forward hopefully to the time when reason and knowledge should rule the world. When that day came, they believed that the cultural perfection of mankind would be at hand. Rousseau, on the contrary, had no faith in their dream because he did not believe that the advance of scientific knowledge alone would bring about the regeneration of society. From a purely practical point of view, the ideal of the Encyclopedists seemed to him to be a pure chimera. As a moralist, Rousseau could not see that the moderns had made any further progress toward perfection than the ancients had done before them. Indeed, he was inclined to believe that, if anything, there was evidence of retrogression. But retrogression was to be ascribed to the pursuit of false gods and false ideals rather than to any *grand penchant à dégénérer* inherent in the human race as a whole. That being so, he saw no reason for adopting an unduly pessimistic attitude. On the contrary, he was convinced that the progress of mankind towards perfection depended upon a sound political, ethical and educational system. The system that the Encyclopedists had worked out was one-sided, whereas Rousseau believed that the only sound system was that which was based on a knowledge of the fundamental characteristics of man, that took into account all aspects of human nature, and did not exalt knowledge at the cost of character. To the *philosophes* he pointed out that it was not sufficient to teach men what was good in order to make them practise it. They had to be brought to love it in order to touch the springs of human action. 'To know good is not to love it,'[3] he asserted; but as soon as man's reason perceived the good, his conscience would encourage him to love it. And from a love of the good would emerge a desire to put it into practice. It was therefore as important to foster man's conscience as it was to foster his reason. But as the effectiveness of moral and educational systems depended upon the political order, it seemed to Rousseau that it was of first importance to evolve a wisely ordered political system. However, that system would be wisely ordered only if it was firmly based upon the general will, the objective order that Rousseau recognized as a constituent part of human society. Progress would again be possible when the general will became the directing force in the life of nations; when its voice was no longer stifled by injustices and the pursuit of selfish aims.

To Rousseau, as to his contemporaries, progress meant essentially a computation of the advance of the human mind as reflected in its achievements, as compared with the achievements of past ages.[4] From this point of view, the scientific discoveries of the seventeenth century placed the accomplishments of the eighteenth century in a particularly rosy light. This not only gave men a feeling of enthusiasm and justifiable pride, but also encouraged them to carry forward the cultivation of the arts and sciences. But Rousseau's thought belonged essentially to the era that preceded the formulation of the doctrine of evolution. It was analytic and static in character, whereas the thought of the historical school which followed became both dynamic and evolutionary. And although at times, as in the *Lettres de la Montagne* and his later political writings, Rousseau showed a firm grasp of the more modern historical viewpoint, it was only rarely that he regarded the development of society as a dynamic process. The paradoxical form which much of his thought assumed told its own story of his struggle to reach the newer ground. Nevertheless, the deep imprint of Calvinistic doctrine that characterized his conception of human progress led him to a belief in the emergence of an ordered system in human society. He believed that God would use men and nations toward that end, even if man himself was wayward. For according to Calvin's teaching, man was made in the image of God, and it was ultimately his destiny to become like Him in character. Thus out of chaotic conditions, order would eventually come, and the destiny of mankind would be found in the achievement of that order. In the background of the physical universe as well as of society was the eternal creative power, whose operation was to be traced in and through the order of the universe. 'That love of order which creates order we call goodness,' Rousseau explained, 'and that love of order which preserves order we call justice.'[5]

In the general will he found the instrument through which the divine will functioned, making possible an ordered society. But if the general will had a meaning for a people, Rousseau had before him the task of showing how it operated in the life of a state and also of indicating the means by which it found expression. The validity of his theory, therefore, hinged upon the reality of the general will. In point of fact, Rousseau was too much of a realist to postulate a mere figment of the imagination. Its intangible nature did not necessarily make the general will any the less real; it merely served to make Rousseau's task of exposition more difficult. His chief difficulty was that its nature was such as to defy clear analysis throughout, and this circumstance led him into error at several important points. However in the broad sweep of the life of a nation, its operation could be traced clearly enough, and from his first presentation of the concept of the general will in the article on *Économie politique* in the fifth volume of the *Encyclopédie* in 1755 to his last political writings Rousseau concerned himself with the elucidation of this 'grand and luminous principle'.[6]

The germ of his doctrine of the general will was present even in the *Discours sur l'inégalité*, in which Rousseau was still mainly concerned with the destruction of false or inadequate doctrine. But when he wrote his second *Discours*, his thoughts were turning towards his own constructive doctrine, which he was to commit to paper in the article on *Économie politique* and also in the first draft of the *Contrat Social*, which was written about the year 1755.[7] Thus in the *Discours*, when discussing the nature of the fundamental contract of all governments, he pointed out that as far as their social relationships were concerned, the people had 'united all their wills in one'.[8] The organic nature of the social will was the starting-point for his own doctrine.

In the *Économie politique*, Rousseau presented a clear-cut description of the general will. He began by personifying the state: it could be regarded as 'an articulated body, living and similar to that of man'.[9] It was a moral being that possessed a will. This will was the general will, and right was its basic principle. The general will tended to the preservation and well-being of the whole body politic as well as of each part of it. It was the 'source of the laws' and the 'rule of the just and unjust' for all the members of the state. And just as the state had a general will, so also had the 'large town of the world'.[10] For the world, the law of nature was the general will, and the relationship of the different states to it was the same as that of the individual citizens to the state to which they owed allegiance. Until he rejected the appeal to the law of nature and recast the foundations of the general will in the light of more mature thought, Rousseau felt that he was basing it firmly upon the eternal constitution of things by making it rest upon natural law.[11]

The rule of justice in national, as in international, affairs was difficult to secure owing to the fact that duties and interests clashed. In that conflict, the voice of duty was not as loud as the voice of interest, and consequently the rule of justice was imperilled. Also interest tended to predominate as the citizen entered into associations that were narrower and less sacred than that of the wider, more remote association of the state. This observation was for Rousseau 'invincible proof' that the 'most general will' would always be the most just, and that consequently the voice of the people would be practically the voice of God.[12]

Rousseau had already recognized that the general will would always operate in the interests of the common good, and for that reason it was an 'important maxim' of government to follow the general will in everything. But in order to do so, the legislator had to know the general will and had to distinguish it clearly from the individual will. In addition, he had to reconcile public liberty with the authority of the government because will had no meaning unless the individual or the state was free to exercise the right of choosing between different alternatives. In order to establish that right, Rousseau fell back upon Locke's doctrine of the basis of the social contract. The motives that led men to unite in civil society, he asserted, were to obtain security for their goods, their lives and liberties through mutual protection of the whole. Otherwise, he asked, how could one oblige men to defend the liberty of the individual, if it were not connected with their own? [10] It was to law alone that men owed justice and liberty, and it was the first duty of the legislator to make the laws conform to the general will. There were two infallible rules that would guide the legislator in this task. These were the spirit of the law and the general will. The former would assist him in dealing with unforeseen circumstances; while the latter would supplement the laws and should always be consulted when the laws failed. If legislators and citizens were just, they could be sure that they were following the general will. And as virtue was 'only the conformity of the individual to the general will', the general will would operate if virtue reigned. [11]

Wise legislators would know that 'the spring of public authority' was to be found in the hearts of the citizens. But it was not enough to exhort the citizens to be good; they had to be taught to be so. However, the task of making citizens could not be accomplished in a day; and, in order to have men, it was necessary to begin teaching them while they were children. Thus public education was one of the fundamental maxims of a democracy. It was part of Rousseau's dream that if children were brought up on a basis of equality, if they were imbued with respect for the laws of the state and for the maxims of the general will, and if they were constantly reminded of the 'tender mother' that nourished them, they would in return love each other as brothers, they would will nothing that was contrary to the will of society, and would become in time the defenders and fathers of their country. [14] By such a process, patriotism would glow warmly within them and would lead them on toward their destiny.

In the *Contrat Social*, Rousseau's central problem was the philosophical interpretation of the general will. He had accepted it as a fact in his article on *Économie politique*, and had described its nature and mode of operation in simple, clear terms. Between the article for the *Encyclopédie* and the final draft of the *Contrat Social* (1762), he had devoted much time to political philosophy. He realized that his own thought turned upon the concept of the general will rather than upon the doctrine of contract. Consequently he used the contract fiction to stress his fundamental contention that the only legitimate basis for the state was the free consent of the citizens, but allowed the concept of contract to recede into the background in order to devote his attention to the analysis of the doctrine of the general will. He found it far from easy to avoid defects in analysis, partly because he was presenting an original conception, and partly because of the interplay of its subjective and objective aspects, both of which had to be taken into careful consideration.

Rousseau's starting-point in the *Contrat Social* was his observation of the fact that relationships of a fundamental and organic nature subsisted between the various aspects of the life of the state. Thus he was able to postulate a state which was a 'moral and collective person' and in so doing he made a signal advance upon the work of earlier thinkers, to whom these aspects had remained scattered and, to a certain extent, unconnected truths. In identifying the general will with the will of that moral person, Rousseau was in a position to base it upon an organic conception of society, and through his use of personification to stress the fundamental nature of that organic unity. He saw in the general will a unifying principle which not only could give coherence to the body politic in all its aspects, but could also give meaning and direction to the whole life of the state. He recognized it as a constructive, integrating principle operating in and through society, although its essence was to be looked for not so much on the surface as in the substrata of the life of society. His problem was therefore to transfer this principle to the service of the state. To that end he had, on the one hand, to trace its operation through society both in the motivation and social attitude of the people, and also through legislation which for him was its characteristic means of expression. And the ideal he kept before him in the *Contrat Social* was that of a free people, guided by the general will, choosing the right and the just, and giving expression to that choice in its laws and institutions. Through the acceptance of the supreme authority of the general will, each citizen became an integral part of the state. Rousseau recognized the first expression of the general will in the desire of a people to live together in an ordered society based upon freedom and justice, so that from their mutual association they could enjoy benefits that were beyond their reach as separate individuals. But such a desire could be realized only because there were interests which all shared in common.

'If the opposition of particular interests has rendered necessary the establishment of civil societies', Rousseau pointed out, 'it is the agreement of these interests which has made it possible. The common element in these different interests forms the social bond. If there were not some point in which all interests were in agreement, society could not exist.' [15]

Because there were common interests and because men found it possible to form political society on a basis of those interests, a bond of union was established through which the citizen found himself no longer 'isolated', but became a member and integral part of the corporate body of the state. From that membership emerged a sense of the solidarity of society, and of the fundamental unity within the group of all the individuals composing it. The only way of assuring stability to that bond was through a mutual agreement that it should be founded upon the principle of justice. But in so doing, the citizens enthroned the general will as supreme, because it was through the agency of the general will that justice became effective. In addition, Rousseau believed that it was an 'incontestable maxim' that the general will was alone competent to assume direction of the common good. When once the social bond was rendered stable, it could be strengthened through the active co-operation of the citizens in fostering the common good. It was out of the enthusiasm and interest of the citizens, born of the advantages and the utility they found in the body politic, that good laws and good institutions were created and that their state flourished. That which each contributed to the common good served to enrich it; and because this was the result, sharing did not decrease, but rather increased the good of the individual citizen. Man, in point of fact, could make progress only through society; the isolated man simply stayed as he was.[16]

When all the citizens acknowledged the supreme authority of the general will, the state could function. The common good was sufficiently broad and inclusive to make an adequate sphere for its activity. Moreover, the general will concerned itself exclusively with the common good. And because it was in a position to devote itself exclusively to the common good, it was able to give a measure of stability and security to that good that the citizens individually could not give. For the citizens were interested in their own private affairs as well, and consequently their attention was not constantly upon the common good as such. In referring their interests to the common good, the citizens had to distinguish between their 'true' and their 'private' interests. Their 'true' interests would not be found to be at variance with the common good at any point; whereas their 'private' interests had no reference whatsoever to the common good. Private interests were those which belonged to the individual citizen exclusively; and because they were his property, they could not be shared by others and so could not enrich the common good. The 'true' interests of the citizen were more fundamental than his 'private' interests, and could be implemented by wise political action. Not only would he benefit by such action, but others would share directly or indirectly in the augmented common good. Because their particular interests tended naturally to draw the will of the citizens away from the common good toward their private concerns, the general will of the state, not concerned with those particular interests, was in a position to safeguard the common good and to see that the citizens could not reap unfair advantages over each other. From its nature, the general will favoured all alike, and drew its strength from the fact that it was as just as it was impartial.

Rousseau recognized that the wills of the citizens would not accord constantly with the general will, and indeed did not expect them to do so.

'If it is not impossible for a particular will to agree on some points with the general will,' he commented, 'it is at least impossible for this accord to be lasting and constant; because the particular will tends by its nature to preferences, and the general will, to equality.' [17]

Nevertheless, the general will was the standard for the individual will, and it alone was competent to direct the individual will toward the common good. It was particularly important to recognize this fact, because sovereignty was the exercise of the general will, and Rousseau looked to the sovereign people to carry through the exceedingly difficult task of self-government. For on Rousseau's view, sovereignty could never be alienated. The exercise of the general will was the distinctive as well as the supreme prerogative of a people. The moment a people agreed to place the direction of its destinies in the hands of anyone else, it alienated thereby that which made it truly a body politic. Rousseau stressed the fact that if a people promised simply to obey, by that very act it dissolved itself and lost that which made it a people. 'The moment a master exists', he declared, 'there is no longer a Sovereign, and from that moment the body politic has ceased to exist.' [18]

Willingness to guide its own destinies and to assume responsibility for its own actions was, from Rousseau's point of view, the essential characteristic of a body politic. Hobbes had not believed that a people could assume such responsibility, and for that reason he had placed the sovereignty in the hands of a prince, who assumed the responsibility for the people. From the time of Hobbes onward, however, political experience had led an increasing number of serious-minded thinkers to realize that while the incompetency of a people to assume the sovereignty was the familiar argument used in favour of absolutism and 'benevolent despotisms', it was not necessarily true. And before noteworthy pages were written in American history to prove that a nation could grow strong when it defied the forces of oppression and asserted its determination to direct its own destinies, the belief had already grown that, left to himself, man would strive towards virtue; while left to their own collective wisdom, peoples would govern themselves probably better and certainly no worse than priests and kings had ever governed them. Rousseau was firmly convinced that self-government was the only way that nations could free themselves from tyrants and could seek their own happiness and welfare. For that reason he insisted that under no circumstances could a body politic retain its status if the people relinquished the exercise of the general will. It could delegate to others the work that had to be done in order to carry its will into effect, but in so doing, it was in no sense placing itself under the direction of a master. Neither could such a delegation be regarded as a renunciation of its initiative, for in its constructive capacity alone the general will could remain in any real sense the supreme guide for the people.

And as the general will could not be alienated, so also it was indivisible. For will either was, or was not, general; it was either the will of the body of the people, or only of a part of the people. But to this statement Rousseau added a note in which he pointed out that to be general, a will need not always be unanimous; but every vote had to be counted. From the point of view of a people, the exercise of the general will was essentially the expression of their social will when directed to its proper sphere, which was the common good. Whether unanimous or not, so long as the citizens were conscious of their solidarity as a group and voted from the one objective common to them all, the majority vote would register the general will.

While Rousseau had enumerated some of the fundamental characteristics of the general will for the guidance of the sovereign people, he was nevertheless aware that human affairs were often so complex that the general will could be elicited only with difficulty. After he had expressed his judgement and to the best of his ability had voted for the common good, the citizen had to leave it to time to discover whether or not his will had been for the good of the people as a whole. If it had not been altogether wrong, time would still be required quite as much as insight to remove contradictions and irrelevancies and to bring it into harmony with the steadfast objectives of the body politic. In other words, it had to be moulded to the personality of the state, and it had to harmonize with the general will. From that process of experience, the citizen gained wisdom. But the general will of the state, on its part, gained both depth and content. It became, as it were, a well into which experience poured that which had shown itself to be for the good of the whole body politic; a repository to which additions could always be made, and which would serve to strengthen whatever superstructure the citizens wished to build upon it.

The general will could be depended upon as an infallible guide; but it did not necessarily follow that in their deliberations, the citizens would recognize it. They willed their own good, but did not always see what it was. It was consequently possible for them to mistake their own good and to will something that was hurtful to the common good. The general will was the constant choice of the good, but Rousseau recognized that as far as the citizens were concerned, circumstances might arise which, in addition to insufficient knowledge, would serve to obscure yet further the nature of that good. But if the citizens were not able to give expression to the general will, they could register the will of all as a result of their deliberations.

There were differences of a fundamental nature between the will of all and the general will. In the first place, the will of all was simply the sum of the individual wills of the citizens; whereas the general will was the will of the moral person known as the state. The general will was the organized social will; while in contrast, the will of all was the mass of disorganized particular wills and did not exclude selfish or even corrupt wills. Furthermore, the general will looked solely to the common good; whereas the will of all recorded that which each citizen took to be his particular interest or good. But when the general will eluded the citizens, it seemed to Rousseau that out of the wills of all, a process of refinement or of social logic would produce a result that would be the same as the general will. There would be a general element in the vote taken, for without it there could be no consensus. In other words, the matter in question would be of interest to all the citizens and would therefore fall within the competency of the general will. The result of their vote would record their assent or dissent to the proposal in question, and if they agreed, even for different reasons, the fact of their agreement would enact the general will, although it would not express it. Or arguing from the somewhat debatable assumption that out of the clash of differences a process of cancellation would remove contradictions and votes that had least reference to the common good, Rousseau concluded that the dominant good would emerge. This good, which would be what was left as the will of all became integrated, would be in effect the same as the general will. Only the general will would have indicated it by a much more direct method. Those who had thought definitely of the welfare of the state would find at the end of this process that their wills counted in the final result, while the wills of those who had followed their own interests had neutralized each other. For the common good was the enduring good of a people; whereas in contrast individual interests were fleeting. In a last analysis, the will of all could only give expression to the momentary and passing good of a people, and only in so far as that good contained an element of the enduring good could the will of all establish its affinity with the general will.

Rousseau laid such strong emphasis upon the motivation of the citizen because he believed that in the long run right motives would triumph over errors in judgement. He believed that if the citizen followed in the path of the general will, his will would be social and would ultimately lead him in the right direction. But if his judgements and his voting were determined by the effort to himself as a private individual, and not by the effect upon the community as a whole, his will would be that of the particular and not of the citizen who was conscious of the fact that he was an 'integral part of the whole'. If he and others voted for a tariff because it was in the interests of their particular businesses, their votes could only be the sum of particular wills, or the will of all. But it might so happen that a tariff was also for the good of the country, in which case the general will would coincide with the will of all. Nevertheless, the result would simply record the fact that on this particular matter, the majority of the citizens voting were desirous of establishing a tariff, and that they wanted it for their own purposes, and not from any thought of public interest. From the point of view of the state, the difference in motivation was profoundly significant. In the first place, the general will implied a unity of purpose and of interest on the part of the citizens without which there could be no state ; whereas the will of all merely recorded the agreement of the citizens upon individual matters, and in no wise implied a consciousness of unity of purpose and interest such as that which characterized the general will. But it was in the consciousness of that unity and that common interest that the will of the citizens became general. In Rousseau's words, 'what makes the will general is less the number of voters than the common interest uniting them'.[19]

As the distinguishing characteristic of the organized life of the state consisted in the presence of various institutions through which it endeavoured to meet the needs of the citizens by providing them with the necessary channels for their activities, Rousseau had to take into consideration the relationship of the wills of these institutions to the general will of the state. He was frankly hostile to these institutions, which he termed 'partial associations', because they seemed to him to remove the will of the citizen from the direct guidance of the general will of the state. If the general will was to express itself, he insisted, it was essential 'that there should be no partial society within the State, and that each citizen should think only his own thoughts'.[20] Instead of remaining a simple direct relationship, the intrusion of these partial associations rendered that relationship complex. Each association possessed a will that was particular in relation to the general will of the state, but was general in relation to its members. Apart from this consideration, however, there was also a more intimate relationship between the individual and the 'partial' association than between the citizen and the broader and more inclusive interests of the state, and Rousseau feared that the smaller association would absorb the interests of the individual at the cost of the state. Even more, he feared the dominance of these associations, should they become centralized and powerful.

Therefore if man could not refrain from his institution-building propensities, Rousseau would have him establish as many partial associations within the state as possible, in order to avoid the dangers of undue strength and influence.* But in clinging to the uninfluenced and independent judgement of the citizen, Rousseau was in point of fact

'ensuring the exact reverse of what he professes to aim at. He is appealing from the organized life, institutions, and selected capacity of a nation to that nation regarded as an aggregate of isolated individuals. And, therefore, he is enthroning as sovereign, not the national mind, but that aggregate of private interests and ideas which he has himself described as the Will of All.' [21]

This bias in Rousseau's mind, which showed itself also in his rejection of representative government and in his preference for federations of relatively small units rather than for the great nations of the modern world, did not detract greatly from the significance of his thought. Indeed, by keeping to the simple, as opposed to the complex, he was able to emphasize and to safeguard the organic unity of the state as it was reflected in

---

* In so far as the totalitarian state can claim to make effective the organized national will, it may be said to realize Rousseau's political ideal. The functioning of the state as an organic whole, as a *persona*, and its direction by the unified national will, are in keeping with his doctrine. The elimination of parties, or 'partial associations', tends to the simplification of the political structure, to which Rousseau would give his unqualified approval. He also stated specifically that much valuable time was lost in deliberation by public assemblies, and that the secret of success in politics was to be able to act promptly and effectively.

But at the same time, the manner in which the totalitarian state actually finds expression, either in communism or fascism, is opposed to the whole spirit of Rousseau's thought. His *Contrat Social* was not an exaltation of the state; it was an attempt to reconcile the rights of the individual with those of the state. Although the 'total alienation' of the citizen to the state of which he spoke in the fundamental pact could lead to the totalitarian state, nevertheless the complete subservience of the individual to the state demanded in the authoritarian state is as foreign as extreme individualism to Rousseau's essential teaching. The totalitarian state is in point of fact the realization of one of his greatest fears: namely, that if partial associations should become centralized and powerful, they would dominate the life of the state. Totalitarianism is essentially the domination of the state by one party which is powerful enough to eliminate all other parties and does eliminate them. It is central in Rousseau's doctrine that the general will should become clarified through the free interplay of social forces, that is, through historical process, and that the citizens should play their part in that clarification through the adoption of a public-spirited attitude and through the full and free discussion of their thoughts. In the totalitarian state the supreme governing body assumes the function of clarifying the national mind; it alone has the right to freedom of thought and action, which it exercises before "the party has spoken" and it alone assumes the right to that creative activity which Rousseau regarded as the right of the whole nation. In other words, the methods of the totalitarian states are directly opposed to Rousseau's political ideals.

the relationship of the general will to the citizens on the one hand and to legislation in which it found embodiment on the other. The social contract had given life to the body politic, but it remained for the general will to give it movement and direction. The general will spoke through laws, and thus it was through the function of legislation that it determined what ought to be done for the welfare and preservation of the state. But this was simply another way of saying that the sovereign people had to legislate in accordance with the general will, for otherwise it would place the well-being of the state in jeopardy. Hence it was of first importance to discover the nature of the general will and how the will of the citizen could be brought to reflect it, so that when he was engaged in the all-important task of initiating legislation for his country, he would have a standard to guide him in his deliberations.

Rousseau's anxiety to bring the will of the citizen into conformity with the general will suggested that the will of the individual might clash with the will of the state. Although there was a fundamental relationship between them, Rousseau made it clear that the will of the state was not subject to the passing whims of the citizens. 'The constant will of all the members of the State is the general will,' he asserted; 'by virtue of it they are citizens and free.' [22] The implication was clearly that the 'constant will' of the citizen might be something he would not recognize; that it was his 'real' will as opposed to the 'actual' will which he recognized as his own everyday will. Just as the will of all had to pass through a process of correction before it could serve as a guide for the state, so also the will of the individual citizen required a certain amount of organizing and correcting before it could represent his 'real' will. In ordinary life, immediate interests might lead the will in one direction; whereas if those interests were viewed in the light of the ultimate good, the longer view might well take the will in a completely different direction. In other words, the aims and interests of the moment might not be in accordance with the good which the individual willed. But that he would will his own good could be taken for granted, since he would scarcely desire to compass his own harm. Consequently, what he willed at any given moment might not be what the logic of his will implied. It might not be the good toward which his life was directed. Therefore the choices that he made could lead to harmful results because he could not see the good he willed. This was understandable because life itself was a constant process of becoming, of creative activity, and could not be surveyed in its entirety. It was exceedingly difficult for the individual to tell exactly what was hidden beyond life's distant horizons, and what ultimately was the goal toward which his life was leading. Nevertheless, either through experience or insight, or through both, he would gain knowledge of the direction in which his true good was to be found. If he could not see the whole way, as a rule it would be possible for him to see the next step forward. But if his 'real' or constant will was at one with the general will, then in spite of the possibility of clashes between his own will and the will of the state, it was to the state that he had to look in order to find his greatest good.

If the individual found it difficult to direct his own life toward his own good, he would find it even more difficult to legislate for the body politic. Rousseau fully recognized the difficulty. Laws were, properly speaking, only the conditions of civil association, he explained. But

'the people who are subjected to the laws, ought to be their author; it belongs only to those who associate together in society to regulate the conditions of their association. But how are they to regulate them? Will it be by common agreement, by a sudden inspiration? Has the body politic an organ to declare its will? Who will give it the necessary foresight to formulate and announce its acts in advance? Or how will it announce them in time of need? How can a blind multitude, that often does not know what it wills, because it rarely knows what is good for it, carry out for itself so great and difficult an enterprise as a system of legislation? Of itself the people always wills the good, but of itself it does not always see it. The general will is always in the right, but the judgement which guides it is not always enlightened. . . . The individuals see the good they reject; the public wills the good it does not see. All are equally in need of guides. The former must be compelled to conform their wills to their reason; the latter must be taught to know what it wills. . . .' [23]

This, Rousseau concluded, made a legislator necessary.

The legislator was an 'extraordinary' person in the state. He had no official authority, but he was chosen because of his genius and insight to elucidate the general will for the people and to lead them toward their own good without becoming in any sense their master. The idea of the legislator appealed to Rousseau for two important reasons. In the first place, he was anxious for his state to have a sound constitution. He disliked the way in which the laws of the different European countries were made up of shreds and patches.[24] One law was made to remedy the abuses of another, until at length in the multiplicity of laws, legislation lost its vitality. In the second place, Rousseau wanted a guiding spirit who could accomplish what Moses, Lycurgus, and Numa had done in the past.[25] He looked back with unfeigned admiration to the way in which Moses had turned wandering tribes into a free people. When they had had not so much as a stone upon which to rest their heads, he had implanted the seeds of nationhood so successfully that the Hebrew people had remained a nation, in spite of being conquered and losing their country. Lycurgus had had a different kind of problem. His work had been to transform the Spartans from a degraded and enslaved people into a noble race that gave its laws to the whole of Greece. In the light of such achievements the essential problems confronting the modern legislator could hardly be regarded as insurmountable. If the nascent people of his ideal state were to be in a position to relish sound principles of political theory and to follow the fundamental rules of statecraft, 'the effect would have to become the cause', he stated paradoxically. 'The social spirit, which should be created by those institutions, would have to preside over their very foundations; and men would have to be before law what they should become by means of law.'[26] And the legislator, unable to appeal to either reason or force, had to resort to divine sanctions in order to 'constrain by divine authority' those whom human prudence could not move.

It was precisely because man possessed those qualities which could be developed by legislation and political institutions into a social spirit that the problem of the legislator admitted of solution. Man created laws in order to help him in his strivings toward the good, while laws and institutions played their part by making more clear to him the nature of that good and by providing the necessary means for the attainment of it. As the nature of that good became more explicit, through the agency of the general will which operated whenever the social spirit sought to find the good, laws and institutions could be improved, and progress would be possible for both man and the state.

The kind of people that would benefit most from the work of the legislator would be one which had progressed to a point at which it had evolved bonds of unity from 'origin, interest, or convention', but which had not felt the 'real yoke' of law. It would not have either customs or superstitions deeply ingrained, and while it would not stand in fear of invasion, it would be able to resist enemies if necessary. It would be sufficiently compact for the members to know each other, and it would not impose upon any man burdens that were too heavy to be borne. It would be independent; neither rich nor poor, but self-sufficient. Furthermore, it would unite the solidarity of the Greek city state with modern youthfulness of spirit. Rousseau concluded his description of the kind of people worthy of the services of the lawgiver by paying a graceful compliment to Corsica—the one country left in Europe that he regarded as capable of being given laws.

Liberty and equality, Rousseau pointed out, were the two main objects of every system of legislation. Liberty was desirable from the point of view of the state 'because all particular dependence means so much force taken from the body of the State'; while without equality, liberty could not exist. By equality, Rousseau did not mean that 'the degree of power and riches are to be absolutely identical for everybody'; but that power should never be great enough for oppression and that it should always be exercised by virtue of rank and law; also that as far as riches were concerned 'no citizen shall ever be wealthy enough to buy another, and none poor enough to be forced to sell himself'.[27] In addition to these two principles common to all legislative systems, every nation had 'in itself something that gives them a particular application, and makes its legislation peculiarly its own'.[28] But the legislator had to work in accordance with nature if the constitution of a state was to be really solid and enduring. If he mistook his object and adopted a principle other than the circumstances naturally directed:

'if his principle makes for servitude while they make for liberty; or if it makes for riches, while they make for populousness; if it makes for peace, while they make for conquest—the laws will be observed to lose their influence insensibly; the constitution will change, and the State will have no rest from disturbance until it is either destroyed or altered, and invincible nature has resumed her sway.' [29]

There were four kinds of laws with which the legislator would be occupied. The first were the constitutional laws, known as 'political' or 'fundamental' laws. Agreeing with Montesquieu that there was only one good system of laws for each state, Rousseau advised any nation that was fortunate enough to be in possession of that good system to hold fast to it. But if, on the other hand, the established order was bad, 'why should laws that prevent men from being good be regarded as fundamental?' [30] In any case, he argued, a people was always in a position to change its laws, no matter how good they might be. Even if it chose to do itself harm, he added, who had the right to stop it? After the constitutional law, the legislator had to think of civil and criminal law, but there was a fourth kind of law that was even more important than any of the others. It was not 'graven on tablets of marble or brass', but on the hearts of the citizens. This was the real constitution of the state. Every day it assumed new powers. When other laws decayed or died out, it restored them or else took their place. It kept a people in the ways in which it was meant to go, and almost unnoticed it replaced authority by the force of habit.

'I am speaking of morality, of custom,' Rousseau explained, 'and above all of public opinion, a power unknown to political thinkers, but on which none the less the success of all the others depends. With it, the great legislator concerns himself in secret, although he seems to limit himself to particular regulations; but these are no more than the arc of the arch, while manners and morals, slower to arise, form in the end its immovable keystone.' [31]

Thus the real constitution of the state was to be found, not so much in the tablets of marble or brass, but deeply embedded in the moral nature of the citizens themselves. When the legitimate authority of the state called for so little justification in the minds of the people that they were prepared to accept it as a matter of course, Rousseau recognized that it had found a secure abiding-place in the substrata of the life of society. And because it was able to establish itself in the foundations of society, it was also able to find expression in the social forces with which the people were most familiar and which touched them more closely than their legal systems. Thus it came to permeate their customs, their manners, and their morals, and to mould itself to their particular circumstances in such a way that it became a part of themselves.

Of all these social forces, however, the legislator singled out public opinion for special attention, because it was through public opinion that the general will found its greatest source of strength. It was a 'power unknown to political thinkers' because the kind of state in which it could function most effectively was only beginning to emerge. It was practically unknown under feudalism, which Rousseau scathingly denounced as 'that iniquitous and absurd system which degrades humanity and dishonours the name of man',[32] where privilege and a ruling caste imposed so-called laws and government. But when that system was cast aside for a political association more in keeping with the dignity of man's nature, public opinion would be able to take its rightful place. It was, in point of fact, only able to emerge in a state which seriously attempted to govern itself in accordance with the general will. When the people were allowed to give full and free expression to their ideas, Rousseau believed that a public opinion would crystallize that would not only help to clarify the national mind, but would support that which was good in national life as well. It would do so because that which a people accepted as right guided its judgements and determined the nature of its opinions. And recognizing that his art consisted to a large extent in establishing a fundamental accord between the legislation and that conception of right upon which public opinion was based, Rousseau's legislator saw the wisdom of 'concerning himself in secret' with that public opinion. Legislation could not be looked upon as firmly established until it had finally been ratified by public opinion, and therefore the legislator could not regard his task as completed until he had secured that ratification. He would have to anticipate some difficulty in this owing to the fact that there was an element of uncertainty in public opinion, in that it could be swayed by the demagogue or the subtle propagandist. He had consequently to keep constant vigil in order to save public opinion from the snares that were set for it, some of which he could foresee and therefore could guard against.

Rousseau did not expect any particular individual to solve the complicated problems that were the special care of his legislator. For the legislator to whom he looked was one of the rarest of persons, and in so far as either institutions or individuals possessed the necessary qualities of insight and leadership to fit them for his special work, Rousseau would have them undertake it. But while they could fulfil the most important service the state could ask of any individual or any group of people, Rousseau would not allow them to become masters of the state. They were to work through the constitutional agencies provided by the state, or through the social forces which supported those agencies in the life of the state. With their greater insight into the general will and into the means through which it found expression, they were to teach the people not only the nature of the good, but what principles would have to be applied in order to secure it. The gifts possessed by the prophet and the teacher were required by those who would assume the duties of Rousseau's legislator.

Although men as individuals were born free, every form of society did not permit the realization of social freedom. Rousseau acknowledged that 'liberty, not being a fruit of all climates, is not within the reach of all peoples'.[33] There were peoples to whom the work of the legislator would not have any real value. Where decadence and external circumstances conspired to kill all desire for freedom, there would be no vitality left in the nation. Consequently it would not be an encouraging task to try to revive its laws and bring back life to its body politic. But in the kind of community which

Rousseau described as that which was most suitable for the services of the legislator, the qualities existed which would enable the people to give their state a suitable form, and by following the general will to establish a living constitution. As the 'life principle' of the body politic was to be found in the sovereign authority, such a people could be taught to use it aright so that the state would live and the general will would remain their surest guarantee against tyranny and oppression.

One of their first enactments would be to establish their government and to decide what form it should take. In this, they would have to be guided by circumstances, and Rousseau would admit as legitimate any form of government in which the general will, or the laws through which the general will found expression were recognized as supreme. The simple forms of government which he recognized were democracy, aristocracy, and monarchy. Democracy could not be considered as a suitable form for men as it called for a degree of virtue and excellence to be found only among the gods. A monarchy was the natural form assumed by powerful and wealthy peoples. At heart a republican, Rousseau distrusted kings because of their notorious love of power and their ambition, but his objection to the monarchy rested mainly upon the fact that it was the furthest removed from his ideal of an egalitarian society. Intermediate orders, with princes, personages, and nobility to compose them, had to be established in order to make a link between the monarchy and the people, for without that link there was no bond of union in the state.[34] The king was too far removed from the people. Of the three forms that aristocracy could assume, elective aristocracy came nearest to his ideal. Wise government was made possible through the election of men of upright character and of experience. Virtue was needed in an elective aristocracy as in a democracy, but moderation also was necessary. With the elective aristocracy, Rousseau insisted upon the sovereignty of the people, for while aristocracy was 'the best of governments', it was also 'the worst of sovereignties'.[35] Thus the popular sovereignty and the elective aristocracy which Rousseau described as the best combination for the state were subsequently linked together under the modern meaning of the word 'democracy'.

Strictly speaking, however, there was no such thing as a 'simple' government. Rousseau agreed that a monarch required the assistance of magistrates, while a democratic people needed a leader.

The distinctions between the different forms of government were of minor importance for Rousseau owing to the fact that he insisted upon the assembling of the sovereign people before any valid legislation could be enacted. 'The sovereign,' he declared, 'having no force other than the legislative power, acts only by means of the laws; and the laws being solely the authentic acts of the general will, the sovereign cannot act save when the people is assembled.'[36] The sovereignty was indivisible and inalienable, and therefore it was only when the sovereign people had met together for the purpose of deliberation that the general will could speak through the laws.

'Sovereignty,' he continued emphatically, 'for the same reason as makes it inalienable, cannot be represented; it lies essentially in the general will, and will does not admit of representation. . . . Every law a people has not ratified in person is null and void—is, in fact, not a law.'[37]

From Rousseau's point of view, it was the legislative power rather than the laws themselves which preserved the vitality of the state. So long as the legislative power existed to enact new legislation when the usefulness of old laws had gone, the state would be safe. The sovereign alone had the function of making the laws, and while yesterday's laws could not be regarded as binding to-day, yet if they were good, they would remain in force by tacit consent. But to be good, a law had to be an expression of the general will upon some matter affecting the common good. It could not fit into Rousseau's definition of law if it dealt with anything outside the common good. Thus particular interests as such were outside the scope of law. Neither could a wise measure be accepted as a law if it had not been enacted by the sovereign people when they met together for the purpose of deliberating upon the common good. Rousseau acknowledged that the majority vote would count when the deliberations of the sovereign people were properly constituted and were carried out in the spirit of the general will, and that the law which was enacted as a result of that vote would express the general will, because under such conditions the voice of the people would be the 'voice of God'.[38]

But in leaving the laws at the stage of majority decision, Rousseau took them only a part of the way toward their ultimate destination in the living constitution, and consequently was not true to the deeper insight that characterized his understanding of the subtle processes of social logic through which the general will became clear and at last found permanent embodiment in the laws and institutions of the state.

Fundamentally Rousseau was dealing with the problem of how to find a way of reflecting the national mind in legislation. Enlightened states were turning to representative government which, with all its defects, seemed to present the most natural channel for their legislation. But Rousseau rejected it as incompetent to resolve the problem. His indictment of it was based upon sound criticism, for the representative government that he had seen as an outside observer was no more than an adaptation of feudal privilege,[39] and consequently it could in no wise be regarded as a satisfactory medium for the exercise of sovereignty in the only sense in which sovereignty had significance for him. His insistence that the sovereign people should make the laws in person was in the interests of an undivided and unlimited sovereignty. It was of the essence of sovereignty that it could not be limited. If it was not supreme, it was worthless.[40] And while he clung to this fundamental conviction as basically sound, he nevertheless gave a clear demarcation of the province of law in constitutional government which effectively, and rightly also, limited the competency of his sovereign. To be valid, political law could not invade the domain of the particular, but had to remain general in its object. 'Law cannot by its nature have a particular and individual object,'[41] he wrote in the course of a résumé of his fundamental principles. But he restrained political law yet further by linking it to moral law through his stipulation that the only authentic acts of the general will were those which were directed to the common good. Hence the only kind of law that the sovereign could recognize was 'a public and solemn declaration of the general will upon an object of common interest. I say, on an object of common interest, because law would lose its power and would cease to be legitimate if it did not concern all.' [42] And as the general will was concerned solely with the common good, the common interest became a matter affecting the welfare of all, and the sovereign could accept as legitimate, not the laws which harmed the people, but only those which were for their welfare.

The means through which the sovereign people gave expression to its will was in the first instance through the vote. Rousseau invested his sovereign people with the right of voting, not on the basis of the right of universal suffrage, but because their moral and intellectual qualities fitted them for freedom. But in addition to the right of voting, the sovereign people could give free expression to their opinions. Out of this right, public opinion was born. Thus there were two powerful weapons in the hands of the citizens, which together could preserve for them the direction of their own affairs. It was this right to be masters of their own destinies that Rousseau was primarily interested in securing for the sovereign people. And incidentally through the effective use of those two weapons, modern democracies have been able to reconcile representative government with popular sovereignty. As Rousseau's legislator recognized, laws were not a part of the living and enduring constitution until they had passed through the fire of public opinion and had finally won their right to a place in the fundamental law of the state. In other words, a majority decision had to win its way to general assent. It had to pass through the stage of controversy and undergo purging in the fierce light of public opinion if it was to become the true reflection of the national mind, and hence the voice of the general will that the sovereign recognized as law. If it could pass through this rigorous test, it would then be able to take its place in that living code of law to which the citizens looked with pride and affection as the constitution of their country.

CHAPTER VIII

THE BRITISH CONSTITUTION

'OUR constitution is like our Island, which uses and restrains its subject Sea; in vain the waves roar,' Edmund Burke told his fellow-members of Parliament with a glow of patriotic pride in his speech on Reform of Representation in the House of Commons in 1782, as he gave expression to his sentiments regarding the constitution that had been bequeathed to them by their liberty-loving ancestors.

'In that Constitution I know, and exultingly I feel, both that I am free, and that I am not free dangerously to myself or to others. I know that no power on earth, acting as I ought to do, can touch my life, my liberty, or my property. I have that inward and dignified consciousness of my own security and independence, which constitutes, and is the only thing, which does constitute, the proud and comfortable sentiment of freedom in the human breast. . . .' [1]

Rousseau had thought of the constitution of his ideal state in terms of the general will, and had concerned himself with an analysis of its fundamental principles. Burke, on the other hand, looked upon the constitution of his country, not as a philosophical principle, but as the concrete fabric that liberty had built, for which he felt profound reverence and respect. A sense of awe, of wonder and of boundless admiration suffused his mind as he contemplated the intricacies of the constitutional machinery of his country, the harmonious working of which secured that freedom which he and all other Englishmen alike enjoyed. In striking contrast to the warmth and colour of Burke's sentiment, Rousseau's attitude was one of calm, philosophic detachment.

Yet curiously enough, Burke's deep attachment for the constitution of his country was based fundamentally upon the fact that he saw in it the beneficent operation of those very principles which Rousseau had regarded as the fundamental constituents of the general will. Therefore, instead of crushing Rousseau's teaching, as he had set out to do in the days of the

French revolution, he gave eloquent proof that, when put into practice, the principles of the general will actually would guarantee the liberty and welfare of a free people. The irony of this situation was due primarily to the fact that Burke had missed entirely the significance of Rousseau's doctrine. He preferred so much the writers who dealt with concrete fact, that he could never bring himself to do justice to the 'framers of imaginary commonwealths', and in Rousseau's case this prejudice was supplemented by personal dislike. But when forced back upon his own fundamental articles of faith in defence of the constitution of his country, he based his arguments upon principles that were substantially at one with those of the despised author of the *Contrat Social.*

For Burke, the British constitution was a living form, in which the Anglo-Saxon race had embodied the principles of justice and liberty, and which when allowed to function properly conferred the greatest of human blessings and benefits upon all who owed allegiance to it. The abstract reasoning of theorists was not only visionary, but inasmuch as it led to constant attacks upon the constitution, it was also dangerous. His resentment against these attacks was intense. 'The Constitution of England is never to have a quietus,' he complained, in defending it against the attempts of liberals to introduce reforms in representation some years before the French revolution. 'It is to be continually vilified, attacked, reproached, resisted; instead of being the hope and sure anchor in all storms, instead of being the means of redress to all grievances, itself is the grand grievance of the nation, our shame instead of our glory.' [2] England had faced serious economic problems during the period in which Burke had been a member of Parliament, and out of the disturbed conditions had grown a feeling of discontent that had shown itself in a critical attitude towards the constitution which Burke felt was not altogether justified. He was concerned primarily with the stability of the established order of society and of the constitution, but he failed to appreciate some of the important factors that were disturbing them. He believed that the theorizing radicals of the age had so impressed upon men's minds the defects of their constitution, that they had become blind to any virtues it might possess.

As he observed the lengths to which discussion and criticism were going, he saw that there was genuine danger of a rift in the constitution; that the bonds of 'unsuspecting confidence' which had linked the people to it, were being weakened perceptibly. He loved liberty, but he would never agree with Milton or Rousseau, or with the great champion of liberty of speech who was yet to come, John Stuart Mill, that full and free discussion was salutary—least of all when it assumed the form of ungenerous criticism and casuistry, for then it seemed to him that liberty had turned to licence. 'It has been the misfortune (not as these gentlemen think it, the glory) of this age, that everything is to be discussed,' [3] he exclaimed some years later in criticism of the radicals as he surveyed the ruin that had followed in the wake of unlimited discussion and theorizing in France. What he disliked so intensely was not so much the frank discussion of political affairs as the irresponsible raising of fundamental issues, the constant questioning of the principles of the constitution, and the incessant demand that they should be brought to terms with the abstract theories in which the radicals had unbounded faith.

'Whilst they are possessed by these notions', he confessed, 'it is vain to talk to them of the practice of their ancestors, the fundamental laws of their country, the fixed form of a constitution, whose merits are confirmed by the solid test of long experience and an increasing public strength and national prosperity. They despise experience as the wisdom of unlettered men. . . .' [4]

From his wide knowledge of constitutional principles, gained not only from his studies at the Middle Temple, and from the careful attention he had devoted to the most important writers on the subject from Aristotle to Montesquieu and Blackstone, but also from his own experience as a statesman, Burke was satisfied that the British constitution was sound in principle and was in addition a most effective safeguard for the rights and liberties of the people. That it never could guarantee the enjoyment of the sweeping 'natural' rights and the perfection of liberty that the radicals demanded of it, was only to be expected and in no wise detracted from its value. When, in the closing years of his life, he watched the French attempt to constitute their state upon such a basis, he was able to prove the truth of his contention that a constitution never could guarantee sweeping natural rights and the perfection of liberty by the disasters and the terror that attended the revolution. The British constitution, on the other hand, had enabled men to enjoy a large measure of freedom and was essentially conducive to their happiness. It had gradually emerged as the means by which the British people had secured their liberty, and its history had been marked by the building up of checks and balances to prevent the inroads of injustice and oppression upon the life of the nation. And because he appreciated its worth so thoroughly, Burke became almost morbidly sensitive to the dangers that confronted it. For that reason his attention was constantly absorbed in safeguarding it from what he regarded as foolish attempts of would-be reformers to introduce radical change into it at a time when he believed such change to be unnecessary. Of this desire to preserve intact the constitution of his country were born his attempts to teach the people of England to understand and to love it as he himself did, a task for which no one was more admirably fitted than he was. And by teaching them to show it that 'filial' respect which he felt toward it, he hoped incidentally to strengthen once more the bonds that linked the people to their country.

In undertaking a project of such a nature, Burke fully recognized that one of the chief difficulties he had to encounter was the misapprehension that existed in people's minds regarding constitutional principles generally and the constitution of England in particular. From the nature of the criticisms advanced and from the kind of demands that were made, he had no doubt that the abstract theorists were principally to blame for the wrong ideas that had gained popular acceptance. But if those wrong ideas were to be uprooted, it was necessary for him to show them wherein their fallacy lay, and to replace misconception by showing the way in which the constitution actually worked. And although he was at times inclined to take too seriously the possible menace to established institutions that lurked behind popular critical comment, he was nevertheless able to expound the principles of the constitution so brilliantly and so clearly that he was soon in a position to influence national thought profoundly. He made his first efforts to defend the constitution at the time of the American revolution, but it was only with the French revolution that he felt that all his energies would have to be put forth in its defence. He made no attempt to give any systematic study of the constitution because he preferred to show immediate problems in their relationship to the enduring principles upon which the constitution was based, and so to keep it in its true setting. Thus he kept clearly before them the idea that the constitution was not in any sense a set of abstract principles to be refuted at will, or changed for another set whenever the fancy took them, but that it was in fact the living, concrete form in which the eternal principles of justice, liberty, and right had been moulded in accordance with the particular circumstances and the temperament of the British people. Consequently he was able to play a conspicuous part in guiding England through a particularly trying period of transition, and indeed his work was done so effectively that when later the time came for radical change, the people had a much clearer knowledge of the nature of the complicated machinery with which they had to deal and were therefore in a better position to carry forward the work begun so auspiciously by Parliament in 1688.

In addition to the necessity for correcting error due to ignorance, however, Burke was confronted with a problem of a much more subtle nature, owing to the fact that the radicals had derived their strength from the blind faith that men reposed in arguments that were logically sound and apparently in accordance with common sense. It was taken for granted that politics could be reduced to a science, and that the constitutional system which was devised scientifically and in accordance with the principles of reason would be the best. In that faith, they had advanced arguments to the effect that the constitution should be simplified in the interests of liberty, which could be more fully enjoyed if it were more systematic and more in accordance with enlightened ideas. To the ordinary man, unfamiliar with the necessarily complex nature of the constitutional system, these arguments carried conviction.

In order to show the factors which had been left out of consideration, Burke pointed out that fundamentally the effectiveness of the constitution depended upon the art of government and that without that art, the most enlightened ideas the theorist could devise would be ineffectual. Government was essentially a practical matter, and was concerned with given situations. These situations were often more complex and might vary radically in character. Consequently a method which would be effective in one given set of circumstances might fail entirely in another. In other words, 'nothing universal can be rationally affirmed on any moral, or any political subject'. Pure metaphysical abstraction, upon which the arguments of the theorists were based, did not belong to the political world.

'The lines of morality are not like the ideal lines of mathematics,' Burke explained in giving expression to convictions he had always held. 'They are broad and deep as well as long. They admit of exceptions; they demand modifications. These exceptions and modifications are not made by the process of logic, but by the rules of prudence. . . . Metaphysics cannot live without definition; but prudence is cautious how she defines.' [5]

By this he did not mean that the statesman could dispense with sovereign reason, but that reason, when it dealt with human actions, must constantly check its judgements against the facts of experience in a way that was not necessary in a purely abstract science such as mathematics.

'I do not vilify theory and speculation—no, because that would be to vilify reason itself,' he said in making his position clear on the subject. 'No; whenever I speak against theory, I mean always a weak, erroneous, fallacious, unfounded, or imperfect theory; and one of the ways of discovering that it is a false theory, is by comparing it with practice. This is the true touchstone of all theories, which regard man and the affairs of men—does it suit his nature in general;—does it suit his nature as modified by his habits?' [6]

But there was yet another demand that had to be made of theory before it could become the auxiliary of politics. It had to fit itself not only to human nature, but also to the great empire of circumstance which was the domain of which the statesman had to be master. For a statesman, theory had to assume the form of a principle.

'Without the guide and light of sound well-understood principles,' he pointed out, 'all reasonings in politics, as in everything else, would be only a confused jumble of particular facts and details, without the means of drawing out any sort of theoretical or practical conclusion.'

Whereas a professor in a university had to take a 'general' view of society, the statesman had

'a number of circumstances to combine with those general ideas, and to take into his consideration. Circumstances are infinite, are infinitely combined; are variable and transient; he, who does not take them into consideration, is not erroneous, but stark mad—*dat operam ut cum ratione insaniat*—he is metaphysically mad.'

And while the theorist, following the light of reason, might make errors in his logic to the detriment of his conclusions, 'a statesman, never losing sight of principles, is to be guided by circumstances; and judging contrary to the exigencies of the moment, he may ruin his Country for ever'.[7]

If the theorists would take these facts into consideration, Burke was certain that they would be on the highway to understanding how intricate a constitution had to be, and particularly the constitution of a free country. Moreover, they would not be so eager to suggest radical reformation of it as they would see the difficulties and dangers involved in all change of an organic nature. 'We are members for a free country,' he wrote; 'and surely we all know, that the machine of a free constitution is no simple thing; but as intricate and as delicate, as it is valuable.'[8] England was a 'great and ancient monarchy', and through the checks and balances that safeguarded the liberties of all within the realm, a complicated structure had been built up that was technically known as a mixed constitution. It was composed of monarchy, aristocracy, and democracy, each principle being so equally balanced in power that any change might work untold havoc to the whole.

'Our constitution stands on a nice equipoise, with steep precipices and deep waters upon all sides of it,' he stated in one of his favourite descriptions of it. 'In removing it from a dangerous leaning towards one side, there may be a risk of oversetting it on the other. Every project of a material change in a government so complicated as ours, combined at the same time with external circumstances still more complicated, is a matter full of difficulties; in which a considerate man will not be too ready to decide; a prudent man too ready to undertake; or an honest man too ready to promise.'[9]

But in addition to the fact that 'a constitution made up of balanced powers must ever be a critical thing',[10] and was therefore to be interfered with as little as possible, Burke pointed out that through all its complexities, it unified and bound together the different parts of the nation and established the liberties of the people upon a sure foundation. Its whole policy was to 'prevent any one of its principles from being carried as far, as taken by itself, and theoretically, it would go'. And from this point of view, most of the faults with which it was charged would appear to be

'not imperfections into which it had inadvertently fallen, but excellencies which it has studiously sought. To avoid the perfections of extreme, all its several parts are so constituted, as not alone to answer their own several ends, but also each to limit and control the others: insomuch that, take which of the principles you please—you will find its operation checked and stopped at a certain point. The whole movement stands still rather than that any part should proceed beyond its boundary.' [11]

From thence it resulted that in the British constitution there was a 'perpetual treaty' and compromise going on, sometimes openly, sometimes indirectly, but through that process of compromise, a 'steady direction' was given to the state, and liberty was rendered secure. Thus it became apparent that liberty depended not so much upon enlightened theory as upon the harmonious working of that system of checks and balances.

It was equally important, however, to take into account the fact that a nation followed a vast number of ends, all of which had to be provided for by the constitution. It was impossible to simplify those ends, while it was not wise to simplify the machinery which enabled them all to be followed as far as possible. 'The nature of man is intricate; the objects of society are of the greatest possible complexity,' Burke emphasized, and therefore no 'simple direction' or 'disposition' of power could be looked upon as suitable to man's nature, or to the quality of his affairs. The dynamic quality of Burke's thought was obscured, if not completely lost, in face of the threats to society implicit in the French revolution. 'When I hear the simplicity of contrivance aimed at and boasted of in any new political constitutions, I am at no loss to decide that the artificers are grossly ignorant of their trade, or totally negligent

of their duty.' And to say no worse of them, simple governments were 'fundamentally defective'. For, he explained,

'if you were to contemplate society in but one point of view, all these
simple modes of polity are infinitely captivating. In effect each would
answer its single end much more perfectly than the more complex is able
to attain all its complex purposes. But it is better that the whole should
be imperfectly and anomalously answered, than that, while some parts
are provided for with great exactness, others might be totally neglected,
or perhaps materially injured, by the over-care of a favourite member.' [12]

Moreover, it had to be remembered that the *a priori* method of
reasoning presented the state and its institutions in a false
perspective. For the states of the modern world had grown
to their present magnitude in a great length of time, and by a
great variety of accidents. They were the product of the
ages, and they had been improved in the course of time with
greater or less degrees of felicity and skill. But none of them
had been formed upon a regular plan, nor yet with any thought
of conformity to design.

'As their constitutions are not symmetrical', Burke continued, 'they
have not been directed to any *peculiar* end, eminently distinguished, and
superseding every other. The objects which they embrace are of the
greatest possible variety, and have become in a manner infinite.'

In all these countries, the state had been made to the people,
and not the people to the state.

'Every state has pursued, not only every sort of social advantage, but it
has cultivated the welfare of every individual. His wants, his wishes, even
his tastes have been consulted. This comprehensive scheme, virtually
produced a degree of personal liberty in forms the most adverse to it.
That liberty was found, under monarchies styled absolute, in a degree
unknown to the ancient commonwealths. From hence the powers of all
our modern states, meet in all their movements, with some obstruction.'

Thus it was in the interests of liberty that obstructions had
been put in the way of the full power of the state. Of all the
states of the modern world the British state was 'without
question, that which pursues the greatest variety of ends, and
is the least disposed to sacrifice any one of them to another, or
to the whole'.[13] The British state, moreover, aimed at taking
in the entire circle of human desires, and securing for them

their fair enjoyment. And personal liberty, which in other European countries had been preserved through the manners and customs of the people, was in England the direct object of the government. But in order to adapt themselves to the important function of safeguarding the liberties of the people, 'the parts of our constitution have gradually, and almost insensibly, in a long course of time, accommodated themselves to each other, and to their common, as well as to their separate purposes'.[14]

Burke touched upon a favourite theme as he stressed the significance of history in the evolution of the constitution. Nations had developed slowly and as their needs had grown, so also had they found it necessary to improve their political institutions. As national life emerged and became integrated, it bore the imprint of the social processes through which it had passed, and which could be traced through historical study.

'Political arrangement, as it is a work for social ends, is only to be wrought by social means,' Burke said as he described in his own way the operation of that social logic through which Rousseau had believed the general will found expression in the life of a people. 'There mind must conspire with mind. Time is required to produce that union of minds which alone can produce all the good we aim at. . . . By a slow but well-sustained progress, the effect of each step is watched; the good or ill success of the first, gives light to us in the second; and so, from light to light, we are conducted with safety through the whole series.'

It was necessary to see that the different parts of the constitution did not clash. The evils latent in the most promising 'contrivances' could be provided for as they arose, and in this manner, it was possible to sacrifice one advantage to another as little as possible.

'We compensate, we reconcile, we balance. We are enabled to unite into a consistent whole the various anomalies and contending principles that are found in the minds and affairs of men. From hence arises, not an excellence in simplicity, but one far superior, an excellence in composition. . . .'[15]

'Our Constitution is a prescriptive Constitution,' Burke explained, 'it is a Constitution, whose sole authority is, that it has existed time out of mind.' And in spite of the fact that the radicals had no sympathy for the claims of prescription, Burke was certain that it was 'the most solid of all titles', not only to property, but to government, which was to secure that property. Moreover, prescription was accompanied by 'another ground of authority in the constitution of the human mind', namely, presumption.

'It is a presumption in favour of any settled scheme of government against any untried project, that a nation has long existed and flourished under it. It is a better presumption even of the *choice* of a nation, far better than any sudden and temporary arrangement by actual election.'

Furthermore, it was

'a choice not of one day, or one set of people, not a tumultuary and giddy choice; it is a deliberate election of ages and of generations; it is a Constitution made by what is ten thousand times better than choice, it is made by the peculiar circumstances, occasions, tempers, dispositions, and moral, civil, and social habitudes of the people, which disclose themselves only in a long space of time. It is a vestment, which accommodates itself to the body. . . .' [16]

As he fought for the constitution of his country against those who would introduce the French system, he repeated what he had said about the length of time it had taken to build up the British constitution. If he could not impress his readers with the fact that prescription was as valid a basis for authority as any they could bring forward, and that it was ultimately nothing more than their habitual acceptance of established and legitimate authority in the state, then at least he hoped to make them understand that the prescriptive government of England had been solidly established, with its roots far away in the past of the nation's history. The British constitution had not been

'struck out at a heat by a set of presumptuous men, like the assembly of pettifoggers run mad in Paris,' he asserted. 'It is the result of the thought of many minds, in many ages. It is no simple, no superficial thing, nor to be estimated by superficial understandings.'

And he followed up his contrast with a characteristic warning.

'An ignorant man, who is not fool enough to meddle with his clock, is however sufficiently confident to think he can safely take to pieces, and put together at his pleasure, a moral machine of another guise, importance and complexity, composed of far other wheels, and springs, and balances, and counteracting and co-operating powers. Men little think how immorally they act in rashly meddling with what they do not understand. . . .' [17]

For in a last analysis, the constitution of a country was a 'moral' machine, and as such it claimed both the respect and reverence of men. In keeping with the idea of prescription, it had been the uniform policy of the constitution 'to claim and assert our liberties', Burke declared, 'as an *entailed inheritance* derived to us from our forefathers, and to be transmitted to our posterity'. By this means it had preserved a unity in the great diversity of its parts, a fact that he could not emphasize sufficiently. 'We have an inheritable crown ; an inheritable peerage; and a house of commons and a people inheriting privileges, franchises, and liberties, from a long line of ancestors.' [18]

To those who condemned inheritance as a preposterous and unjust survival of feudalism, Burke replied that the policy of the constitution seemed to him to be rather 'the result of profound reflection; or rather the happy effect of following nature, which is wisdom without reflection, and above it'. A spirit of innovation was usually the accompaniment of small intellects and selfishness. 'People will not look forward to posterity, who never look backward to their ancestors.' But as far as the British people were concerned, they knew that the idea of inheritance furnished a sure principle of conservation and of transmission, 'without at all excluding a principle of improvement'. Thus 'by a constitutional policy, working after the pattern of nature, we receive, we hold, we transmit our government and our privileges, in the same manner in which we enjoy and transmit our property and our lives'. The political system was placed in a 'just correspondence and symmetry' with the order of the world, and with the 'mode of existence decreed to a permanent body composed of transitory parts', wherein

'by the disposition of a stupendous wisdom, moulding together the great mysterious incorporation of the human race, the whole, at one time, is never old, or middle-aged, or young, but in a condition of unchangeable constancy, moves on through the varied tenor of perpetual decay, fall, renovation, and progression.'

And thus, by preserving the 'method of nature' in the conduct of the state, 'in what we improve we are never wholly new; in what we retain, we are never wholly obsolete'. By following the course set by their forefathers, they were guided not by the 'superstition of antiquarians', but by the 'spirit of philosophic analogy', and by so doing they had given to their polity

'the image of a relation in blood; binding up the constitution of our country with our dearest domestic ties; adopting our fundamental laws into the bosom of our family affections; keeping inseparable, and cherishing with the warmth of all their combined and mutually reflected charities, our state, our hearts, our sepulchres, and our altars.' [19]

Through the same plan of a conformity to nature in their institutions, 'and by calling in the aid of her unerring and powerful instincts, to fortify the fallible and feeble contrivances of our reason',[20] they had derived other important benefits from regarding their liberties as an inheritance. 'Always acting as if in the presence of canonized forefathers, the spirit of freedom, leading in itself to misrule and excess, is tempered with an awful gravity.' The idea of a liberal descent inspired them with a sense of habitual native dignity, and by this means 'our liberty becomes a noble freedom'. Moreover, 'we procure reverence to our civil institutions on the principle upon which nature teaches us to revere individual men; on account of their age, and on account of those from whom they are descended'.[21] Even more, the ancestors to whom Burke looked with such reverence had set the standard of virtue and wisdom for the nation to follow. And, he challenged,

'all your sophisters cannot produce anything better adapted to preserve a rational and manly freedom than the course that we have pursued, who have chosen our nature rather than our speculations, our breasts rather than our inventions, for the great conservatories and magazines of our rights and privileges.' [22]

But doubtless there would have been more than a passing sense of mortification if, in his triumph, he had known that the *Contrat Social* had proclaimed that the constitution of a country had to fulfil these conditions if it was to live and endure.[23]

To prove that he had not elaborated a theory of his own regarding the constitutional principles and practice of England, Burke turned to the history of the constitution itself. The successive measures by which the rights and privileges of the British people had been established, and also the grounds upon which they had been claimed, were to be found in the great statutes and also in the records and journals of Parliament. The last and greatest of the charters of liberty was the Declaration of Right, which Burke looked upon as the cornerstone of the British constitution. It was the final statement of the principles upon which the liberties of the nation were based and by which legislation and parliamentary procedure were regulated. In that solemn statute, through which the Whigs of 1688 had asserted the traditional rights and liberties of the nation, which had been trampled under foot by the Stuarts, but which subsequent monarchs were sworn to protect, the constitution was 'reinforced, explained, improved, and in its fundamental principles for ever settled'. [24]

From Magna Charta, the first of the nation's great charters of liberty, down to the Declaration of Right, the fundamental principle of prescription had been definitely and clearly asserted, so that it could be regarded as the established constitutional policy of the realm. If at any time there had been an opportunity to vary that principle of prescription, it was at the time of the revolution of 1688. But in order to restore the balance of the constitution, the legislature was particularly careful to adhere to it. For the 'glorious' revolution was made, Burke declared,

'to preserve our *ancient* indisputable laws and liberties, and that *ancient* constitution of government which is our only security for law and liberty. ... We wished at the period of the revolution, and do now wish, to derive all we possess as *an inheritance from our forefathers.*' [25]

The revolution of 1688 had been caused by a 'breach of the original contract' implied and expressed in the constitution of the country as a scheme of government 'fundamentally and inviolably' fixed in king, lords, and commons. No changes were made in the unimpaired parts of the constitution, so that when the 'deficient' part was regenerated, it was possible for the organic unity of the constitution to be restored. The crown was taken out of the immediate line of inheritance, but the new line was derived from the same stock, and the only qualifications placed upon the right of succession to the throne were that the monarch should be a Protestant and that he should subscribe to the Declaration of Right. Thus the two principles of conservation and correction, inherent at all times in the spirit of the constitution, played an important part in resolving the difficulties the Stuarts had caused through the usurpation of powers that did not rightfully belong to them. Consequently, when the revolution was an accomplished fact, it was found that the whole frame of the government had been restored unhurt. No one part of the constitution had been altered or had suffered the least damage. On the contrary, the whole had received new life and vigour.

In the new order, the king became the constitutional monarch with definite legal rights, which it was the duty of Parliament and the people alike to respect. For those rights formed the 'key-stone that binds together the noble and well-constructed arch of our empire and our constitution'. [26] And while for the most part Burke disapproved strongly of the policies of George III, he nevertheless believed that the monarch should not be allowed to become a mere figurehead. It was essential to the welfare of the nation for the monarch to play an active part in the delicately-poised system of constitutional checks and balances if that system was to retain its validity. The tyranny of the French revolution, however, caused Burke to become more emphatic about the importance of the monarchy to the constitution. In the fourth *Letter on a Regicide Peace*, he asserted that the British constitution was formed upon 'the principle of jealousy to the crown'. Even more emphatically, he declared that 'it must keep alive some part of that fire of jealousy eternally and chastely burning, or it cannot be the British constitution'.[27] It would no longer be the British constitution, when loyalty to the hereditary monarch no longer existed.

The House of Lords, the second important member of the British constitutional system, represented the aristocracy and the property of the nation.

'I am no friend to aristocracy, in the sense at least in which that word is usually understood,' Burke stated early in his career. 'If it were not a bad habit to moot cases on the supposed ruin of the constitution, I should be free to declare, that if it must perish, I would rather by far see it resolved into any other form, than lost in that austere and insolent domination.' [28]

Years later, he repeated much the same sentiments.

'I am accused, I am told abroad,' he wrote, 'of being a man of aristocratic principles. If by aristocracy they mean the Peers, I have no vulgar admiration, nor any vulgar antipathy towards them; I hold their order in cold and decent respect. I hold them to be of an absolute necessity in the Constitution; but I think they are only good when kept within their proper bounds.' [29]

But on the other hand, he looked upon the nobility as the class that had risen to distinction and wealth through outstanding public service, and as such it claimed his profound respect. In the British constitutional system it was expected to accept responsibility and to exert a stabilizing influence upon the Crown on the one hand, and upon the House of Commons on the other. Through it, the inherited property of the nation as well as the aristocracy of intellect spoke, and it was consequently the class to which the nation had to look for responsible guidance and leadership. Its members included some of Britain's most distinguished sons, who had not only built up the great traditions of the nation, but had also become the founders of families. With their titles, their illustrious names, their honours and their property, they formed the 'Corinthian capital of polished society', for which Burke had a genuine admiration. But that which appealed to him most of all was the fact that the aristocracy of the country was in a unique position to carry forward the great tradition of duty and service, and that it possessed the necessary means to fit it for that particular function in the life of the nation. Men who were born and bred as they were had the advantage of being accustomed to public affairs; they understood public opinion; they were able to take enlightened and lofty views of national concerns, and they had the leisure to read, to reflect, and to converse. In addition to being in a position to foster the arts and sciences and all that pertained to the cultural side of national life, they were trained to carry responsibility, and to scorn danger in the pursuit of duty and honour. Indeed, without such a class, there would be no nation. Yet much as the 'natural' aristocracy appealed to his imagination, Burke did not think of it altogether as holding exclusive rights to leadership, rank, and privilege in the nation. Wherever wisdom and virtue were found combined with eminent talents, they had the 'passport of heaven' to human place and honour, although, as Burke knew from bitter experience, the path to that eminence for such was all too often paved with rough, uneven stones.

Burke's views of the functions of the natural aristocracy, and of the representatives of the people who composed the House of Commons and who were also heirs to the highest traditions of the nation, illustrated in point of fact the way in which Rousseau's legislator assumed reality in the constitutional system of a country. That it would manifest itself in a typically English mode of realization was only to be expected since Rousseau had thought that each nation would evolve its own particular methods and forms.

While the aristocracy of England was more conservative and settled, the legislative class in the House of Commons was essentially creative and progressive. Furthermore, the members of the House of Commons, who possessed the privilege of initiating legislation, were in closer touch with the people whom they represented than the peers were. Thus they were in a position to observe the first signs of changes in the economic and social systems of the country, and also to know the nature of evils that aroused discontent and resentment against government. And while their legislative measures were based upon this special knowledge, they had to present their proposals to the House of Lords for approval. In this way, national legislation had the benefit of the judgement of the peers as well, who were expected to examine it carefully to make sure that it was not the hasty expression of immature opinion, but that it reflected wisdom and sane judgement. Finally, legislation had to pass through the hands of the King, whose signature was necessary before it could become law.

But if the House of Commons had to satisfy the Lords and Crown before its measures could become law, it also had to gain the approval of the nation as a whole before its work could be regarded as successful. For unless its legislation was a true reflection of the course that national life was taking, it would prove ineffectual if not actually harmful, and would therefore fail. Consequently, it was necessary for the House of Commons to make itself so sensitive to the needs and desires of the people as a whole that it could anticipate exactly the course that would be most helpful in guiding the nation towards its proper interests. But in so doing, it would give 'a direction, a form, a technical dress, and a specific sanction, to the general sense of the community',[30] which was what Burke regarded as the true end of legislation, and Rousseau as the expression of the general will.

Whereas Rousseau had defined law as the voice of the general will, Burke had thought of it essentially as legislation, bearing a definite set form, which had passed through the Houses of Parliament where it had been modified by full and free debate in the two Houses, and when finally signed by the monarch, took its place in the statute books. He thought of it as the expression of justice and equity not unbending like the laws of the Medes and Persians, but 'severe and awful', and a steadfast auxiliary to manners, customs, morals, and religion in the life of a people. For laws were the outcome of conflicting interests which necessarily arouse within the state. Those conflicting interests rendered deliberation, not a matter of 'choice' but of 'necessity', because they made all change a subject of compromise, 'which naturally begets moderation', and therefore made laws so many added securities to liberty. It was one of the great advantages of the British system of government that members of Parliament, although elected by different constituencies, were legislators for the nation, and not for a section of the people only.

'Parliament is not a *Congress* of ambassadors from different and hostile interests,' Burke explained; 'which interests each must maintain, as an agent and advocate, against other agents and advocates; but parliament is a *deliberative* assembly of *one* nation, with *one* interest, that of the whole; where, not local purposes, not local prejudices ought to guide, but the general good, resulting from the general reason of the whole. You choose a member indeed; but when you have chosen him, he is not member of Bristol, but he is a member of *parliament*.' [31]

In accordance with this viewpoint, Burke liked to think of the laws as the highest expression of the legislator's gifts, exercised for the good of his country.

The legislator for Burke was no personification, but the faithful representative of the people who had a highly responsible office to fulfil. His function was essentially to promote the 'common happiness of all those who are, in any degree, subjected to our legislative authority', and to bind together in 'one common tie of civil interest and constitutional freedom, every denomination of men amongst us'.[32] But he could accomplish such a difficult task only if he brought to it steadfastness of purpose and a deep sense of trust. He had to be strong enough in character to maintain his intellectual integrity, so that he could be a 'pillar of state', and like Burke, would not flinch from standing before his electors and declaring that

'I did not obey your instructions: No, I conformed to the instructions of truth and nature, and maintained your interest, against your opinions, with a constancy that became me. . . . I am to look, indeed, to your opinions; but to such opinions as you and I must have five years hence.' [33]

While the ability to distinguish correctly the enduring interests of the people was the supreme distinction of the legislator, Burke also looked to the members of Parliament to possess a sound knowledge of the art of government, which he regarded as of fundamental importance. The function of the people was to make known their wants. But, he pointed out,

'we are the expert artists; we are the skilful workmen, to shape their desires into perfect form, and to fit the utensil to the use. They are the sufferers, they tell the symptoms of the complaint; but we know the exact seat of the disease, and how to apply the remedy according to the rules of art.' [34]

Burke was firmly convinced that the wisdom shown in good government was of greater importance than the laws, for through that good government it was possible to gain the respect and loyalty of the people, which constituted the surest support for the laws. When the people gave their confidence to their representatives in Parliament, there was no need for concern as to the fate of the laws.

Burke did not think of the people as making their own laws.

Indeed, the very thought of it was repugnant to him in the extreme, and he would not discuss the subject until he was finally driven to do so in the closing years of his life. He believed that the legislating class was drawn essentially from that 'natural' aristocracy, which by training, tradition, and environment was ideally equipped to undertake the exceedingly difficult task of law-making. For legislation was a highly complicated matter, the success of which depended upon the ability of the legislators to follow faithfully 'the great principles of reason and equity', as well as 'the general sense of mankind'. It was a task entirely beyond the reach of the ordinary, untrained person. Burke realized that those among his fellow-members of Parliament who were best fitted for their work had not only spent long years of study in order to fit themselves for their careers, as he himself had done, but that they represented the finest of the nation's intelligentsia. While he looked with no great respect on the great majority of members of Parliament, he had conceived an ideal type of parliamentarian who was not only well trained for his work, but who was also distinguished by unselfish devotion to the service of his country. And because he was so certain that the harmonious working of the constitution depended upon the skill of his fellow-members as statesmen quite as much as upon their wisdom as legislators, he resisted all movements for reform in representation that might bring about an organic change in the constitution. He feared that the demand for redistribution of seats and for extension of the franchise might exclude from Parliament some of those most eminently fitted by training and talents, for whom seats were found under the existing system. He feared a threat to the property and security of the nation, which were safeguarded by the revolution settlement. But he also feared the triumph of the spectacular demagogue and the plausible opportunist at the polls only less than he feared the great, if not irreparable injury that might be done to the art of government.

With the French revolution, Burke realized that the question of the people's right to govern themselves was the most absorbing topic of popular interest, and that it could no longer be brushed aside impatiently. The doctrine of the sovereignty of the people presented a grave challenge to the British consti-

tutional system because it confounded, he declared, 'in a
manner equally mischievous and stupid, the origin of a government from the people with its continuance in their hands'.[35]
He was definitely resentful as he recalled the fact that it was
Rousseau's legacy to political thought. But when he found
that the doctrine was being accepted by members of the Whig
party, he knew that the time had come to show clearly the
implications of that doctrine, and to indicate how radically it
differed from British constitutional practice.

'I have often endeavoured to compute and to class those who, in any
political view, are to be called the people,' he wrote in his *Letters on a
Regicide Peace*. 'Without doing something of this sort we must proceed
absurdly. . . . In England and Scotland, I compute that those of adult
age, not declining in life, of tolerable leisure for such discussions, and of
some means of information, more, or less, and who are above menial
dependence, (or what is virtually such) may amount to about four hundred thousand. . . . This is the British public; and it is a public very
numerous. The rest, when feeble, are the objects of protection; when
strong, the means of force. They who affect to consider that part of us
in any other light, insult while they cajole us. . . .'[36]

It was to this public of four hundred thousand that Burke as a
member of Parliament looked for the information he needed in
order to play his part efficiently in the formulation of legislation. While that British public elected the members of Parliament, its office following the election of those members was
essentially in making explicit the needs of the nation as a whole
and in discussing intelligently the effect of the government's
actions. Thus Burke looked to it to take an active part in the
creation of public opinion, but he would put up impassable
barriers between it and the halls of Westminster. He would not
concede to it the right of bringing pressure to bear upon members of Parliament, although following the Wilkes agitations,
other members of Parliament realized that they could no longer
stand aloof from their constituents.

Fundamentally, however, Burke objected so strenuously to
the doctrine of the sovereignty of the people with its claim that
the people should assume the direction of their own destinies,
because it seemed to destroy entirely the organic structure of
national life. He saw not only legislation and the art of government sacrificed to it, but he also saw the disruption of society

itself implicit in its demands. Viewed from the standpoint of historical evolution, the British state had developed naturally into the form in which Burke knew it. The aristocracy of the nation had risen naturally to the rank and cultural background that had enabled it to help the British people onward to the highest achievements in all fields of human endeavour, while it had also the property and the traditions needful to make its position stable and enduring. The middle and lower classes were in the strata of society to which their ideas, their capacities, and their inclinations naturally fitted them. Moreover, while these ranks were clearly defined in the British state, they were not exclusive. Distinguished service, high ideals, virtue, and merit enabled men to rise to the highest places of honour in the nation; failure to live up to the standards demanded by tradition inevitably dragged them down. But the evolution of their political institutions had placed the British people in a particularly fortunate position. As long as their constitution endured, they knew that however humble or exalted their status, the full force of the law was exerted to protect their rights, their liberties, and their property. The law in its turn was secure so long as the people's representatives kept watch and ward faithfully. Moreover, instead of being a menace to their liberty, their monarch was the sworn defender of all their traditional rights and liberties. But it was precisely this established order in the British state that Burke saw menaced in the assertion of the doctrine of the sovereignty of the people. It was based on the claim that 'the *people*, in forming their commonwealth, have by no means parted with their power over it'.[37]

'Discuss any of their schemes,' Burke wrote in anger, '—their answer is—it is the act of the *people*, and that is sufficient. Are we to deny to a *majority* of the people the right of altering even the whole frame of their society, if such should be their pleasure? They may change it, say they, from a monarchy to a republic to-day, and to-morrow back again from a republic to a monarchy; and so backward and forward as often as they like. They are masters of the commonwealth; because in substance they are themselves the commonwealth. The French revolution, say they, was the act of the majority of the people; and if the majority of any other people, the people of England for instance, wish to make the same change, they have the same right.'[38]

But it was a right that Burke indignantly refused to concede to them. They had no right to act 'merely by their will' in any matter connected with duty, trust, engagement, or obligation, and to presume to do so was to 'subject the sovereign reason of the world to the caprices of weak and giddy men'.[39]

Their presumptuous claim struck in two directions. On the one hand, the state was essentially part of the moral order of the universe; justice and right were the basis of the constitution, and the body politic was the outcome of a long process of historical development. And as history was the 'known march of the ordinary providence of God', it became evident to Burke that men were not placed in authority or obscurity by their own volition, but that on the contrary,

'the awful author of our being is the author of our place in the order of existence; and that having disposed and marshalled us by a divine tactic, not according to our will, but according to his, he has, in and by that disposition, virtually subjected us to act the part which belongs to the place assigned us.' [40]

For them to take the fate of the state into their own hands and to destroy it at their will, was therefore to flout that divine tactic—to subject the sovereign reason of the world to the caprice of 'weak and giddy' men. But on the other hand, the claim that the people were masters of the state was supported by the doctrine that all men were free and equal by nature, and that the ranks and orders of society were consequently arbitrary. On the basis of this abstract theory, the French had levelled all ranks and had destroyed their nobility. Out of their egalitarian ideal had emerged, not an organized state, but a disbanded people in which men were merely 'loose counters'.

A number of men in themselves had no corporate capacity, Burke explained. The idea of a people was the idea of a corporation. It was an association of men bound together by ties of an organic nature, who when so associated, agreed mutually to the establishment of their political institutions. But when men broke up their original agreement which gave its corporate form and capacity to their state, as the French had done, they could no longer be regarded as a people. They were simply a number of 'vague, loose individuals', and nothing more. They had to begin over again to create their state, and 'Alas!' Burke added, 'they little know how many a weary step is to be taken before they can form themselves into a mass, which has a true politic personality.'[41] They had to become organized once more; they had to establish relationships once more upon a basis of justice and right, which was the only kind of basis upon which a body politic could rest; and they had to make those relationships secure through law which all were bound to respect. But that could only come about through a 'state of habitual social discipline, in which the wiser, the more expert, and the more opulent, conduct, and by conducting enlighten and protect the weaker, the less knowing, and the less provided with the goods of fortune'.[42] It was a simple matter of fact that a people had to have 'chiefs' because the ordinary man, belonging to 'a sort of equestrian order', followed a leader loyally and through preferring to steer a middle course, kept things from going to excess. But when called upon to assume leadership, he failed because of irresolution and timidity. And in a body politic the leaders belonged to the ranks of the 'natural' aristocracy. Consequently, until that aristocracy was restored to its proper place and function in the body politic, and until the other people also fell into their natural ranks, Burke could not see an organized society that could function as a state. For that aristocracy 'is the soul to the body, without which the man does not exist', but when in their rightful place, the men who composed it were the natural 'leading, guiding, and governing' part of the state. And to give no more importance in the social order to such men than that of so many units was a 'horrible usurpation'.[43]

Unless men were united in a body politic, it was idle to talk about acting by majorities. Among 'disbanded' men, there could be no such thing as majority or minority, neither was there power vested in any person to bind another. The power of acting by a majority presupposed two things. In the first place, there had to be an 'incorporation produced by unanimity', or, in other words, a body politic established by a social contract; while in the second place, there had to be also a unanimous agreement that the act of a 'mere' majority, even of one, should be accepted by all as the act of the whole group. Thus Burke, reverting curiously enough to contract fiction in order to refute the arch-individualists of France and England who wished to translate the doctrine of the sovereignty of the people into fact, presented Rousseau's version of contract. For Rousseau had insisted upon an association as the basis of the body politic, and also upon the necessity for all to recognize the supremacy of the general will which alone could bind every one and therefore render majority decisions valid, which Burke supplemented with the practical observation that 'the mind is brought far more easily to acquiesce in the proceedings of one man, or a few, who act under a general procuration for the state, than in a vote of a victorious majority in councils in which every man has his share in the deliberations'.[44] It was therefore necessary, Burke continued, that this mode of decision should be the result of a special convention, 'confirmed afterwards by long habits of obedience, by a sort of discipline in society, and by a strong hand, vested with stationary permanent power, to enforce this sort of constructive general will'.[45] What organ it was that should declare the 'corporate mind' was so much a matter of positive arrangement, that some states had required a proportion of voices much greater than a mere majority before their acts could be accepted as legally valid.

But whatever positive arrangements were made in different states, Burke insisted basically that there must be a body politic that was an organic unity; that it must evolve a 'natural' aristocracy, and that the constitution framed by its legislators must be based upon the great principles of reason and equity and also upon the 'general sense' of the people. Rousseau, arguing from the abstract doctrine of contract, had stipulated the same fundamental requirements for the body politic. Although he had not expressed himself in historical terms, he had recognized no less clearly than Burke that the building up of a body politic was not something that could be achieved suddenly, but that it was evolved in a long course of time and through a long process of social discipline. Nor was there any fundamental contradiction between Burke's idea of a natural aristocracy and Rousseau's ideas. While Rousseau's ideal tended more naturally towards an egalitarian society, Burke's love of the established order of England caused him to turn his attention to the dangers which threatened it through the doctrine of the sovereignty of the people, and to overlook the fact that a natural aristocracy could be evolved in an egalitarian state as well. Indeed, Rousseau's legislator was the personification of this aristocracy. And finally, where Burke would avoid the necessity for revolution by seeing that the British constitution functioned effectively, Rousseau would limit change to that which was for the welfare of the nation, for that alone carried the sanction of the general will.

CHAPTER IX

THE PRINCIPLES OF GOVERNMENT

IN the *Contrat Social*, Rousseau emphasized the fact that men must 'always be ready to sacrifice the government to the people, and not the people to the government'.[1] Similarly, in the *Letter to a Member of the National Assembly*, Burke insisted that

'I must see the things; I must see the men. Without a concurrence and adaptation of these to the design, the very best speculative projects might become not only useless but mischievous. Plans must be made for men. We cannot think of making men, and binding nature to our designs.'[2]

One of the chief dangers of an age such as the eighteenth century, which was so preoccupied with abstract speculation, was that of losing touch with reality. Theories of natural rights and utility alike were based upon metaphysical assumptions and upon a rationalistic psychology without reference to 'man in the concrete'. Thinkers were so wrapped up in their theories of progress, that they forgot that perhaps man might not bend to their systems. And although his thought was essentially abstract, Rousseau realized fully that it was necessary to keep it at all times in the closest touch with life. He saw that failure to do so was one of the chief weaknesses of current thought and was also responsible for much of the misconception that existed in men's minds regarding man and human nature.

'Gentlemen,' he wrote to Mirabeau, one of the leading Physiocrats, 'permit me to tell you that you give too much importance to your calculations, and not enough to the inclinations of the human heart and to the play of the passions. Your system is excellent for Utopians; it is worthless for the children of Adam.'[3]

His own problem in the *Contrat Social*, which he compared to that of the quadrature of the circle in geometry, was to see whether it was possible to find a form of government which would place law above man. But he rescued his attempt to formulate a theory of government from the *pays des chimères* through his full recognition of the essential fact that government was made for man, and not man for the government. Thus he repudiated definitely the *étatisme* with which Burke and others have charged the *Contrat Social*. For much as he would have loved to find a simple formula that would have made a perfect system of government, yet he feared so greatly the danger of creating an instrument of tyranny that might be used to crush humanity that he immediately made those qualifications in his theory that would protect human beings from the oppression of government. That his practical suggestions were frequently weak or even futile in no wise detracted from the great strength which came from his fundamental recognition of the fact that whatever form a government assumed, its essential function was to further man's welfare and that it had to mould itself not to abstract theory, but to circumstances, to human nature, and to human needs.

So also through all Burke's utterances on the subject of government, the plea ran like a constant refrain that man should be governed in accordance with his nature and not according to abstract theories. When he first entered Parliament, he discovered that the attitude of the ministers of the Crown, and of members generally, was determined, not by an understanding of the needs and problems of the people, but by theories of sovereignty and the legal rights of government. With a much clearer insight into the nature of true statesmanship, Burke insisted that people had to be governed 'in a manner agreeable to their temper and disposition', and not in any other way. For nations, like people, were governed by a knowledge of 'their temper' and a 'judicious management' of it. 'The question with me is, not whether you have a right to render your people miserable; but whether it is not in your interest to make them happy,' he told the House of Commons in his speech on *Conciliation with America*. 'It is not, what a lawyer tells me, I *may* do; but what humanity, reason, and justice, tell me, I ought to do.'⁴ Some years later, he informed the sheriffs of Bristol that he was persuaded that government was 'a practical thing', made for the happiness of mankind, and that it was not to 'furnish out a spectacle of uniformity, to gratify the schemes of visionary politicians'.[5] But even further, he believed that as the Sabbath was made for man, and not man for the Sabbath, so also government 'in its exercise at least, ought to conform to the exigencies of the time, and the temper and character of the people, with whom it is concerned', and that their rulers should not always attempt 'violently to bend the people to their theories of subjection'.[6] It was the tyranny inherent in those abstract theories that caused Burke to regard them as so serious a menace to the welfare of mankind. And the further away from reality the theorists got, the more unbending their theories seemed to become, until at last in desperation Burke exclaimed that he could think of nothing 'more hard than the heart of a thoroughbred metaphysician'. For 'these philosophers, consider men in their experiments, no more than they do mice in an air pump, or in a recipient of mephitic gas'.[7] And although he had classed Rousseau with those 'modern philosophers', who were everything that was 'ignoble, savage, and hard-hearted', yet Rousseau had recognized as fully and as clearly as Burke had that if a theory of government was at variance with human nature and the needs of mankind, it was fundamentally defective, to say the least.

Rousseau and Burke not only adopted the more modern viewpoint that government had to be for the welfare of the people and that the interests of the governed had to be recognized as of paramount importance, but they also did much to strengthen the bonds that linked the people to their governments. When rulers governed in their own interests, and when political philosophy was still struggling with the fundamental antagonism between the interests of the individual on the one hand, and those of the state on the other, it was only to be expected that a wide gap would exist between governors and the governed. Rousseau bridged the gap as far as political thought was concerned by discarding individualistic doctrine with its fundamental antagonism to government, and by basing his political theory upon the idea of self-government. The 'real' will of the citizen found its counterpart in the general will of the state, and thus the antagonism between the individual and the state was resolved in a higher synthesis. That the gap had remained in political life until a late date was apparent from

Burke's eulogy of his fellow-member of Parliament, Sir George Savile, whose great distinction was that 'he has taught that grand lesson to government and subject,—no longer to regard each other as adverse parties'.[8] Burke himself never wearied in his attempts to bury that antagonism and to build up a better understanding and a deeper sympathy between the members of Parliament and the people. He knew that 'obedience is what makes government, and not the names it is called',[9] and he believed that obedience would come more readily from citizens who knew from the actual conduct of the government that their interests were being constantly cared for. 'I am sure', Burke said confidently in his *Speech on American Taxation*, 'the natural effect of fidelity, clemency, kindness in governors is peace, good-will, order and esteem, on the part of the governed'.[10]

The first practical step towards bridging that gap between the government and the people for Rousseau as for Burke consisted in making certain that the government would be both stable and just and that it would be beyond the reach of arbitrary human wills and passions. Without the steady rule of justice and a reasonable measure of stability, both knew that there could be neither liberty nor security. 'Those who subject the laws to human passions', Rousseau declared in the *Lettres de la Montagne*, 'are the true destroyers of governments'.[11] Burke, on his part, preferred by far to live 'under the jurisdiction of severe but steady reason' than to be subjected to 'the empire of indulgent, but capricious passion'.[12] Even more emphatically, he stated in his *Letter to a Noble Lord* that he had ever abhorred, since the first dawn of his understanding

'to this its obscure twilight, all the operations of opinion, fancy, inclination, and will, in the affairs of government, where only a sovereign reason, paramount to all forms of legislation and administration, should dictate. Government is made for the very purpose of opposing that reason to will and to caprice, in the reformers or in the reformed, in the governors or in the governed, in kings, in senates, or in people.' [13]

And both Rousseau and Burke looked to constitutional government to provide the rule of law and reason, and to exclude arbitrary human will and passion to which nations had been subjected under absolute governments.

Rousseau desired above all that the citizens of his ideal state should not be subjected at any time to any human being who might possibly tyrannize over them either individually or collectively. He believed that if the sole authority in the state was the general will, then the people would be subject only to laws that were declared, enduring and just, and that were in final analysis the expression of their 'real' will. And their freedom would be assured, no matter what their form of government, if in whoever governed, they saw not 'the man, but the organ of the law'.[14] Under such conditions, dependence on men could become as safe and as sure as dependence on things had been in the state of nature, and with all the advantages that civil society had to offer, man could rise to virtue and could find happiness under government.

But in order to secure the rule of reason and law, there had to be a relationship of a most intimate order between the legislative and executive functions of government. Legislation, which was the special function of the sovereign people, was no more than the declaration of their will, and it had to be supplemented by an executive agent whose special function was to carry out that will. And just as every action of a free individual involved two co-ordinating elements, one moral in the will which determined the nature of the act, and the other the physical power to carry the act into effect, so also the will of the state needed an executive agent, which could 'bind together' the public force, and set it to work under the direction of the general will. This agent had to serve as a 'means of communication between the state and the sovereign', and had to do for the moral and collective person of the state, 'more or less what the union of the soul and body does for man'.[15] 'Here', Rousseau added, 'we have what is, in the State, the basis of government, often wrongly confused with the Sovereign, whose minister it is'.[16] The government itself was an 'intermediate body' set up between the subjects and the Sovereign, 'to secure their mutual correspondence', while at the same time it was charged with 'the execution of the laws and the maintenance of liberty, both civil and political'.[17]

While legislation was the most important function in the state, Rousseau recognized with Montesquieu that there had to be a separation of powers in government if there was not to be tyranny of the worst kind. Legislation itself had to remain in the hands of the sovereign people. Rousseau rejected representative government partly because he failed to see its possibilities as a legislative body which could actually interpret and reflect the national mind, but partly also because he insisted that the sovereign people were alone competent to seek to elicit the general will, which was the supreme authority in the state, and to give expression to it in their legislation. In the *Contrat Social*, therefore, the citizen body was expected to convene in accordance with established convention, in order to carry out directly the function of legislation. And while he would not allow the legislation to be taken out of the hands of the sovereign people, he also stated emphatically that it was most unwise for those who made the laws to execute them as well. Legislation was concerned solely with matters of general interest, and consequently the laws the sovereign people enacted could only assume the form of a statement of the principles to be followed in the state. The execution of the laws, on the other hand, involved the application of those principles to particular cases. If the people as a whole turned their attention to particular objects, which would be unavoidable if they assumed executive as well as legislative duties, it would not be easy for them to keep a 'general' view before their minds constantly when they had to turn to legislation. And because there could be nothing fraught with more danger to the welfare of the state than for private interests to intrude upon public affairs, Rousseau safeguarded the legislator from corruption by insisting that the executive should be placed in other hands.

Both the executive and the judiciary had to work under the supreme direction of the general will, and the magistrates who served on these bodies had to be appointed by the sovereign as its special ministers entrusted with the sacred duty of administering the laws. But at the same time, Rousseau recognized fully that they had to be separate and independent bodies within the state and had to be allowed to carry out their duties without undue interference from the legislature, for otherwise they could not function properly. Moreover, both the executive and the judiciary had special duties to fulfil that fell outside the province of the people. Thus the people had to leave such matters as foreign affairs to the executive, because

'the great maxims of state are not within their reach; they must refer them to their chiefs. . . . That which essentially concerns each citizen is the observation of the laws within (the state), the ownership of property, and the security of the individuals.' [18]

Although Rousseau did not have a great deal to say about the judiciary, he recognized fully that it had to be placed in the hands of properly qualified magistrates. The condemnation of a criminal was a particular act, and for that reason it could not be regarded as a function of the sovereign. Nevertheless, 'it is a right the sovereign can confer without being able itself to exert it'.[19] But to place either the judiciary or the executive in the hands of the people was to risk the worst abuses of democracy.[20]

The different functions of government not only had to be separate, but Rousseau recognized that they also had to be balanced. In that balance the secret of good government was to be found, and although he was critical in many ways of British political methods and institutions, Rousseau was prepared to join with other political thinkers of his day in paying tribute to the British government as a 'model of the exact balance of the respective powers'.[21] What government, he asked, in turning his attention to the constitution of Geneva, could be better than that in which all the parts were balanced in a perfect equilibrium, 'where individual citizens cannot transgress the laws, because they are subject to judges? and where the judges cannot transgress them either, because they are constantly watched by the people?'[22] The legislator, eternally vigilant, watched the good effects or the abuse of the laws; he saw whether they were being followed or transgressed, and whether interpreted in good or bad faith.

For a government to function effectively, however, it was necessary for it to have a corporate personality of its own. Like the state, of which it was an integral part, it had important duties to fulfil, which could only be performed satisfactorily if it possessed the strength, initiative and unity that were inherent in an organic body. So that it could have a 'true existence', and a 'real life' to distinguish it from the rest of the state, and so that all its members could act together harmoniously and thus fulfil the end for which it was instituted, it was necessary for the government to have a 'personality of its own, a feeling shared by all its members, a power and a will of its own'.[23] For then, and then only, could there be the close harmony between the legislature and the executive bodies that was necessary if there was to be the rule of law and reason in the state.

When constituted along such lines, Rousseau believed that a government would possess the qualities necessary to secure liberty, which for him was the fundamental objective of government. Indeed, liberty was the *summum bonum*; it was to be preferred to all other advantages that came in the train of good government. To Rousseau, it was a vital force that gave value to the state and meaning to all human endeavour. When the Poles sighed for tranquillity after long years of suffering caused by internal dissension as well as foreign aggression, he told them that they were worthy of liberty because they loved it, but that they could not have both liberty and tranquillity. The two things were incompatible, and it was therefore necessary to choose between them. Nothing could be more fatal to liberty than the relaxation of effort that went with tranquillity, or the peace that accompanied stagnation. But if a people really loved liberty and right, Rousseau believed that incidental disadvantages would count for nothing. Corruption might raise its head within the state, but as corruption was an abuse of liberty, its presence was for Rousseau a proof that liberty still existed. Moreover, he pointed out that a people which would never misuse governmental powers would never misuse independence; a people that would always govern well would not need to be governed. It was ultimately through continual struggle with human imperfections that an individual as well as a nation won liberty.

Burke was scarcely prepared to accept Rousseau's ideal as either desirable or practicable from the point of view of the statesman. Liberty through self-government could be obtained only through the sacrifice of some of those bonds which Burke regarded as of the greatest importance not only in welding a people together but also in maintaining the authority of the government. While not denying for a moment that a people should be free, or that its government should foster that freedom by every means within its power, Burke nevertheless exalted good order as the statesman's ideal—the good order that came through the harmonious working of the constitution. 'Good order', he declared, 'is the foundation of all good things.' [24] Indeed, liberty itself could not flourish without it. The only liberty that genuinely appealed to Burke was 'a liberty connected with order; that not only exists along with order and virtue, but which cannot exist at all without them. It inheres in good and steady government, as in its substance and vital principle.' [25] And that liberty was not limited to the few; it belonged to the whole nation. The liberty that belonged to only a section of the people was 'a most invidious mode of slavery', against which he resolutely set his face. 'Liberty, if I understand it at all,' he wrote to the sheriffs of Bristol, 'is a *general* principle, and the clear right of all the subjects within the realm, or of none.' [26] But the liberty that belonged to the nation and was a sacred heritage from the past, was neither an unlimited freedom nor an abstract speculation. Social and civil freedom, like all other things in life, was 'variously mixed and modified, enjoyed in very different degrees, and shaped into an infinite diversity of forms, according to the temper and circumstances of every community', and had nothing in common with the propositions of geometry and metaphysics 'which admit of no medium, but must be true or false in all their latitude'. For 'the *extreme* of liberty (which is its abstract perfection, but its real fault) obtains nowhere, nor ought to obtain anywhere. Because extremes, as we all know, in every point which relates either to our duties or satisfactions in life, are destructive both to virtue and enjoyment.' For that reason, liberty had to be limited in order to be possessed. Nevertheless, it was not possible to state precisely how much limitation should be placed upon it. But, Burke added, it should be the constant aim of every wise public council to find out 'by cautious experiments, and rational, cool endeavours, with how little, not how much of this restraint' the community could subsist; for liberty was a good to be improved, and not an evil to be lessened. 'It is not only a private blessing of the first order, but the vital spring

and energy of the state itself, which has just so much life and
vigour as there is liberty in it.' [27] In other words, as long as
liberty remained a restrained and ordered principle within the
framework of the constitution and found expression in good
order and steady government, it was to be respected and
fostered as a blessing to all within the state.

But in so far as Rousseau's ideal of liberty tended to the disruption of the established order, Burke both disliked and
feared it. Where Rousseau had regarded the fullest expression
of public opinion and the frequent election of magistrates as
the necessary concomitants of political liberty, Burke thought
of them with deep concern as profoundly disturbing elements
in the life of the nation. He disliked elections intensely on
account of the public disturbances that invariably accompanied
them, while he desired to bring the expression of public opinion
within well-defined limits. It seemed to him that full and free
discussion of national affairs might easily become a disin-
tegrating force within the state. He clung to prescription not
only as the principle which gathered together the most powerful stabilizing forces in the life of the nation, but also as the
surest foundation for stable government; whereas Rousseau
would have summarily rejected it as an undesirable fetter upon
liberty, if not actually antithetical to it.

Fundamentally the liberty of Rousseau's ideal demanded
more than Burke was prepared to admit. He saw with alarm
that the demand for greater liberty of thought and action in
political affairs would inevitably break down some of the bonds
of 'unsuspecting confidence' that he regarded as the mainstay
of all stable government and that it would tend to take authority away from the governing classes and place it in the hands of
the people. While he had faith in the ability of the 'natural'
aristocracy to carry forward the great national traditions of
statesmanship and enlightened government, he had no faith in
the political wisdom of the people as a whole nor in their ability
to become the arbiters of their own destinies. Not only were
the people for the most part at least half a century behindhand
in their politics, but the 'mere vulgar' were entirely disqualified
by their 'violence and instability'. And far from receiving
instructions from the people, it was the duty as well as the

privilege of their representatives in Parliament to decide what was best for the nation.

'Faithful watchmen we ought to be over the rights and privileges of the people,' he wrote in making clear his position on this vital issue. 'But our duty, if we are qualified for it as we ought, is to give them information, and not to receive it from them; we are not to go to school to them to learn the principles of law and government. In doing so, we should not dutifully serve, but we should basely and scandalously betray, the people, who are not capable of this service by nature, nor in any instance called to it by the Constitution.' 'I reverentially look up to the opinion of the people, and with an awe, that is almost superstitious,' he continued, but 'I should be ashamed to show my face before them, if I changed my ground, as they cried up or cried down men, or things, or opinions; if I wavered and shifted about with every change, and joined in it, or opposed, as best answered any low interest or passion; if I held them up hopes, which I knew I never intended, or promised what I well knew I could not perform.' [28]

Under the established government of England, Burke knew that there could be both liberty and security for the people if good faith and confidence existed between them and their representatives in Parliament. But to take literally the ideal of liberty and self-government was to challenge the foundations of that established government as well as to jeopardize the peace and good order of the whole nation. After the outbreak of the French revolution, he became more than ever convinced that he was right on this important issue.

Because Burke believed that it was of vital importance to the welfare of the nation that the great principles of government for which his party stood should not be sacrificed to the demands of the people, he turned aside from the ideal that Rousseau had regarded as most desirable and took his stand on the doctrine of Whig trusteeship. Thus, in the interests of good order and steady government, he deliberately allied himself with conservative tradition rather than with progressive liberalism. He did not know whither the ideals of emergent democracy would lead, whereas he knew that in adhering to the principles of 1688, he would be on the well-trodden highway of constitutional practice. The doctrine of Whig trusteeship, which reflected the ideals of the 'glorious' revolution, recognized a constitutional monarchy and the existence of a governing class in Parliament, in whose hands the rights and liberties of the people were to be placed in trust. The essence of the doctrine as understood by the ordinary Whig member of Parliament was given in simple terms by Burke in the *Thoughts on the Present Discontents*, when he wrote that

'the king is the representative of the people; so are the lords; so are the judges. They are all trustees for the people, as well as the commons; because no power is given for the sole sake of the holder; and although government certainly is an institution of divine authority, yet its forms and the persons who administer it, all originate from the people.' [29]

Whig trusteeship was in point of fact a stepping-stone to the great Reform Bill of 1832, when full recognition was given by Parliament to the right of the British people to self-government. In the period of gradual transition to self-government, it gave a sense of responsibility to the Whig party, and set a high standard for statesmanship to which high-minded men such as Burke responded wholeheartedly. For Burke took to his duties not only a deep religious faith, but also high ideals and a sincere appreciation of the art of government. And in his hands the doctrine of Whig trusteeship was raised from an oligarchical tradition to an inspiring set of political principles that had affinity with the coming age of self-government rather than with the Walpole and Bolingbroke era in which it had become firmly rooted in British political thought.

Between the Walpole era and Burke's political career, however, forces had stirred in the life of the nation which made a profound impression upon Burke and his outlook on life. With the dawn of the age of romanticism, of humanitarianism, and of religious revival, a new emphasis was placed upon the meaning and value of human life. Consequently it became customary to contemplate man in a different light. While the romanticists were becoming aware of the fact that man was a creature endowed with imagination, emotions, and sentiments, the humanitarians were discovering that he was suffering acutely and often unnecessarily. On every side they saw important work they could do to bring about an improvement in social conditions. Moreover, the reawakening of religious sentiment fostered a strong spirit of brotherly love and of mutual helpfulness. A deep sense of pity, and an intense desire to wipe out some of the most glaring social abuses, gradually suffused men's minds as they awoke to a new social consciousness and inspired them with a longing for a new and better day when mankind would not be subjected to needless pain. Burke carried this spirit of the new age into the field of politics. It was the motivating force behind all that was finest and best in his long career. He was so deeply sensitive to human suffering that he could not stress sufficiently the fact that government was a sacred trust to be exercised in the disinterested service of humanity. 'The poorest being that crawls on earth,' he solemnly asserted, 'contending to save itself from injustice and oppression, is an object respectable in the eyes of God and man.'[30] The sufferings of the humblest claimed his solicitude quite as readily as the tortured Queen of France, whose fate caused him to exclaim that the age of chivalry had gone, and that the glory of Europe was extinguished for ever.

It seemed to Burke that fundamentally the welfare of a country depended mainly upon the men who held public office. If they possessed high ideals and a deep sympathy with the people and their problems, they would not be prepared to allow the cry of suffering to go unheeded, nor yet would they fail to foster all that was for the good of the nation. But they could render effective service to their country only if, in addition to high ideals and a sympathetic understanding, they brought to their task a mastery of the art of government. The right use of that art was, in point of fact, the whole secret of good and wise government. And if the principles upon which political art was based were those of liberty and justice, Burke believed that the people would not only be able to enjoy the greatest measure of freedom and security compatible with the highly complex conditions of modern society, but that they would not be allowed to endure unnecessary suffering. Believing, as he did, that it was the duty of the statesman to follow in the path of the fundamental principles upon which the British people had been governed from time immemorial, which he saw reflected in the doctrine of Whig trusteeship, he would have him apply these principles in accordance with the dictates of expediency, prudence, and wisdom. The great traditions that had come down through the ages embodied the wisdom of the British race, and Burke felt sure that in following them, the statesman would build upon a solid and enduring foundation. And if legislators and people alike could be taught to use the 'arguments of states and kingdoms' instead of the metaphysical jargon of the schools, it would be possible for government to become as wise and as just as human skill could make it.

Owing to the nature of the problems with which government had to deal, the statesman who would truly serve his country had need above all of a 'sagacious, powerful and combining' mind. Within the framework of the state, the forces of good and evil, of liberty and oppression, of justice and injustice contended with each other, and it was the function of government to foster and develop those forces which operated for the welfare of humanity, and to exclude as far as possible those which led to injustice and oppression. Out of the confusion and strife of conflicting interests and opinions through which those forces operated, it was the duty of the statesman to bring harmony and concord. To that end, he had first of all to distinguish those trends in national life which actually tended to the welfare of the nation as a whole, and having recognized them, he had to make use of the political machinery at his command in order to co-ordinate them in such a way that they could operate effectively for the good of the people. Then in order to achieve his purpose, the statesman not only required to understand 'the things which facilitate or obstruct the various ends which are to be pursued by the mechanism of civil institutions,' but he had also to gain the good will and co-operation of the people, which could be done only through 'a deep knowledge of human nature and human necessities'.[31] The legislators who framed the ancient commonwealths, Burke pointed out, knew that they could not succeed with no better equipment than the 'metaphysics of an undergraduate'. They had to deal with men, and consequently they were obliged to study human nature.

Thus, if his work was to be effective, the statesman had need not only of wide knowledge of men and affairs, but of practical wisdom as well. He had to know what was expedient, in the light of circumstances, and he had to know what methods to

adopt in order to gain his end. The wise prince, Burke wrote
to the Chevalier de Rivarol, would study the genius of his
people.

'He will indulge their humours, and will preserve them in their privileges, he will act upon the circumstances of his states as he finds them,
and whilst thus acting upon the practical principles of a practical policy,
he is the happy prince of a happy people.' [32]

And if he followed such a statesmanlike course, he would
not need to trouble himself about what the 'Condorcet and
the Raynal, and the whole flight of the magpies and jays of
philosophy', might think about him.

But, as Burke fully realized, it was not altogether possible to
ignore entirely what the 'magpies and jays' of philosophy had
to say, because they had taught most assiduously their doctrine
of government in accordance with the rights of man. While he
readily acknowledged that government was deeply interested
in securing man's rights, he pointed out that rights, like liberties, were not unlimited. They were not sweeping abstract
rights, but on the contrary were in a 'sort of *middle*, incapable
of definition, but not impossible to be discerned'. The rights of
men in government were their advantages. But as it was necessary, according to times and circumstances, to choose between
advantages, it would be found that the real rights of men were
often 'in balances between differences of good; in compromises
sometimes between good and evil, and sometimes, between
evil and evil'. For political reason was a computing principle,
'adding, subtracting, multiplying, and dividing, morally and
not metaphysically or mathematically, true moral denomin-
ations'.[33] In other words, it was not rational to imagine that
any one could enjoy an unlimited number of advantages. As
the individual had to choose between alternatives, so also the
legislators had to make a similar choice for the nation. In that
choice, they had to be guided by expediency, because circumstances would dictate what methods had to be chosen in order
to gain the ends they desired. And even the measure of good
that was practicable was limited owing to the fact that inconveniences hampered the operation of every political principle.
Consequently, it was necessary to modify those principles

themselves in accordance with circumstances in order to obtain some good. In point of fact,

'all government, indeed every human benefit and enjoyment, every virtue, and every prudent act, is founded on compromise and barter,' Burke asserted. 'We balance inconveniences; we give and take; we remit some rights, that we may enjoy others; and, we choose rather to be happy citizens, than subtle disputants.' [34]

And if Burke stood charged with being 'too fond of the right to pursue the expedient', it was because he believed that ultimately only that was expedient which was also right. Moral right had to be linked to political right before the expedient could become completely satisfactory.

The standard of expediency by which the statesman could be guided was that which was 'good for the community, and good for every individual in it'.[35] But that good, as Burke never wearied of stressing, was not necessarily the apparent good of the moment; it was the more enduring good that the statesman's insight enabled him to recognize, and that was to be found beneath the surface of the clash of conflicting purposes and desires in the everyday life of the nation. It was the common good that Rousseau had regarded as the objective of the general will and that he had thought would be found by processes of social logic similar to those which Burke described.

The statesman, in search of the expedient, had to judge of the value of political tenets by their practical consequences. In other words, he had to find out by the experience gained through trial and error what tenets were valuable, and he had to link them on to his own political principles on the one hand, and to expediency on the other. However, he would make a fatal error if he thought that political problems were concerned with truth or falsehood. They were concerned with good and evil, and not with logical propositions. 'What in the result is likely to produce evil, is politically false,' Burke asserted; while 'that which is productive of good, politically true'.[36]

Although the principle of expediency was simply a knowledge of the wisest and best course to pursue under given circumstances, it was not merely another name for opportunism.

In the first place, expediency was linked to principles and was employed by the statesman so that national life could be directed towards definite objectives. The opportunist lacked that conception of an end to which Aristotle maintained all human activity should be directed, whereas the statesman's actions were constantly directed towards a purposive end. And while the opportunist might happen to seize upon a favourable opportunity, he would fail to turn it to enduring good for the nation for the simple reason that he had no co-ordinated plan of action into which it could be fitted. The statesman, on the contrary, possessed the vision which enabled him to see the possibilities for good in any opportune moment, while in addition he knew how to turn them to advantage for the welfare of his country. Moreover, with an intimate knowledge of the circumstances of national life, he was in a position to judge with a reasonable degree of accuracy what would be the most expedient as well as the wisest course to follow. Under his guidance the nation could make progress, whereas the lack of the necessary qualities for true leadership would ultimately render the activities of the opportunist ineffectual.

So that expediency might not degenerate into opportunism, however, it was necessary for it to be supplemented by high ideals and the practical virtues. Thus the way of the statesman was essentially that prescribed by prudence and wisdom and by sound judgement. Because government and legislation were matters of reason and judgement, Burke looked to the wise statesman to form his judgement upon principle rather than upon theory. For he regarded a principle as something more enduring and more substantial than mere theory. It was, in point of fact, that practical reason which had stood the test of time and had become embodied in tradition, and had also been moulded to fit into the habitual mode of thought of a people. Such qualities characterized the principles of the British constitution and also the doctrine of Whig trusteeship. Theory, on the other hand, had no sounder basis than logic, which Burke mistrusted completely as a guide for the statesman. Until theory had been tested by experience, Burke believed that the statesman should exercise the utmost caution in placing any reliance upon it. But he regarded that judgement as sound which accepted well-established principles, and in the light of them followed the dictates of prudence and wisdom.

Of all the political virtues, Burke regarded prudence as the most important. 'Prudence is not only the first in rank of the virtues political and moral,' he declared, 'but she is the director, the regulator, the standard of them all.' [37] Her lessons were written upon the pages of history, where Burke looked, not for political principles, but for the precepts of prudence. 'History is a preceptor of prudence, not of principles,' he informed the Bishop of Chester. 'The principles of true politics are those of morality enlarged. . . .' [38] The general principles of moral prudence never varied, and consequently were an unfailing guide for the statesman. But the circumstances which were under the dominion of that prudence were 'perpetually variable', and for that reason it was necessary for the statesman to have a sound grasp of the principles of prudence so that he could apply them to the most varied situations. Moreover, the prudence to which Burke looked was not a 'false, reptile prudence'; it was the result of caution and not of fear.

Burke exalted prudence because it gathered together the various political virtues which guided the statesman aright in the exceedingly difficult problems with which he was confronted in the course of his work. Because questions of state were moral, and not abstract, in nature, they called for the well-informed judgement of the statesman rather than for the logic of the metaphysician. Indeed, Burke believed that nothing could be more absurd than to discuss them, or to regard them, as matters of metaphysical speculation. They were essentially practical problems that demanded practical solutions. 'Abstractedly speaking,' Burke conceded that government, as well as liberty, was good. But, he demanded,

'is it because liberty in the abstract may be classed among the blessings of mankind, that I am seriously to felicitate a mad-man who has escaped from the protecting restraint and wholesome darkness of his cell, on his restoration to the enjoyment of light and liberty? Am I to congratulate a highwayman and murderer, who has broke prison, upon the recovery of his natural rights?' [39]

Presenting his argument from another angle, he asked what was the use of discussing a man's abstract right to food or medicine? 'The question is upon the method of procuring and administering them. In that deliberation I shall always advise to call in the aid of the farmer and the physician, rather than the professor of metaphysics.' [40] In other words, every political problem involved a careful consideration of the attendant circumstances, and a knowledge of what measures would be most efficacious in dealing with them. Because all political problems were of such a nature, it was impossible to prescribe any hard and fast rules for dealing with them.

'No lines can be laid down for civil and political wisdom,' Burke asserted. 'They are matters incapable of exact definition. But, though no man can draw a stroke between the confines of day and night, yet light and darkness are upon the whole tolerably distinguishable.'

By the same token, it was not impossible for a prince

'to find out such a mode of government, and such persons to administer it, as will give a great degree of content to his people; without any curious and anxious research for that abstract, universal, perfect harmony, which while he is seeking, he abandons those means of ordinary tranquillity which are in his power without any research at all.' [41]

For these reasons, Burke believed that politics must for ever remain an art, and must be left under the supreme jurisdiction of prudence and wisdom.

The success of the art of politics depended upon other important factors as well as upon the rules of prudence. It depended also upon the breadth of vision possessed by legislators and legislative assemblies, and upon a due sense of responsibility on the part of those who administered the affairs of state. The best rules that could be devised would fail unless the men who were to apply them had the necessary intellectual and moral stature.

'My observation has furnished me with nothing that is to be found in any habits of life or education, which tends wholly to disqualify men for the functions of government,' Burke wrote, 'but that, by which the power of exercising those functions is very frequently obtained, I mean a spirit and habits of low cabal and intrigue; which I have never, in one instance, seen united with a capacity for sound and manly policy.' [42]

He had known merchants with the 'sentiments and abilities of great statesmen', and he had also seen 'persons in the rank of

statesmen, with the conceptions and character of pedlers'.[43]
And after the colonists in America had declared their independence, Burke attributed England's troubles very largely to
the fact that members of Parliament had not had constantly
before their eyes 'a general, comprehensive, well-connected,
and well-proportioned view of the whole of our dominions
and a just sense of their true bearings and relations'. Remem-
bering that 'a great empire and little minds go ill together', he
pointed out that

'if we make ourselves too little for the sphere of our duty; if, on the contrary, we do not stretch and expand our minds to the compass of their
object, be well assured, that everything about us will dwindle by degrees,
until at length our concerns are shrunk to the dimensions of our
minds. . . .' [44]

But in addition to having wide and comprehensive views
before their minds, it was necessary for them to assume the
responsibilities of their office and to take into account the
consequences of the measures they proposed adopting. 'It is
the direct office of wisdom to look to the consequences of the
acts we do; if it be not this, it is worth nothing, it is out of place
and of function; and a downright fool is as capable of government as Charles Fox.' [45] It was essentially because government
called for men who were trained to hold enlightened views and
to assume moral responsibility that Burke believed democratic
government would fail. 'How can he get wisdom that holdeth
the plough, and that glorieth in the goad,' he quoted pertinently
from *Ecclesiastes*, '. . . and whose talk is of bullocks?' [46] And
although he was deeply disturbed by the shortcomings of
fellow-members of Parliament, he firmly believed that the
welfare of the country depended upon arousing them to a sense
of their duties and responsibilities rather than upon allowing
the people as a whole greater political power.

The statesman after Burke's own heart was the man who
realized the sacredness of the trust that had been placed in his
hands, and who had a 'disposition to preserve, and an ability to
improve'.[47] It was upon such qualities that he believed the
foundations of all true statesmanship rested, without which no
country could hope to prosper and become great. The states-

man who recognized the importance of disturbing the orderly course of national life as little as possible, and who was able to make constructive plans out of the materials he found at hand, was the one to whom the country had to look for true leadership. For such a man could not only develop the latent possibilities of his country, but he could so organize and co-ordinate national life that all its complex parts would work together harmoniously for the good of the whole. In this way, the varied activities of a people would fall naturally into their proper niche in the vast and all-embracing scheme of national affairs. Thus progress would be achieved in 'the silent lapse of events', and it was a progress that Burke regarded as far more certain and quite as valuable as that achieved by the more violent means of revolution. But in order to keep national life upon an even tenor and at the same time to keep abreast of the forward march of events, the statesman required all the political wisdom that he could gain from 'the bank and capital of the ages', as well as from his own experience. In looking to the past for its lessons, he would be in a position to mould the materials provided by both 'nature and chance', so that the present could enjoy to the full the blessings of good government, while the future could build with confidence upon his foundations.

Because Burke recognized that history was a dynamic process, he realized that the work of reformation must necessarily be an ever-present concern of government. But he was certain that the only kind of reformation that would prove enduring was that which was woven into the orderly course of national life. For that reason, he believed that it was highly undesirable for the control of national affairs to be taken out of the hands of those most fitted by nature to govern. If, however, the statesman was allowed to follow the course dictated by prudence without undue interference from outside, Burke believed that he would be able to accomplish far more than would otherwise be possible. While he would regard it as no inconsiderable part of wisdom to know how much of an evil could be left undisturbed in national life, he would also know when it was prudent to institute reform. For early reforms were 'amicable arrangements with a friend in power', while late reformations were 'terms imposed upon a conquered enemy'.[48] The wise statesman would not allow a spirit of grievance and hostility to grow up in the nation, because in addition to making his task more difficult, it would also injure the prestige of the government itself. And as it was in the interest of government that reformation should be early, so also it was in the interest of the people that it should be temperate.

'It is in their interest,' Burke reasoned, 'because a temperate reform is permanent; and because it has a principle of growth. Whenever we improve, it is right to leave room for a further improvement. It is right to consider, to look about us, to examine the effect of what we have done. Then we can proceed with confidence, because we can proceed with intelligence. . . .'[49]

Moreover, the statesman who followed such a policy would discover that he had an unfailing ally in Nature. For Burke had found that 'never, no, never, did nature say one thing and wisdom say another'.[50] Thus wise statesmanship and temperate reform could keep national life in harmony with the natural order, which Burke regarded as of fundamental importance. For the accord with Nature enabled political law to be joined to moral law, and thereby secured progress for the nation upon sound lines, while at the same time it provided the means for the attainment of the highest good, and therefore the ultimate happiness, of every individual within the state. When the principles of statesmanship were linked to the natural order on the one hand, and to human nature, to habits, prejudices and affections, and to all that was most deeply rooted in national life, on the other, Burke saw them firmly and securely established. Under such conditions, the art of the statesman could procure the greatest blessings that good government could confer upon mankind.

Rousseau's conception of the end of government was in fundamental agreement with Burke's views. He did not possess Burke's deep understanding of the art of government, nor yet did he realize its possibilities as fully. Nevertheless, he had a remarkable grasp of the nature of the principles which operated in the world of affairs, and like Burke, he looked upon the principle of expediency as that which had to be respected in the domain of fact. But at the same time, he believed that political law had to be regulated by morality, and for that reason he expected expediency to conform to the ideal of Right. For whereas Right was an absolute and unbending universal principle, expediency was a relative principle which could degenerate into acquiescence with imperfection, if not with evil.

While his *Contrat Social* was the work of the fearless thinker, the deeply conservative side of Rousseau's nature became apparent when he came to apply his ideas to actual states. He desired to disturb the trend of national life as little as possible, and he appreciated as much as Burke the importance of taking circumstances fully into consideration if the fundamental stability of the state was to be preserved. Thus when asked to 'trace the plan of a political system' for Corsica, he took pains to gather together the necessary facts regarding the circumstances of the people, their occupations, their sources of wealth and their cultural background, as well as the principal geographic facts concerning the island. The Corsicans were mainly agriculturists, and on the grounds of expediency, he advocated a republican state for them because it was least expensive, and a democratic administration because it was most suitable for an agricultural community. He advocated a 'mixed' government rather than a 'pure' democracy, because he recognized that modern conditions were entirely different from those of the ancient world, when free men had the necessary leisure time to devote themselves exclusively to the service of the state. With the same regard for 'political fact', he pointed out in his *Considérations sur le Gouvernement de Pologne*, that the liberation of the peoples of Poland was a great and worthy project, but at the same time it was also 'risky, dangerous, and not to be attempted without thought'.[51] Among the important precautions to be taken was one which would require time, but was nevertheless indispensable. 'It is, before everything else, to make the serfs whom you wish to liberate worthy of liberty and capable of maintaining it.' He frankly recognized that it was useless to advocate the liberation of a whole class of people without being assured first of all that they had the character which would make them prize and desire to foster their liberty when once they were given it.

The spirit of caution which led Rousseau to counsel the Poles never to lose sight of the important maxim 'not to change anything without necessity, neither to take away nor to add . . .' [52] also animated his conception of the methods by which practical reform should be instituted. His fear of drastic change and of revolution made him cautious even to the point of timidity. Indeed, he believed that liberty itself was bought at too great a price if it involved the sacrifice of even a single life. He preferred to follow the more pacific method of preparation and training for greater privileges as well as for greater responsibilities.

Rousseau's starting-point as a reformer was with the correction of false ideas. Like Burke, he attempted to present the corrective to current misconceptions and to clarify ideas that were but imperfectly understood. He was firmly convinced that man was good by nature and that it was institutions which made him bad. His ideas on the influence of institutions upon human nature were in harmony with the tendency of eighteenth-century writers to over-emphasize the significance of political institutions. For them, man's imperfections were the result of external influences; if he could be surrounded by the right kind of social institutions, he would overcome his defects. This belief was the logical consequence of Locke's psychology, upon which their thought was based, and it was also intimately linked to the current conception of perfectibility. No account was taken of heredity or of evolutionary process as important factors in the moral development of man. Consequently, it seemed rational to suppose that if men could be brought gradually to a clearer understanding of what political institutions should be and of what might be expected of them, they would desire to improve them upon sound lines. And when institutions were rectified, Rousseau believed that man's nature would be able to expand once more under the salutary influence of the right art.

While the correction of mistaken ideas was undertaken on a grand scale in the *Contrat Social*, it also became an important aspect of Rousseau's later political writings. Thus in his *Projet de Constitution pour la Corse*, he chided the Corsicans for their wrong conception of a nation. They had filled their protests against the Genoese with the injuries that had been inflicted upon their nobility, which they had resented bitterly. 'The Genoese only wanted to bring the nobility into disrepute,' Rousseau pointed out, whereas, 'you wish to ennoble the nation'. [53] To place the dignity of the state in the titles of several of its members was to take the shadow for the substance. Counselling them to leave titles to other states, Rousseau pointed out that the fundamental law for the Corsicans ought to be equality. 'The state should not give distinctions for anything except merit, virtues, or services rendered to the nation; and these distinctions should be no more hereditary than the qualities upon which they were founded.' [54] Rousseau was firmly convinced that the true dignity of a country did not depend upon the existence of marquises and counts, but rather upon the virtue and nobility of character of the individuals who together composed the nation. Like the Encyclopedists, Rousseau looked upon work as ennobling. Agriculture appealed to him particularly because it was a pursuit which enabled a people to remain self-contained, while at the same time it fostered both virtue and liberty. 'Commerce produces wealth,' he acknowledged, 'but agriculture assures liberty.' [55] And his economic ideal was that form of activity which enabled a people to live with a moderate degree of comfort; which encouraged virtue and simplicity of life, but which left no room for idleness nor for the accumulation of great wealth. Unlike Burke, who believed that 'if wealth is the obedient and laborious slave of virtue and of public honour, then wealth is in its place, and has its use. . . . If we command our wealth, we shall be rich and free : if our wealth commands us, we are poor indeed,' [56] Rousseau was so greatly concerned with the evils that accompanied wealth and luxury that he was inclined to condemn them altogether. If the Corsicans wished to enjoy to the full the advantages of their constitution, it was necessary for their government to encourage them to work by showing them that it was the way to their welfare and that it offered them great advantages, of which the greatest was not wealth.

But it was not sufficient for a government to care only for the economic and social welfare of a people. It had also to foster a spirit of patriotism, and to weld the people together by a common bond of affection for their country, their national institutions, and their national ideals. For then, and then only, could a nation become a spiritual unity, conscious of the destiny that lay before it. In protest against the cosmopolitanism of the age, which failed to recognize the importance of true patriotism to the welfare of a nation, Rousseau became an ardent champion of nationalism. There were no longer any Frenchmen, Germans, Spaniards, or even Englishmen, he lamented—there were only Europeans. 'All have the same tastes, the same passions, the same manners. . . . In the same circumstances, all will do the same thing. . . .'[57] When, however, a people had a distinctive national character, there was something upon which legislation could be engrafted. The citizens 'will obey the laws, and will not seek to elude them, because they will suit them, and will have the internal assent of their wills', he explained in elaborating the advantages of nationalism. 'Loving their country, they will serve it zealously and with all their hearts. With this sole sentiment, even bad legislation will make good citizens. . . .'[58] With Tennyson, Rousseau believed that

> That man's the true cosmopolite
> Who loves his native country best.

Without a people's genuine love for its country, there could be no deep-rooted loyalties upon which a government could rely for support and for stability. And not loving their country, it would be scarcely possible for men to extend their affections to other countries. The cosmopolitan spirit which knew no loyalty was therefore the real object of Rousseau's attack, as it was in later years of Burke's as well.

But Rousseau's appeal to patriotic sentiment had an even deeper significance, and it is important to remember that it was basic in all his political thought.[59] If the liberty which was the ideal of his political philosophy was to leave scarcely anything more than the 'cash nexus' which Carlyle found so deplorable, Rousseau recognized that it was essential to have a deep-rooted national sentiment that could replace the undesirable shackles imposed by 'meagre, stale, forbidding' custom and by outworn tradition. For that reason, he desired that the citizens should regard their country as symbolic of all that was finest and most ennobling in national life and aspirations, and that they should give to it the loyal attachment which alone was strong enough to replace the traditions of the past. In the consciousness of the destiny and the patriotic spirit which they shared in common, Rousseau hoped to build new loyalties for the people, which would firmly re-establish their sense of fundamental unity as well as the stability of national life, and at the same time would allow the spirit of freedom the latitude that was necessary if it was to thrive.

In order to build wisely for the future, Rousseau recognized that a programme of education was essential.

'There can be no patriotism without liberty, no liberty without virtue, no virtue without citizens. . . .' he had declared in his article on *Économie politique*. 'But to form citizens is not the work of a day; and in order to have men, it is necessary to educate them when they are children.' [60]

Through education, the author of the *Émile* hoped to form the 'natural' man so that he could take his rightful place and assume his rightful duties in a free society. For education not only gave a 'national bent' to a people, but it also went a long way towards removing many of the difficulties that Burke regarded as insurmountable obstacles in the way of democratic government. The gradual lessening of illiteracy; the wider political experience which came with a greater share in political affairs; the dignity and efficiency which came with the ideal of work; and the enriching of life which came with the democratic ideals of liberty, happiness, and peace, not only resolved Burke's main objections to democratic methods of government, but also saw the triumph of Rousseau's most cherished ideals.

It must, however, be admitted that education itself must be free if it is to function effectively. Experience has shown that by controlling the subject-matter of instruction and by the use of propaganda, education can become the instrument of a party and not the agent of the general will. Nevertheless, it is true that liberty and education are inseparably connected and that a free state must always provide media both for the expression of enlightened opinion and for the training of the minds of the people so that they can grasp the essential issues upon which the well-being of the commonwealth depends. It need scarcely be added that this, like every other ideal, is difficult of achievement. The right and the practical do not always coincide, and for that reason the choice of instruments of government must frequently be determined by the principle of expediency, which, as Burke clearly stated, must always aim at establishing that which is for the good of the people. Rousseau, the theorist, emphasized the ideal right with which expediency must come to terms; Burke, the statesman, laid stress upon the best attainable in the light of particular circumstances and tried to bring expediency to terms with the right.

CHAPTER X
STATESMAN AND *PHILOSOPHE*

BY a curious irony of fate, it has happened more than once in the course of human history that men whose ideas and work were really based upon the same fundamental principles have regarded each other as bitter opponents. When Edmund Burke thundered forth his vitriolic denunciations of Rousseau, he had no conception of the fact that they were both dreaming of the better society in which men would be free and would be willing to assume the responsibilities of citizenship in a state dedicated to liberty. Yet the real gulf which separated him from Rousseau was not fundamental difference in principle, but was rather a difference in tradition which showed itself in their mode of thought and in the methods they used for the presentation of their basic ideas. Rousseau had used the methods of the passing age of Cartesianism in order to present the constructive political philosophy that was to mould the future. Unfortunately, his thought was narrowed and distorted by a generation of enthusiasts who believed that with the French revolution the dream of liberty which had inspired his writings would be realized. And Burke, who belonged to the newer historical school, fought desperately for the preservation of the old order because it seemed to him that true liberty as well as all that was of greatest value in national life and traditions were being trampled under foot by the triumphant doctrinarianism of emergent democracy. He based his criticisms of Rousseau mainly upon those misinterpretations of the doctrine of the *Contrat Social* which, in the era of the French revolution, were proclaimed as the 'gospel according to Jean Jacques'. But in doing so, Burke fell back upon the same fundamental principles as Rousseau himself had held.

One of the few contemporaries who was able to see an affinity in their thought—because he stood sufficiently aloof from the spirit of partisanship that Burke aroused through his fierce denunciations of the French revolution and of Rousseau as the author whose works were its main source of inspiration,—was a German journalist, Friedrich Gentz. When translating Burke's *Reflections* into German, Gentz pointed out that both Rousseau and Burke felt the same toward two of the fundamental problems of the day, although they developed and expressed their ideas in totally different ways. In the first place, they both wished to counteract a one-sided appreciation of and admiration for the present with its manifold advantages, virtues, and pleasures. They did this by showing in contrast the charm and virtue of former times. Hence Rousseau's idyllic description of the state of nature, the golden age of·the past, and Burke's powerful apology for the Middle Ages. Also they both turned from the evil that was inevitably mingled with a high degree of culture and found inspiration in a past age in which there was evil, to be sure, but not the same as they saw around them. In both Rousseau and Burke, this awoke a sentimental longing for what was past and gone. But Gentz hastened to add that he did not believe either had any desire to halt the progress their contemporaries wished to make; they only wished 'to steer the winged chariot on the steep slope of cultural perfection'. Thus Rousseau, who knew the advantages of civilization as well as any one else, depicted the simplicity, purity, and unalloyed happiness of the 'natural' man, not in order to preach a crusade into the woods and forests of the Orinoco or of the Mississippi, but on the contrary, with the purpose of arousing an ardent desire for that felicity in ordinary life. By making people ashamed of their obvious inferiority, despite all their greatness and culture, Rousseau had hoped to make them desirous of incorporating into their lives as many of the advantages of the state of nature as possible, without loss of the advantages of cultured society. Burke, whose imagination led him to appreciate profoundly what was good in the ancient modes of thought, in ancient customs and manners, wanted to weave that good into the highest culture of his own day. He sought to prevent a proud, one-sided, intolerant, despotic philosophy from narrowing the reason, destroying customs, and killing all seeds of improvement past hope of regeneration, while it rocked its followers in a sick delusion of imaginary perfection, proclaiming audaciously that the ruling opinions, principles, maxims, and procedures were the climax of all human achievement.

But there were even more fundamental grounds of agreement between Rousseau and Burke than Gentz had observed. These two outstanding figures of eighteenth-century political thought also had a profound sense of the reality of those unseen forces which worked together for good in society. Like Cowper, they believed implicitly that 'God moves in a mysterious way, His wonders to perform', and their thought was deeply tinged with mysticism as they contemplated the divine and realized man's oneness with God. They had complete faith in God as the moral ruler of the universe, and in that objective moral order which held all things 'fast in their place'. Furthermore both believed that the state was the means appointed by the Author and Founder of Society through which man could find virtue and the perfection of which his nature was capable. And because the state fitted into the comprehensive scheme of the moral order of the universe, it seemed to them that in accepting the guidance of Nature man would find happiness.

Nature was the ideal to which both Rousseau and Burke looked. It was essentially the personification of the forces of justice and virtue, and because it represented the moral order of the universe, it would prove an infallible guide. But while it was a high ideal to place before mankind, it was not one that necessarily required great erudition in order to strive toward it. It was rather an ideal that called for the wisdom that was born of goodness and that could be found by following conscience, the intuitive perception of what was right, which had been implanted in the soul of every human being. As opposed to the ideal of knowledge which the age of reason had fostered, it presented the ideal of virtue. And while both recognized with Goethe that *es irrt der Mensch, so lang er strebt*, they nevertheless had implicit faith in the ultimate rightness of the human race. 'The species is wise,' Burke declared, 'and when time is given to it, as a species, it almost always acts right.' This faith in mankind was justified on the assumption that man was constantly striving to become what the Author of Nature intended he should be.

As far as political philosophy was concerned, the acceptance of the ideal of nature involved the recognition of two things. In the first place, it laid emphasis on the Aristotelian conception of nature as the attainment of man's highest good; while it also involved the acceptance of the principle that morals must not be divorced from politics. To found the state upon any other basis than right would bring about a conflict with the order of nature, and as Burke warned the French revolutionary leaders, 'Whilst you pique nature against you, you do unwisely to trust to duty.' In other words, political obligation had to be based upon the principles of justice and right. Moreover, both Rousseau and Burke were convinced that there could be no state in any true sense of the term unless virtue, wisdom, and justice were present. Without them there could be no such thing as liberty, and to take away liberty was to deny to man his moral nature. There was, however, a more immediate significance in the emphasis placed upon the need for liberty within the state. Long centuries of oppression had led to an intense desire for a political order which would leave men as free as possible so that they could seek their own highest good in whatever way they saw fit. Rousseau appreciated the desire for liberty even more than Burke, because he had experienced the evils and persecution that had to be endured under absolutism, whereas Burke had lived in England where the tradition for liberty was strong and where there was relatively little personal tyranny. And if Rousseau became the prophet of nature, it was, as Höffding pointed out, because nature was for him, first and last, freedom.

When the question arose how nature was to be followed in the modern state, the sharp divergences between the two men and their methods began to appear. It seemed to Rousseau that the first step to take was to find out what was implied in the idea of following nature. He was certain that actual states were not governed in accordance with justice and right; but before offering any criticisms of existing political conditions, he thought it was wise to have a clear conception of what ought to be. Therefore he planned his *Contrat Social* in accordance with the principles of Right, which for him was the path that nature and freedom followed. His political philosophy bore the stamp of idealism that had also characterized

Plato's *Republic*. It was devoted to the formulation of first principles and was not intended to be an historical investigation because, like Plato, Rousseau was mainly interested in the presentation of a rational ideal towards which actual states and peoples could strive.

Following nature implied an entirely different method of procedure for Burke. Indeed, he could not denounce Rousseau's Utopia-building loudly enough. He argued that states had not been built according to theories but had emerged through the processes of history. In addition, he believed that idealistic theories were fraught with danger to the state because they might appeal so strongly to men's imaginations that, in a misguided endeavour to realize Utopia, people might be led to destroy the real advantages they enjoyed under established government. In the French Revolution Burke saw, not the breakdown of an outworn system of absolutism, but the wilful destruction of a powerful empire so that a new state could be constructed according to enlightened theory. 'They build their politics, not on convenience, but on truth,' he complained, 'and they profess to conduct men to certain happiness by the assertion of their undoubted rights.' Indeed, in everything they did, it seemed to Burke that they had strayed out of the highway of nature, and as a consequence they had found not liberty and happiness, but disorder and tyranny. The course that nature dictated, however, was that by which nations had grown great. The institutions that had been constructed in the course of the ages in order to meet the changing and growing needs of the people were those which he regarded as best suited to the habits and customs of the people. They were like the vestment that shaped itself to the body, and they fitted because they had been shaped, not by the wisdom of one person, but by the wisdom of generations. History, in other words, was the process through which nature found expression. It was essentially a process of growth and slow development, through which national institutions and national character took definite shape and form. Through that slow process of growth, the forms of government became established; while customs, traditions, and economic, civic, cultural, and religious ideals became woven into the texture of national life.

The harmonious development of national life was not altogether the result of chance. Burke pointed out that it was
partly the work of art and that the happiest results had been
obtained through the right use of the right art. It had been
fostered by the high-minded leadership of those to whom the
responsibilities of government and statesmanship had fallen.
But it had also developed through the deep-rooted desire of the
race to preserve that which it regarded as its highest good.
Thus the rights and liberties which Englishmen prized so
highly as their sacred heritage had been won only at the cost of
centuries of determined resistance to oppression and by the
gradual building up of the necessary governmental machinery
to safeguard them. Because Burke knew that it was necessary
for the present to foster the heritage it had received from the
past, his thoughts were constantly concentrated upon what
ought to be done so that the present would faithfully discharge
its trust. Indeed, he was so concerned with what ought to be
that he frequently lost touch with reality. But his idealism was
that which built itself up from facts and from the possibilities
he saw latent both in people and in institutions, and he justified
it accordingly. It was the idealism which preserved all that
was fine in national life and which consequently enabled the
nation to follow nature in the truest sense of the term. For
'nature is never more truly herself, than in her grandest form.
The Apollo of Belvedere . . . is as much in nature, as any figure
from the pencil of Rembrandt, or any clown in the great rustic
revels of Teniers'. [1] The nature which represented the finest
expression of the national mind and which was nurtured by the
greatest skill of the statesman and the devoted service of the
patriot was therefore also true.

Because Rousseau's idealism was that which worked from
principles and presented an ideal standard towards which the
actual might strive, Burke regarded it with the deepest distrust and misgivings. Although it would probably achieve
somewhere about the same result as Burke's method, Burke
could not bring himself to accept it. Logic of itself was too
flimsy a basis for political ideals, and it seemed to Burke that
no Englishman would feel himself called upon to place implicit
trust in it. Indeed, the Englishman's distrust of logic was a

deep-rooted national prejudice. 'We Englishmen,' Burke explained, 'stop very short of the principles upon which we support any given part of our constitution or even the whole of it together. . . .' So that in the last analysis, Burke's quarrel with Rousseau resolved itself into a matter of national temperament. For Rousseau, like the French to whom he belonged by family descent as well as by adoption, enjoyed the deep intellectual stimulation of working out thought patterns into logical system. Moreover, as the way was not open for him to take an active part in political life, he chose the most natural means of giving expression to the conclusions of long years of meditation and profound preoccupation with the fundamental problems that confronted his age.

So many deep-rooted divergences sprang from their intellectual as well as their national traditions that it would have been impossible for Burke ever to see eye to eye with Rousseau. The circumstances of their lives were so strikingly dissimilar that even these conspired to make misunderstanding wellnigh inevitable. For Rousseau had belonged to the literary circles of Paris in which the most daring speculative thought of the age was nurtured. And while the *philosophes* aroused Burke's curiosity, they also awakened his most violent antagonism and fear when he came into their midst and saw their attitude toward life. When in Paris in 1773, he had visited the salons where the most distinguished literary men had forgathered in the heyday of the Enlightenment, but he had returned to England with a heart heavy with foreboding. Conscious of the heavy responsibilities that fell to the lot of the statesman, he resented bitterly the irresponsibility of spirit that he believed had animated their writings. In contrast with the ferment of Parisian intellectual life, his own home surroundings seemed settled and peaceful. In London, he enjoyed the friendship of men such as Johnson and Reynolds, whose encouragement had helped him in the days when he was struggling to gain recognition as a statesman. The meetings of the Literary Club, at which Burke and his friends entered into their famous discussions, were vastly different from the salons of Paris or the Grandval home of the Baron d'Holbach, where Rousseau had listened to the eloquent discourse of Diderot,

Grimm, and the other Encyclopedists, who in their 'intellectual paradise of open questions, where God and a future life, marriage and the family, every dogma of religion, every prescription of morality . . . were being busily pulled to pieces', were preparing the way for a 'social pandemonium'.[2]

Although Burke and Rousseau were both deeply religious men, the form in which their religious faith found expression differed as greatly as the circumstances of their lives. Burke was a member of the Church of England, and looked upon himself as an orthodox member of the Established Church. Religious influences had surrounded him from his earliest days, and that of his Quaker schoolmaster had been abiding. He had early settled his religious convictions, and having decided to follow the faith of his father, he turned in derision from contemporary deistic thought.

'Who, born within the last forty years,' he asked scornfully in the *Reflections*, 'has read one word of Collins, and Toland, and Tindal, and Chubb, and Morgan, and that whole race who called themselves Freethinkers? Who now reads Bolingbroke? Who ever read him through? Ask the booksellers of London what is become of all these lights of the world. . . .'

Although Rousseau recoiled in as much horror as Burke from the atheistic tendencies of the age, he had respect for the deistic movement which Burke certainly did not share. Rousseau regarded himself as a theist and reasoned out his religious faith in the immortal, if unorthodox, pages of the *Vicaire Savoyard* in the *Émile*.

In their intellectual background, the same characteristics are to be observed. Both Rousseau and Burke underwent long periods of preparation for their life's work, in the course of which they both mastered the important thought of the classical writers as well as of the moderns. Then in the years when Rousseau was working out his political philosophy and when Burke was making his reputation as the 'brains' behind the Rockingham Whigs, they both turned to Montesquieu and to the classics, yet with very different results. Rousseau had found the corrective to his thought in Montesquieu, the philosopher of the 'empire of climate', and he spent years in attempting to bring his abstract principles to terms with the doctrine of relativity that had been expounded in the *Esprit des Lois*. Burke, on the other hand, followed in the historical tradition of the Montesquieu school of thought. He respected the conservative strain and the statesmanlike attitude that he had observed in Montesquieu's writings; while in the *Appeal from the New to the Old Whigs* he offered the author of the *Esprit des Lois* homage for his admiration of the British constitution. And while they both showed the greatest respect for Aristotle, Rousseau became the whole-hearted disciple of the 'divine Plato', whom Burke criticized as one of the 'framers of imaginary commonwealths'.

The nature of their contributions to political thought was determined by the fact that Rousseau was a *philosophe*, whereas Burke was man of affairs. Also, the striking contrast in the political and social conditions of France and England in the mid- and later eighteenth century played an important part in determining the nature of their work.

The English statesman looked at life from within the framework of a seemingly stable society, and his thought was directed toward its improvement and preservation. Until the French revolution, there had been no serious challenge to that established order. When, however, that challenge came, Burke enlisted the rich store of his political wisdom in a desperate effort to preserve it intact. And although his powerful pen served to retard the cause of progress, so many sober truths shone through his pages that his writings became a veritable manual for the guidance of the magistrate who would play his part wisely in the direction of the destinies of a great and free people. He clothed the principles that had guided his political thinking in powerful, majestic rhetoric, and he clung to them with the energy of desperation. His crucial weakness lay in the fact that he was not an original thinker. He could not see the path that led to serenity in the future, neither could he visualize a changed social and political order for England. His thought lost much of the dynamic quality it had possessed in earlier years and became wellnigh frozen with fear. The historical imagination that had previously led him forward now forsook him, and in his horror he bade time stand still. Because he was a statesman rather than a political philosopher, he chose to become the critic of the revolution. His love of philosophical reflection made him a penetrating critic and saved him from tilting at windmills. He showed the real dangers to the state that were inherent in abstract theory such as Rousseau had expounded. His criticisms not only presented the practical corrective to Rousseau's fundamental principles, but also taught the important lesson that theory must always be brought to terms with circumstances if it was to become of value to the state. It must assume the form most characteristic of the genius of the people, for 'the circumstances are what render every civil and political scheme beneficial or noxious to mankind'. And the statesman possessing historical perspective as well as an insight into human nature will be the best fitted to bring theory to the touchstone of political 'fact' and so to raise it to the dignity of what Burke recognized as principle.

Rousseau was much less concerned with the preservation of the *status quo* than Burke. In fact the social conditions of France, unlike those of England, were in a state of flux in the mid-eighteenth century, and the best minds of the nation were concentrating upon the problem of the reconstruction of their society. Rousseau's political thought was primarily a contribution to that central problem, but it was destined to exert a vital influence far beyond the shores of France—an influence that will live as long as liberty remains the political ideal of democracy. An exile from Geneva, Rousseau had eventually joined the ranks of the *philosophes* in Paris. But unable to accept important aspects of their philosophy, he found himself contemplating life as a lonely outsider. His intellectual awakening had come slowly, but when it came it marked an important turning-point in his life. The painful process of moral regeneration through which he had to go had given an urgency and a penetration to his thought that distinguished his writings from those of his contemporaries. An intuitive thinker rather than a patient observer of fact, Rousseau set out to establish the principles of political right. He began with the concept of nature as the antithesis of society, but in his more mature writings, the spirit of revolt against society gave way before the recognition that it was essential to man. Similarly his concept of the 'natural' man developed from the 'noble savage' of his speculations in the *Discours sur l'inegalité* to the ideal man of the *Émile*. The ideal society of the *Contrat Social* was meant for men who, like Émile, had been educated to assume their rightful responsibilities as citizens. Moreover, the general will constituted the central principle of that society, and through it justice and right became established. The citizens of the *Contrat Social* were motivated by a desire to make the general will a reality in their body politic; while the legislator, through his insight, interpreted it for them.

Although Rousseau had hoped that the *Contrat Social* would 'set the seal' to his reputation, he became increasingly aware of its shortcomings, and towards the close of his life he declared that it was *un livre à refaire*. Many of his ideas were impracticable; while much of his thought was highly abstract. Critics have invariably laid stress upon its abstract nature, and Burke, who began his political career after Rousseau's most important works had been published, was quick to detect its defects from the practical point of view. Yet in spite of all its weaknesses and shortcomings, the *Contrat Social* has not ceased to stimulate thought. The *Émile* was the companion volume to the *Contrat Social*. It linked the ideal of education to that of democracy, and the vision Rousseau left of free men educated to live in a free society in which justice and right were the basic principles inspired the best minds of his own age as well as of subsequent ages. Burke, fearful lest England might lose the real liberty her people enjoyed if she tried to realize Utopia, emphasized the importance of the constitution and the harmonious functioning of the government as the real guarantees of liberty.

Thus Rousseau bequeathed to posterity the constructive principles upon which a free society must be based; while Burke gave warning of the dangers that surrounded a democratic constitution, but at the same time he showed how the people and the government must co-operate if they were to enjoy the priceless heritage of liberty.

NOTES

CHAPTER I

Except where otherwise stated, the references are to C. E. Vaughan's two-volume edition of *The Political Writings of Rousseau*, Cambridge, 1915, and to the sixteen-volume Rivington edition of Burke's *Works*, London, 1803.

[1] J. Prior, *Life of Burke*, Vol. II, p. 45.

[2] Cf. M. Dupont, *Answer to the Reflections of the Right Hon. Edmund Burke*. Had Dupont known the nature of Burke's work, he might have been able 'to prevent one of the warmest friends of liberty in his own country, from ranging himself with the advocates of despotism in mine. ... Yes, Sir, your susceptible and worthy heart has been too strongly affected with the evils that have attended our Revolution, not to fear exposing it to evils still more dreadful, in a manner by involuntarily serving the party which dares to wish for a Counter-Revolution, and which thinks that our Constitution ought to be purified by fire and by blood. ... I am inspired with the highest confidence from the progress of that enlightened spirit which you have so cruelly attacked, and from the liberty of the press, upon which you have not touched, and I am convinced that these economists, these philanthropists, these philosophers, upon whom you speak with so much asperity, will contribute as much by their writings to the support of liberty and the re-establishment of order, as those famous paladins, those knights-errant, whose extinction you deplore, and whose very institution proves that it was always more necessary to oppose armed force to the excesses of a people more formidable in proportion as they were less enlightened. ...' Pp. 4, 14–15.

[3] For an account of Burke's acquaintance with Rousseau's early work, see Mr. Richard B. Sewall's article in *Philological Quarterly*, April, 1938.

[4] *The Political Writings of Rousseau*, Vol. II, p. 24.

[5] *Ibid.*, p. 132.

[6] *Works of Burke*, Vol. VI, p. 39.

[7] G. H. Sabine, *A History of Political Theory*, p. 543.

[8] *Works of Burke*, Vol. II, p. 170.

[9] *Ibid.*, Vol. V, p. 36.

[10, 11, 12] J. Prior, *op. cit.*, Vol. II, p. 45.

[13] *Works of Burke*, Vol. III, p. 185.

[14] J. Prior, *op. cit.*, Vol. II, pp. 40–1.

[15] *The Political Writings of Rousseau*, Vol. II, p. 28.

[16] *Œuvres complètes de Rousseau*, Vol. II, p. 249. Lib. Hachette, 1877.

[17] *The Political Writings of Rousseau*, Vol. II, p. 37.

[18] J. Prior, *op. cit.*, Vol. II, p. 41.

[19] *The Political Writings of Rousseau*, Vol. II, p. 161.

[20] J. Prior, *op. cit.*, Vol. II, p. 41.

[21] C. E. Vaughan, *The Political Writings of Rousseau*, Introduction, Vol. I, pp. 81 ff.

[22] *Ibid.*, Vol. II, p. 204.

[23] *Ibid.*, pp. 234–5.

[24] *Ibid.*, p. 284.

[25] *Works of Burke*, Vol. V, p. 183.

[26] *Ibid.*, p. 309.

[27] *Ibid.*, p. 394.

[28] *Ibid.*, p. 397.

[29] *Ibid.*, p. 332.

[30] *Ibid.*, p. 174.

[31] Cf. Voltaire to M. Damilaville, June 25, 1762: 'This social, or unsocial Contract, is only distinguished by several gross insults to kings from the citizen of the burg of Geneva, and by four insipid pages against the Christian religion. These four pages were only fragments from Bayle. It was not worth while plagiarizing them. The proud Jean Jacques is in Amsterdam, where more fuss is made over a cargo of pepper than over his paradoxes.' Cf. also Voltaire's comments in his copy of the *Contrat Social* (George R. Havens: *Voltaire's Marginalia on the Pages of Rousseau*, pp. 37–71. Ohio State University Studies, 1933) and his remarks in his *Idées républicaines*, where he attempted to show the absurdities and contradictions of Rousseau's work.

[32] *Works of Burke*, Vol. VI, p. 30.

[33] *Ibid.*, p. 30.

[34, 35] *Ibid.*, p. 32.

[36, 37] *Ibid.*, p. 33.

[38] *Ibid.*, p. 34.

[39, 40] *Ibid.*, p. 35.

[41] *Ibid.*, p. 37.

[42] *Ibid.*, p. 38.

[43] *Ibid.*, p. 40.

[44] Sir Brooke Boothby, *Observations on the Appeal from the New to the Old Whigs*, pp. 89–91.

[45] *Works of Burke*, Vol. VI, p. 257.

[46] *Ibid.*, pp. 257–9.

[47–49] *Ibid.*, Vol. VII, pp. 270–1.

[50] *Ibid.*, Vol. VIII, p. 253.

[51] *Ibid.*, p. 256.

CHAPTER II

[1] H. R. Fox-Bourne, *The Life of John Locke*, Vol. II, p. 155.

[2] K. Feiling, *A History of the Tory Party, 1640–1714*, pp. 343–5.

[3] H. R. Fox-Bourne, *op. cit.*, p. 165.

[4] John Locke, *Of Civil Government*, p. 163. § 93. E. P. Dutton ed.

[5, 6] *Ibid.*, p. 127. § 21.

[7] *Ibid.*, p. 184. § 134.

[8, 9] *Ibid.*, p. 143. § 57.

[10] *Ibid.*, p. 182. § 131.

[11] *Ibid.*, p. 189. § 142.

[12] *Ibid.*, p. 190. § 142.

[13] Cf. Montesquieu, *Esprit des Lois*, Bk. XI, ch. 6, pp. 7–26; Bk. XIX, ch. 27, pp. 360–75. Vol. II. *Œuvres de Montesquieu*. Cf. also J. Dedieu, *Montesquieu et la tradition politique anglaise en France*, pp. 160–91, for a statement of Montesquieu's indebtedness to Locke, in which Dedieu shows that Montesquieu's conception of the 'separation' of powers came in a 'straight line' from the essay on *Civil Government*.

[14] M. T. Blauvelt, *The Development of Cabinet Government in England* pp. 71–91.

[15] C. G. Robertson, *England under the Hanoverians*, p. 161.

[16] K. Feiling, *op. cit.*, p. 276.

[17] *Ibid.*, p. 362.

[18] B. Williams, *The Whig Supremacy, 1714–1760*, p. 21. For a brief statement of the limitations of the Crown under the Hanoverians, see *Ibid.*, p. 15.

[19] C. G. Robertson, *op. cit.*, p. 512. George III called Cabinet meetings on June 21, 1779, and on January 19, 1781. For a concise statement of the cabinet system under George I and George II, see B. Williams, *op. cit.*, pp. 34–9.

[20] L. B. Namier, *England in the Age of the American Revolution*, p. 91.

[21] C. B. Realey, *The Early Opposition to Sir Robert Walpole, 1720–1727*, pp. 39–43.

[22] L. B. Namier, *op. cit.*, pp. 55–8. Cf. also D. A. Winstanley, *Lord Chatham and the Whig Opposition*, p. 24. It was also believed that the best interests of the nation were served by promoting rather than hindering the task of government.

[23] Lord Bolingbroke, *Letters on the Spirit of Patriotism and on the Idea of a Patriot King*, p. 36. Ed. A. Hassall, Oxford, 1917.

[24] D. A. Winstanley, *Lord Chatham and the Whig Opposition*, pp. 14, 17.

[25] *Ibid.*, pp. 30–1.

[26] L. B. Namier, *op. cit.*, p. 66.

[27] D. A. Winstanley, *Personal and Party Government*, p. 35. Cf. also L. B. Namier, *op. cit.*, pp. 147–93, for a detailed account of Bute and his rise to power, and for the significance of his tenure of office in constitutional history.

[28] L. B. Namier, *op. cit.*, p. 181.

[29] C. G. Robertson, *op. cit.*, p. 131.

[30] *Works of Burke*, Vol. II, p. 131.

[31] *Correspondence of the Right Honourable Edmund Burke*, ed. Charles William, Earl Wentworth and Sir Richard Bourke, Vol. I, p. 198.

[32] *Works of Burke*, Vol. II, p. 224.

[33] Cf. L. B. Namier, *op. cit.*, p. 183. After presenting evidence to prove that George III was loyal in his support of the ministers of his reign, from Grenville to Lord North, Namier asserts that 'there never was a deliberate system of "double cabinets" as sketched by Burke in a polemical pamphlet, to which he himself might possibly have applied the phrase used by him on a different occasion: "By Gad, Madam, does any one swear to the truth of a song?"—but which has been often treated as if it were an impartial verdict on George III'.

[34] *Works of Burke*, Vol. II, p. 288.

[35] *Ibid.*, p. 335.

[36] R. H. Murray, *Edmund Burke, a Biography*, p. 135.

[37] *Works of Burke*, Vol. II, p. 366.

[38] *Ibid.*, p. 360.

[39] *Ibid.*, p. 432.

[40] *Ibid.*, Vol. III, p. 35.

[41] *Ibid.*, p. 74.

CHAPTER III

[1] For more detailed accounts of the effects of the revocation of the Edict of Nantes upon the Huguenots, see among other works, J. Texte, *J. J. Rousseau et les origines du cosmopolitisme littéraire*; D. Mornet, *Les Origines intellectuelles de la Révolution Française*; and Kingsley Martin, *French Liberal Thought in the Eighteenth Century*.

[2] Cf. G. M. Trevelyan, 'The Age of Johnson', in A. S. Turberville's *Johnson's England* (2 vols.), Vol. I, p. 4. 'The French observed that whereas their own decline dated from the persecution of the Huguenots by the Revocation of the Edict of Nantes, England had never looked back since she had given peace to her own religious discords by the Act of Toleration of 1689.'

[3] L. Ducros, *Les Encyclopédistes*, p. 33.

[4] D. Mornet, *op. cit.*, p. 19, points to the popularity of the works of Grotius, Pufendorff and Locke in the early years of the eighteenth century. There were six editions of Grotius, eight of Pufendorff, and seven of Locke. All of these thinkers exerted a particularly important influence upon the development of Rousseau's political thought; hence the particular significance of the popularity of their works.

[5] Cf. H. Robinson, *Bayle, the Sceptic*, pp. 246–7.

[6] *Œuvres de Fontenelle*, Vol. I, p. 54.

[7] *Ibid.*, p. 60.

[8] *Ibid.*, Vol. II, pp. 184–90.

[9] A. Laborde-Milàà, *Fontenelle*, pp. 138–9. Hachette, 1905.

[10] C. D. Hazen, *The French Revolution*, Vol. I, p. 69.

[11] K. Martin, *op. cit.*, p. 71. I have to acknowledge my indebtedness to the clear and detailed statement of the development of the creed of the

philosophes, contained in Mr. Martin's work, which helped me much in the preparation of the material for this chapter.

[12] *Œuvres de Montesquieu*, Vol. VI, p. 66.

[13] *Ibid.*, p. 66.

[14] It is interesting to note in passing that this Utopia of Cave Dwellers who practised the Golden Rule was Montesquieu's contribution to the 'noble savage' literature.

[15] *Œuvres de Montesquieu*, Vol. VI, p. 216.

[16] *Ibid.*, p. 245.

[17] A. Maurois, *Voltaire*, p. 44. Tr. Hamish Miles, 1932. For the significance of the *Lettres Philosophiques*, see G. Lanson, *Voltaire*, pp. 44-52; also Lanson's edition of the *Lettres Philosophiques*.

[18] Voltaire, *Lettres Philosophiques*, Vol. I, p. 90. Ed. G. Lanson.

[19] *Ibid.*, p. 104.

[20] *Ibid.*, pp. 106-7.

[21] *Œuvres complètes de Voltaire*, Vol. XLI, p. 82.

[22] Sir Isaac Newton, *Opticks*, Bk. III, part I, p. 401. London, 1931. See also W. C. D. Dampier-Whetham, *A History of Science and its Relations with Philosophy and Religion*, pp. 183-4.

[23] C. Becker, *The Heavenly City of the Eighteenth Century Philosophers*, p. 58.

[24] *The Works of Alexander Pope*, Vol. II, pp. 370-1. Ed. Croker, Elwin and Courthope. London, 1871.

[25] Cf. Sir Leslie Stephen, *History of Thought in the Eighteenth Century*, Vol. I, pp. 315-30, for a critical discussion of Hume's *Dialogues concerning Natural Religion*.

[26] K. Martin, *op. cit.*, p. 123.

[27] *Œuvres de Montesquieu*, Vol. II, p. 22; also p. 112.

[28] *Ibid.*, p. 22.

[29] Cf. C. E. Vaughan, *Studies in the History of Political Philosophy*, 'Montesquieu', Vol. I, pp. 260-3, 295-6.

[30] For a full account of the beginnings of the *Encyclopédie* from De Breton's projected translation of Chambers' *Cyclopedia* to Diderot's collaboration with d'Alembert in the great project, see Joseph le Gras, *Diderot et l'Encyclopédie*, pp. 27-47.

[31] On the whole, it is easy to identify the work of the various contributors to the *Encyclopédie*. Diderot's articles were marked with an asterisk, d'Alembert's with an O, and Rousseau's with an S. In Volume I, Rousseau's contributions were confined to brief notes on musical subjects. For example, on page 237, his note on 'air' appeared; on page 282, a note on 'allemande'; on page 321, a note on 'ambitus'. In Volume II the same kind of contributions appeared. His note on 'baton' appeared on pages 144-5; on 'battre la mesure, en musique', on page 155; on 'broderie en musique' on page 434.

[32] *Encyclopédie*, Vol. VII, p. 767.

[33] Sébastien Mercier, *De J.-J. Rousseau considéré comme l'un des premiers auteurs de la Révolution*, Vol. I, p. 186.

[34] J. Morley, *Diderot*, Vol. I, p. 180.

[35] l'Abbé Raynal, *Histoire philosophique et politique des établissements et du commerce des Européens dans les deux Indes*, Vol. IV, p. 161.

[36] Beaumarchais, *Le Mariage de Figaro*, p. 197.

[37] d'Alembert to Voltaire, Paris, July 21, 1757. *Œuvres complètes de Voltaire*, Vol. LIV, p. 24.

[38] L. Ducros, *op. cit.*, pp. 3, 314–74.

[39] C. A. Helvétius, *De l'Esprit*, Discours II. For the development of the utilitarian doctrine of Helvétius into the 'greatest happiness' doctrine of Bentham, see E. Halévy, *La Formation du Radicalisme Philosophique*, Vol. I, pp. 24–30.

[40] E. B. de Condillac, *Traité sur les Sensations*, p. 179.

[41] Joseph Priestley, *Essay on the First Principles of Government*, pp. 4–5.

[42] For a statement of the relationship of Mandeville's work to the doctrines of Helvétius, see F. B. Kaye's introduction to his edition of *The Fable of the Bees*, note, pp. cxliv–cxlv (Vol. I). Cf. also A. Keim, *Helvétius, sa vie et son œuvre*, p. 222 ff., and E. Halévy, *op. cit.*

[43] K. Martin, *op. cit.*, p. 183.

[44] C. A. Helvétius, *op. cit.*, Vol. I, pp. 108–9.

[45] *Ibid.*, p. 261.

[46] P. H. d'Holbach, *Système de la Nature*, Vol. II, pp. 257–8.

[47] *Ibid.*, p. 261.

[48] *The Political Writings of Rousseau*, Vol. II, p. 158.

[49] *Ibid.*, p. 147.

CHAPTER IV

[1] For a statement of Rousseau's conception of perfectibility, see E. H. Wright, *The Meaning of Rousseau*, pp. 25–6.

[2] *Œuvres complètes de J.-J. Rousseau*, Vol. VIII, p. 302. Hachette ed.

[3] *Ibid.*, p. 152.

[4] *Ibid.*, p. 168.

[5] P. B. Lamy, *Entretiens sur les Sciences*, p. 55.

[6] *Ibid.*, p. 122.

[7] *Ibid.*, p. 6.

[8] l'Abbé Prévost, *Histoire de M. Cleveland*, Vol. I, p. 126. Rousseau's account of his interest in Prévost's work is to be found in his poem, *Le Verger des Charmettes*:

> Ou bien dans Cleveland j'observe la nature
> Qui se montre à mes yeux touchante et toujours pure.
>
> (*Œuvres*, Vol. VI, p. 6.)

[9] B. Lamy, *op. cit.*, p. 283.

[10] *Œuvres complètes de J.-J. Rousseau*, Vol. III, p. 44. Hachette ed. A full consideration of the influence of Plato upon Rousseau's thought is to be found in C. W. Hendel, *Jean-Jacques Rousseau, Moralist*.

[11] *The Political Writings of Rousseau*, Vol. II, p. 25.

[12] For a full discussion of the influence of Grotius and Pufendorff upon Rousseau, see C. W. Hendel, *op. cit.*, Vol. I, pp. 141–56.

[13] *Œuvres complètes de J.-J. Rousseau*, Vol. VIII, p. 116. Hachette ed.

[14] *Ibid.*, Vol. VI, p. 12.

[15] *Ibid.*, p. 13.

[16] *Ibid.*, Vol. VIII, pp. 288–9.

[17] *Correspondance générale de J.-J. Rousseau*, Vol. I, pp. 262–3. Ed. Th. Dufour. Letter to Mme de Bezenval, No. 92. Beside Rousseau's indignant letter may be placed Johnson's famous letter to Lord Chesterfield and Burke's *Letter to a Noble Lord*. Unkind treatment from members of the nobility evoked dignified expressions of hurt pride from all three. An interesting parallel between Burke's letter and Rousseau's is to be found when Burke, driven to defend his right to a pension against the attack of the Duke of Bedford, pointed out that the Duke owed his prestige not to his own merits, but to those of his ancestor. 'My merits, whatever they are, are original and personal; his are derivative,' Burke wrote. 'It is his ancestor, the original pensioner, that has laid up this inexhaustible fund of merit, which makes his grace so very delicate and exceptious about the merit of all other grantees of the crown. . . .' *Works of Burke*, Vol. VIII, pp. 36–43.

[18] *Œuvres complètes de J.-J. Rousseau*, Vol. VIII, p. 231. Hachette ed.

[19] *Ibid.*, Vol. II, p. 257.

[20] *Ibid.*, Vol. X, p. 65. Letter to Mme de Francueil, April 20, 1751.

[21] *The Political Writings of Rousseau*, Vol. II, p. 82.

[22] Gerhard Gran, *Jean-Jacques Rousseau*, p. 297.

[23] *The Political Writings of Rousseau*, Vol. I, p. 195.

[24] *Ibid.*, p. 196.

[25] *J.-J. Rousseau, ses amis et ses ennemis*, ed. M. G. Streckeisen-Moultou, Vol. I, p. 263. Voltaire to Rousseau, August 30, 1755.

[26] *The Political Writings of Rousseau*, Vol. I, p. 126.

[27] *Ibid.*, pp. 130–1.

[28] Wordsworth, *Poetical Works*, p. 207. Oxford ed. 1932.

[29] *The Political Writings of Rousseau*, Vol. I, pp. 413–22.

[30] Cf. D. Mornet, Introduction to his edition of the *Nouvelle Héloise*, pp. 87, 117–22.

[31] C. E. Vaughan, *The Political Writings of Rousseau*, Vol. II, p. 196.

CHAPTER V

[1] For a list of the Huguenot surnames of Burke's schoolmates, see A. P. I. Samuels, *The Early Life, Correspondence and Writings of The Rt. Hon. Edmund Burke*, p. 39 n.

[2] J. Prior, *Life of Burke*, Vol. I, p. 39.

[3] A. P. I. Samuels, *op. cit.*, p. 30.

[4] J. Prior, *op. cit.*, p. 52.

[5] A. P. I. Samuels, *op. cit.*, p. 355.

[6] *Ibid.*, p. 331.

[7] *Ibid.*, p. 338.

[8] *Works of Burke*, Vol. I, p. 5.

[9] *Ibid.*, p. 31.

[10] David Hume, *An Enquiry Concerning Human Understanding*, p. 83, sect. 65.

[11] R. H. Murray, *Edmund Burke*, p. 78.

[12] Montesquieu, *Considérations sur les Causes de la Grandeur des Romains et de leur Décadence*, p. 168.

[13] *Works of Burke*, Vol. X, p. 355.

[14] *Ibid.*, p. 201.

[15] *Ibid.*, p. 550.

[16] *Ibid.*, p. 539.

[17] R. Straus, *Robert Dodsley*, p. 257.

[18] Dr. Thomas W. Copeland, in an unpublished doctoral dissertation (Yale, 1933) *Edmund Burke's Authorship of the Book Reviews in Dodsley's Annual Register*, gathered all available evidence for assigning the book reviews in the *Annual Register* to Burke's pen. In an article in *P.M.L.A.*, March, 1939, 'Burke and Dodsley's Annual Register', Dr.Copeland presented evidence, although he does not regard it as complete proof, that Burke wrote and compiled the entire magazine single-handed from its inception in 1757 at least through the year 1763, which of course includes the reviews of Rousseau.

[19] *Annual Register* for 1758, p. 311.

[20] *Ibid.*, for 1759, p. 479.

[21] *Ibid.*, for 1762, p. 225.

[22] J. Boswell, *Life of Johnson*, Vol. II, pp. 515–6. Ed. George Birkbeck Hill.

[23] Horace Walpole, *Memoirs of the Reign of King George the Third*, Vol. II, p. 273.

[24] Burke, *Correspondence*, Vol. I, p. 103. Fitzwilliam ed.

[25] J. Boswell, *Private Papers*, ed. Geoffrey Scott, in Isham Collection, New York, 1928. (12 vols.) Vol. IV.

[26–29] *Works of Burke*, Vol. V, pp. 208–10.

[30] *Ibid.*, Vol. X, pp. 38–9.

[31] *The Miscellaneous Works of Oliver Goldsmith*, Vol. II, p. 107. (4 vols.) London, 1812.

CHAPTER VI

[1] *The Political Writings of Rousseau*, Vol. II, p. 50.

[2] Cf. *Works of Burke*, Vol. II, p. 262. 'The people of a free *commonwealth . . .*' Vol. III, p. 309. 'Individuals pass like shadows; but the

commonwealth is fixed and stable.' Vol. V, p. 181. '. . . leading principles
on which the *commonwealth* and laws are consecrated . . .' Vol. VI,
p. 200. 'The people, in forming their *commonwealth*, have by no means
parted with their power over it. . . .' &c.

³ *The Political Writings of Rousseau*, Vol. II, p. 74.
⁴ *Ibid.*, p. 75.
⁵ *Works of Burke*, Vol. VI, p. 129.
⁶ *Correspondence of Edmund Burke*, Vol. III, p. 146. Fitzwilliam ed.
⁷ *Ibid.*, Vol. II, pp. 291–2. Letter from Edmund Burke to Dr. John
Curry, August 14, 1779.
⁸ *The Political Writings of Rousseau*, Vol. II, p. 161.
⁹ *Ibid.*, Vol. II, p. 32.
¹⁰ Cf. B. Bosanquet, *The Philosophical Theory of the State*, pp. 102 ff.
¹¹ *Œuvres complètes de J.-J. Rousseau*, Vol. II, p. 261. Hachette ed.
¹² *Ibid.*, p. 257.
¹³ *Works of Samuel Johnson*, Vol. III, pp. 365–6.
¹⁴ *Contrat Social*, Bk. II, ch. XI, conclusion. Cf. Georges Beaulavon
ed., p. 204 *n.*
¹⁵ *Works of Burke*, Vol. X, p. 46.
¹⁶ *Ibid.*, Vol. II, p. 435.
¹⁷ *Ibid.*, Vol. III, pp. 422–3.
¹⁸ J. MacCunn, *The Political Philosophy of Burke*, p. 148.
¹⁹ *Works of Burke*, Vol. V, p. 186.
²⁰ *Ibid.*, Vol. VI, p. 218.
²¹, ²² *The Political Writings of Rousseau*, Vol. II, p. 33.
²³ *Ibid.*, p. 44.
²⁴ Cf. E. H. Wright, *op. cit.*, pp. 74–5.
²⁵ *Works of Burke*, Vol. V, pp. 122.
²⁶ *Ibid.*, Vol. X, p. 97.
²⁷ *Ibid.*, Vol. V, p. 184. It is interesting to note in this connexion
that Burke's thought, no less than Rousseau's, was deeply influenced by
the ideal of the Greek city state. The partnership of his definition was
a reality in the polis. For criticism of it in reference to the modern state,
see R. M. MacIver, *The Modern State*, pp. 83 ff.
²⁸, ²⁹ *Ibid.*, Vol. V, p. 184.
³⁰ Burke is here giving expression to Calvinistic doctrine, which is part
of the creed of the Church of England, to which he belonged. His conception of the moral order of the universe was essentially the same as
Rousseau's and was derived from the same doctrine. For an analysis of
the moral order, see A. R. Osborn, *Christian Ethics*, pp. 2–3, 12 ff.
Oxford, 1939.
³¹, ³² *Works of Burke*, Vol. X, pp. 104–5.
³³ *Ibid.*, Vol. III, p. 148.
³⁴ *Ibid.*, Vol. III, p. 191.
³⁵ *Ibid.*, Vol. II, pp. 260–1.
³⁶ *Ibid.*, Vol. III, p. 200. 'The active men in the state are the true
samples of the mass. If they are universally depraved, the commonwealth

itself is not sound. . . .' Cf. also Burke's Letter to a Member of the Bell Club. *Correspondence*, Vol. II, p. 194. '. . . Believe me, it is a great truth, that there never was, for any long time, a corrupt representative of a virtuous people; or a mean, sluggish, careless people that ever had a good government of any form. If it be true in any degree, that the governors form the people, I am certain it is as true that the people in their turn impart their character to their rulers. Such as you are, sooner or later, must parliament be. . . .'

[37] *Works of Burke*, Vol. X, p. 97.
[38] *Ibid.*, Vol. V, p. 312.
[39] *Ibid.*, Vol. VIII, p. 191.
[40] *Ibid.*, Vol. VI, p. 207.
[41] *Ibid.*, Vol. III, p. 367.
[42-44] *Ibid.*, Vol. VI, pp. 204-5.
[45] R. M. MacIver, *op. cit.*, p. 448.
[46-50] *Works of Burke*, Vol. V, pp. 173-8.
[51-3] *Ibid.*, p. 181.
[54] *Ibid.*, p. 186.
[55] *The Political Writings of Rousseau*, Vol. II, p. 128.
[56] *Œuvres complètes de J.-J. Rousseau*, Vol. II, p. 285. Hachette ed.
[57] *Ibid.*, p. 285 *n*.
[58] *Ibid.*, p. 283.
[59] *Ibid.*, p. 263.
[60] *Ibid.*, p. 258.
[61] *Ibid.*, p. 260.
[62] *The Political Writings of Rousseau*, Vol. II, p. 36. 'Afin donc que le pacte social ne soit pas un vain formulaire, il renferme tacitement cet engagement, qui seul peut donner de la force aux autres, que quiconque réfusera d'obéir à la volonté générale y sera contraint par tout le Corps: ce qui ne signifie autre chose sinon qu'on le forcera d'être libre.'
[63] *Ibid.*, p. 36.
[64] For a full discussion of this point, see C. E. Vaughan's edition of the *Contrat Social*, Introduction, pp. xxii-xxxvii. Manchester University Press, 1918.
[65] J. Lemaître, *Jean-Jacques Rousseau*, p. 267.
[66] *Œuvres complètes de Rousseau*, Vol. II, p. 52. Hachette ed.

CHAPTER VII

[1] G. D. H. Cole, Introduction to his translation of the *Contrat Social*, p. xxxv.
[2] Cf. C. W. Hendel, *op. cit.*, Vol. I, pp. 99-108, for a statement of the chief contributions of each of these thinkers to the development of the idea of the general will.

[3] *Œuvres complètes de J.-J. Rousseau*, Vol. II, p. 262. Hachette ed.

[4] The significance of Rousseau's first discourse was essentially in its attack upon the failure of morals to keep in stride with the advance of the arts and sciences. Man was making intellectual progress, but he was, if anything, retrogressing morally. Cf. *Revue de Métaphysique et de Morale*, May, 1912. B. Bosanquet, 'Les idées politiques de Rousseau', pp. 324 ff. Cf. also J. B. Bury, *The Idea of Progress*, pp. 180–3.

[5] *Œuvres complètes de J.-J. Rousseau*, Vol. II, p. 253. Hachette ed.

[6] *The Political Writings of Rousseau*, Vol. I, p. 242.

[7] *Ibid.*, Vol. II, p. 2.

[8] *Ibid.*, Vol. I, p. 188.

[9, 10] *Ibid.*, pp. 241–2.

[11] Cf. *Ibid.*, pp. 441–5.

[12] *Ibid.*, p. 243.

[13] *Ibid.*, p. 245.

[14] *Ibid.*, p. 257.

[15] *Ibid.*, Vol. II, pp. 39–40.

[16] *Ibid.*, Vol. I, p. 355.

[17, 18] *Ibid.*, Vol. II, p. 40.

[19] *Ibid.*, p. 45.

[20] *Ibid.*, p. 43.

[21] B. Bosanquet, *The Philosophical Theory of the State*, p. 109.

[22] *The Political Writings of Rousseau*, Vol. II, pp. 105–6.

[23] *Ibid.*, pp. 50–1.

[24] *Ibid.*, p. 446.

[25] *Ibid.*, pp. 428–9.

[26] *Ibid.*, p. 53.

[27–31] *Ibid.*, pp. 61–4.

[32] *Ibid.*, p. 96.

[33] *Ibid.*, p. 82.

[34] *Ibid.*, p. 78. For a discussion of the relationship of Rousseau's thought to Montesquieu's, with particular reference to the question of intermediate orders, see J. Tchernoff, 'Montesquieu et J.-J. Rousseau', in the *Revue du droit public*, 1903. Vols. XIX and XX; and also E. Faguet, *La Politique comparée de Montesquieu, Rousseau et Voltaire*.

[35] *The Political Writings of Rousseau*, Vol. II, p. 202.

[36] *Ibid.*, p. 92.

[37] *Ibid.*, p. 96.

[38] *Ibid.*, Vol. I, p. 243; cf. also, *ibid.*, Vol. II, p. 256.

[39] Cf. A. Cobban, *Rousseau and the Modern State*, p. 64.

[40] *The Political Writings of Rousseau*, Vol. II, p. 219; Cf. also *ibid.*, p. 33; and G. D. H. Cole, Introduction to his translation of the *Contrat Social*, pp. xxiv–xxvii.

[41, 42] *The Political Writings of Rousseau*, Vol. II, p. 201.

CHAPTER VIII

1 *Works of Burke*, Vol. X, p. 104.
2 *Ibid.*, p. 105.
3 *Ibid.*, Vol. V, p. 175.
4 *Ibid.*, p. 119.
5 *Ibid.*, Vol. VI, pp. 97–8.
6 *Ibid.*, Vol. X, p. 99.
7 *Ibid.*, pp. 41–2.
8 *Ibid.*, Vol. III, p. 21.
9 *Ibid.*, Vol. II, p. 323.
10 *Ibid.*, Vol. III, p. 22.
11 *Ibid.*, Vol. VI, pp. 258–9.
12 *Ibid.*, Vol. V, pp. 125–6.
13 *Ibid.*, Vol. VIII, p. 252.
14 *Ibid.*, Vol. VI, p. 62.
15 *Ibid.*, Vol. V, pp. 305–6.
16 *Ibid.*, Vol. X, pp. 96–7.
17 *Ibid.*, Vol. VI, p. 261.
18–22 *Ibid.*, Vol. V, pp. 78–81.
23 *The Political Writings of Rousseau*, Vol. II, pp. 63–4. 'À ces trois sortes de lois il s'en joint une quatrième, la plus importante de toutes, qui ne se grave ni sur le marbre, ni sur l'airain, mais dans les cœurs des citoyens; qui fait la véritable constitution de l'état; qui prend tous les jours de nouvelles forces; qui, lorsque les autres lois vieillissent ou s'éteignent, les ranime ou les supplée, conserve un peuple dans l'esprit de son institution, et substitue insensiblement la force de l'habitude à celle de l'autorité. . . .'
24 *Works of Burke*, Vol. V, pp. 50–1.
25 *Ibid.*, pp. 74–5.
26 *Ibid.*, Vol. III, p. 22.
27 *Ibid.*, Vol. IX, p. 110.
28 *Ibid.*, Vol. II, p. 246.
29 *Ibid.*, Vol. X, p. 138.
30 *Ibid.*, Vol. III, p. 180.
31 *Ibid.*, p. 20.
32 Burke, *Correspondence*, Vol. II, pp. 216–7. Letter to John Noble, April 24, 1778.
33 *Works of Burke*, Vol. III, p. 374.
34 *Ibid.*, p. 344.
35 *Ibid.*, Vol. VII, pp. 270–1.
36 *Ibid.*, Vol. VIII, pp. 140–1.
37–39 *Ibid.*, Vol. VI, pp. 200–2.
40 *Ibid.*, p. 206.
41 *Ibid.*, p. 211.
42 *Ibid.*, p. 216.
43 *Ibid.*, pp. 218–9.
44, 45 *Ibid.*, pp. 212–3.

CHAPTER IX

1 *The Political Writings of Rousseau*, Vol. II, p. 68.
2 *Works of Burke*, Vol. VI, pp. 53–4.
3 *The Political Writings of Rousseau*, Vol. II, p. 160.
4 *Works of Burke*, Vol. III, p. 75.
5 *Ibid.*, pp. 144–5.
6 *Ibid.*, p. 186.
7 *Ibid.*, Vol. VIII, p. 57.
8 *Ibid.*, Vol. III, p. 393.
9 *Ibid.*, p. 60.
10 *Ibid.*, Vol. II, pp. 379–80.
11 *The Political Writings of Rousseau*, Vol. II, p. 204.
12 *Works of Burke*, Vol. VI, p. 75.
13 *Ibid.*, Vol. VIII, pp. 23–4.
14 *The Political Writings of Rousseau*, Vol. II, p. 235.
15 *Ibid.*, Vol. II, p. 65. Beaulavon points out that while Rousseau's conception of the relationship of the government to the State was essentially mystical, it was also an aspect of Cartesian philosophy. See Beaulavon's ed. of the *Contrat Social*, p. 210, *n.* 3.
16, 17 *The Political Writings of Rousseau*, Vol. II, p. 65.
18 *Ibid.*, p. 220.
19 *Ibid.*, p. 47.
20 *Correspondance générale de J.-J. Rousseau*, Vol. XVIII, p. 103. Rousseau to Coindet, February 9, 1768.
21 *The Political Writings of Rousseau*, Vol. II, p. 266.
22 *Ibid.*, p. 236.
23 *Ibid.*, p. 68.
24 *Works of Burke*, Vol. V, p. 432.
25 *Ibid.*, Vol. III, p. 8.
26 *Ibid.*, p. 146.
27 *Ibid.*, pp. 185–6.
28 *Ibid.*, Vol. X, p. 76.
29 *Ibid.*, Vol. II, p. 288.
30 *Ibid.*, Vol. III, p. 156.
31 *Ibid.*, Vol. V, pp. 123–4.
32 Burke, *Correspondence*, Vol. III, p. 211. Burke to the Chevalier de Rivarol, June 1, 1791.
33 *Works of Burke*, Vol. V, p. 126.
34 *Ibid.*, Vol. III, pp. 110–11.
35 *Ibid.*, Vol. X, p. 100.
36 *Ibid.*, Vol. VI, p. 210.
37 *Ibid.*, p. 08.
38 Burke, *Correspondence*, Vol. I, p. 332.
39 *Works of Burke*, Vol. V, p. 36.
40 *Ibid.*, p. 124.
41 *Ibid.*, Vol. II, p. 269.
42, 43 *Ibid.*, Vol. IV, pp. 14–5.

[44] *Ibid.*, p. 201.

[45] *Ibid.*, Vol. X, p. 58.

[46] *Ibid.*, Vol. V, p. 105.

[47] *Ibid.*, p. 285.

[48, 49] *Ibid.*, Vol. III, pp. 247–8.

[50] *Ibid.*, Vol. VIII, p. 295.

[51] *The Political Writings of Rousseau*, Vol. II, p. 445.

[52] *Ibid.*, p. 456.

[53, 54] *Ibid.*, pp. 314–5.

[55] *Ibid.*, p. 311.

[56] *Works of Burke*, Vol. VIII, pp. 88–9.

[57, 58] *The Political Writings of Rousseau*, Vol. II, p. 432.

[59] Alexandre Choulguine, 'Les Origines de l'Esprit national moderne et Jean-Jacques Rousseau', p. 11. In *Annales de la Société Jean-Jacques Rousseau*, Vol. XXVI.

[60] *The Political Writings of Rousseau*, Vol. I, p. 255.

CHAPTER X

[1] *Letters on a Regicide Peace*, Letter III. *Works of Burke*, Vol. VIII, p. 295.

[2] J. Morley, *Burke*, pp. 110–11.

BIBLIOGRAPHY

(SELECTED)

I. TEXTS

The Political Writings of Jean-Jacques Rousseau, ed. C. E. Vaughan. 2 vols., 1915.

Œuvres complètes de J.-J. Rousseau, 12 vols. Hachette, 1877.

Le Contrat Social, ed. Georges Beaulavon. 1922.

Le Contrat Social, ed. E. Dreyfus-Brisac. 1896.

Le Contrat Social, ed. C. E. Vaughan. 1918.

The Social Contract, tr. and Introduction by G. D. H. Cole. 1930.

Correspondance générale de J.-J. Rousseau, ed. Th. Dufour and P. P. Plan. 20 vols. Armand Colin, 1924–30.

The Works of the Right Honourable Edmund Burke, 16 vols. Rivington ed. 1803.

Burke: Select Works, 3 vols. Introduction and Notes by E. J. Payne, 1888.

Correspondence of the Right Honourable Edmund Burke, 1744–1797, ed. Earl Fitzwilliam and Sir Richard Bourke, 4 vols. Rivington ed. 1844.

Letters of Edmund Burke, ed. Harold J. Laski. The World's Classics.

The Annual Register, years 1758–62.

II. WORKS ABOUT ROUSSEAU

Annales de la Société Jean-Jacques Rousseau, Geneva, 1905– . *In progress.* (A complete Rousseau bibliography, with critical comments, is to be found in the *Annales.*)

Bonnard, R. *Du pretendu individualisme de J.-J. Rousseau à propos de quelques livres récents.* Paris, 1907.

Champion, E. *J.-J. Rousseau et la révolution française.* Paris, 1909.

Cobban, A. *Rousseau and the Modern State.* London, 1934.

Collins, J. C. *Voltaire, Montesquieu and Rousseau in England.* London, 1908.

Courtois, L. J. *Le séjour de Jean-Jacques Rousseau en Angleterre (1766–1767), lettres et documents inédits.* Lausanne, 1911.

d'Escherny, Comte. *Éloge de J.-J. Rousseau,* 3 vols. Paris, 1796.

Dunning, W. A. 'Rousseau's Political Theories', *Political Science Quarterly,* Vol. XXIV. 1909.

Faguet, E. *La politique comparée de Montesquieu, Rousseau et Voltaire.* Paris, 1902.

Faguet, E. *Vie de Rousseau*. Paris, 1911.
— *Rousseau Penseur*. Paris, 1912.
Gran, G. *Jean-Jacques Rousseau*, tr. M. H. Janson. London, 1912.
Havens, G. R. *Voltaire's Marginalia on the Pages of Rousseau*. Ohio State University, 1933.
Haymann, F. *Der Begriff der volonté générale als Fundament der Rousseauschen Lehre von der Souveränität des Volks*. Leipzig, 1897.
— *Jean-Jacques Rousseaus Soẓialphilosophie*. Leipzig, 1898.
Hendel, C. W. *Jean-Jacques Rousseau, Moralist*, 2 vols. Oxford University Press, 1934.
٭ Höffding, H. *Jean-Jacques Rousseau and his Philosophy*, tr. W. Richards and L. E. Saidla. Oxford University Press, 1930.
Hubert, R. *Rousseau et l'Encyclopédie*. Paris, 1928.
Josephson, M. *Jean-Jacques Rousseau*. New York, 1931.
Kreinitz, M. *Das Wesen des Gemeinschaftswillens bei Jean-Jacques Rousseau*. Greifswald, 1925.
Leçons faites à l'École des Hautes Études Sociales, 1912, by G. Lanson, D. Mornet, G. Gastonel, F. Vial, I. Benrubi, G. Beaulavon, F. Baldensperger, and others.
Lemaître, J. *Jean-Jacques Rousseau*. Paris, 1907.
Lindsay, A. D. and Laski, H. J. 'Symposium: Bosanquet's Theory of the General Will.' *Aristotelian Society*, Supplementary Vol. VIII, 1928.
Masson, P. M. *La religion de J.-J. Rousseau*, 3 vols. Paris, 1916.
Mercier, S. *De J.-J. Rousseau considéré comme l'un des premiers auteurs de la révolution*, 2 vols. Paris, 1791.
Morley, J. *Rousseau*, 2 vols. London, 1915.
Plastara, G. *L'égalitarisme de J.-J. Rousseau*, Paris, 1905.
Revue de Métaphysique et de Morale, 1912, by H. Höffding, B. Bosanquet, J. Jaures, L. Levy-Bruhl, and others.
Rodet, H. *Le Contrat Social et les idées politiques de J.-J. Rousseau*. Paris, 1908.
Schinz, A. *La pensée de J.-J. Rousseau*, 2 vols. Smith College Studies, 1929.
Spink, J. S. *Jean-Jacques Rousseau et Genève*. Paris, 1934.
Streckeisen-Moultou, M. G. (Correspondance publiée par). *J.-J. Rousseau, ses amis et ses ennemis*, 2 vols. Paris, 1865.
Texte, J. *Jean-Jacques Rousseau et les origines du cosmopolitisme littéraire*. Paris, 1895.
Valette, G. *Jean-Jacques Rousseau Genevois*. Paris, 1911.
del Vecchio, G. *Su la Teoria del Contratto Sociale*. Bologna, 1906.
Williams, A. T. *The Concept of Equality in the Writings of Rousseau, Bentham and Kant*. New York, 1907.
Wright, E. H. *The Meaning of Rousseau*. Oxford University Press, 1929.

III. WORKS ABOUT BURKE

Cobban, A. *Edmund Burke and the Revolt against the Eighteenth Century.* London, 1929.

Einaudi, M. *Edmondo Burke e l'indirizzo storico nelle scienze politische.* Torino, 1930.

MacCunn, J. *The Political Philosophy of Burke.* London, 1913.

McCormick, C. *Memoirs of the Right Honourable Edmund Burke.* London, 1798.

Morley, J. *Edmund Burke: a historical study.* London, 1867.

— *Burke.* English Men of Letters Series. London, 1923.

Murray, R. H. *Edmund Burke, a Biography.* Oxford University Press, 1931.

Prior, J. *Memoir of the Life and Character of the Right Hon. Edmund Burke,* 2 vols. Boston, 1854.

Samuels, A. P. I. *The Early Life, Correspondence and Writings of the Rt. Hon. Edmund Burke.* Cambridge University Press, 1923.

IV. GENERAL WORKS

d'Alembert, J. la R. *Discours préliminaire de l'Encyclopédie.* Paris, 1912.

Aristotle, *Politics,* tr. B. Jowett, 2 vols. Oxford, 1885.

Barckhausen, H. A. *Montesquieu, ses idées et ses œuvres d'après les papiers de la Brède.* Paris, 1907.

Bayle, P. *Dictionnaire historique et critique,* 4 vols. Amsterdam, 1740.

Becker, C. D. *The Heavenly City of the Eighteenth-Century Philosophers.* Yale University Press, 1932.

Bentham, J. *A Fragment on Government,* ed. F. C. Montague. Oxford, 1891.

Blackstone, Sir W. *Commentaries on the Laws of England,* 4 vols. Oxford, 1765-9.

Boothby, Sir B. *A Letter to Edmund Burke (upon his Reflections on the French Revolution).* London, 1792.

Bosanquet, B. *The Philosophical Theory of the State.* London, 1925.

Boswell, J. *Life of Johnson,* ed. George Birkbeck Hill. Revised and enlarged, ed. L. F. Powell, 4 vols. Oxford, 1934.

— *Private Papers,* ed. Geoffrey Scott, in Isham Collection. 12 vols. New York, 1928.

Bury, J. B. *The Idea of Progress.* London, 1920.

Cole, G. D. H. *Politics and Literature.* New York, 1929.

Condillac, Abbé de. *Traité sur les Sensations.* Paris, lib. Delagrave.

Cook, T. I. *History of Political Philosophy from Plato to Burke.* New York, 1936.

Dampier-Whetham, W. C. D. *A History of Science and its Relations with Philosophy and Religion.* Cambridge University Press, 1929.

Dedieu, J. *Montesquieu et la tradition politique anglaise en France, les sources anglaises de l'Esprit des Lois.* Paris, 1909.

Ducros, L. *Les Encyclopédistes.* Paris, 1900.

Dupont, M. *Answer to the Reflections of the Right Hon. Edmund Burke,* London, 1791.

Encyclopédie, ou Dictionnaire raisonné des sciences, des arts et des métiers, par une société de gens de lettres, 17 vols. Paris, 1751–65.

Fairchild, H. N. *The Noble Savage.* New York, 1928.

Feiling, K. *A History of the Tory Party, 1640–1714.* Oxford, 1924.

Fénelon, F. de S. de la M. *Les Aventures de Télémaque.* Paris, 1920.

Fontenelle, B. de B. de. *Œuvres,* 5 vols. Paris, 1825.

Fox-Bourne, H. R. *The Life of John Locke,* 2 vols. New York, 1876.

Gentz, Fr. von. *Betrachtungen über die französische Revolution, nach dem englischen des Herrn Burke, neu-bearbeitet mit einer Einleitung.* Berlin, 1793–4.

Gibbon, E. *Autobiography.* New York, 1923.

Green, T. H. *Lectures on the Principles of Political Obligation.* London, 1917.

Greig, J. Y. T. *David Hume.* Oxford University Press, 1931.

Grimm, Friedrich Melchior. *Correspondance littéraire, philosophique et critique,* 16 vols. Paris, 1877–82.

Halévy, E. *La Formation du Radicalisme Philosophique,* 3 vols. Paris, 1901.

Hazen, C. D. *The French Revolution,* 2 vols. New York, 1932.

Helvétius, C. A. *De l'Esprit,* 2 vols. Paris, 1758.

Hobbes, T. *Leviathan,* ed. A. R. Waller. Cambridge University Press, 1904.

Hobhouse, L. T. *The Metaphysical Theory of the State.* London, 1918.

d'Holbach, Baron. *Système de la Nature,* 2 vols. Paris, 1821.

Hume, D. *Essays moral, political, and literary,* with preliminary dissertations and notes by T. H. Green and T. H. Grose. London, 1882.

— *Dialogues concerning Natural Religion,* ed. N. K. Smith. Oxford, 1935.

— *Enquiries concerning Human Understanding and concerning the Principles of Morals,* ed. L. A. Selby-Bigge. Oxford, 1902.

Johnson, Samuel. *Works,* 12 vols. London, 1816.

Keim, A. *Helvétius, sa vie et son œuvre.* Paris, 1907.

Lamprecht, S. P. *The Moral and Political Philosophy of John Locke.* Columbia University Press, 1918.

Lamy, B. *Entretiens sur les sciences, dans lesquels on aprend comme l'on doit étudier les sciences, et s'en servir pour se faire l'esprit juste et le cœur droit.* Lyon, 1724.

Lanson, G. *Voltaire.* Paris, 1910.

Laski, H. J. *Political Thought in England from Locke to Bentham.* London, 1925.

le Gras, Joseph. *Diderot et l'Encyclopédie.* Paris, 1928.

Locke, John. *Works,* 10 vols. London, 1823.

Lord, A. R. *The Principles of Politics,* Oxford University Press, 1926.

Lovejoy, A. O. *The Great Chain of Being.* Harvard University Press, 1936.

MacIver, R. M. *The Modern State*. Oxford University Press, 1928.
Mackintosh, Sir J. *Vindiciae Gallicae*. London, 1791.
Mandeville, B. *The Fable of the Bees*, ed. F. B. Kaye. 2 vols. Oxford University Press, 1924.
Martin, K. *French Liberal Thought in the Eighteenth Century*. Boston, 1929.
Montesquieu. *Œuvres*, 8 vols. Paris, 1926.
— *Considérations sur les Causes de la Grandeur des Romains et de leur Décadence*. Paris, 1911.
Morley, J. *Diderot and the Encyclopedists*, 2 vols. London, 1914.
Mornet, D. *Les origines intellectuelles de la révolution française*. Paris, 1933.
— *La pensée française au XVIIIᵉ siècle*. Paris, 1926.
— *Le romantisme en France au XVIIIᵉ siècle*. Paris, 1912.
— *Introduction to La Nouvelle Héloïse*, 2 vols. Paris, 1925.
Namier, L. B. *England in the Age of the American Revolution*. London, 1930.
— *The Structure of Politic. at the Accession of George III*, 2 vols. London, 1929.
Neff, E. E. *Carlyle and Mill*. Columbia University Press, 1926.
Paine, T. *The Rights of Man: being an answer to Mr. Burke's attack on the French Revolution*. New York, 1915.
Plato. *The Republic*, tr. B. Jowett. Oxford, 1888.
— *Laws*, 2 vols. ed. R. G. Bury. New York, 1926.
— *The Statesman*, ed. H. W. Fowler. New York, 1926.
Pollard, A. F. *The Evolution of Parliament*. London, 1926.
Porritt, E. *The Unreformed House of Commons*. Cambridge University Press, 1903.
Prévost, Abbé. *Histoire de M. Cleveland*, 6 vols. Paris, 1808.
Priestley, J. *Letters to Edmund Burke, occasioned by his Reflections on the Revolution in France*. Birmingham, 1791.
— *Essay on the First Principles of Government*. London, 1771.
Pufendorff, S. *Les devoirs de l'homme et du citoyen tels qu'ils sont préscrits par la loi naturelle*, ed. J. Barbeyrac. Amsterdam, 1718.
Raynal, G. T. F. *Histoire philosophique et politique des Établissements et du Commerce des Européens dans les deux Indes*, 7 vols. Paris, 1774.
Realey, C. B. *The Early Opposition to Sir Robert Walpole, 1720–27*. Philadelphia, 1931.
Ritchie, D. G. *Natural Rights*. London, 1895.
Robertson, Sir C. G. *England under the Hanoverians*. London, 1923.
Robertson, J. M. *Bolingbroke and Walpole*. London, 1919.
Robinson, H. *Bayle, the Sceptic*. New York, 1931.
Sabine, G. H. *A History of Political Theory*. New York, 1937.
See, H. *Economic and Social Conditions in France during the Eighteenth Century*, tr. E. H. Zeydel. New York, 1927.
— *Les idées politiques en France au XVIIIᵉ siècle*. Paris, 1920.

Smith, Adam. *An Inquiry into the Nature and Causes of the Wealth of Nations,* 3 vols. Edinburgh, 1806.

Stephen, Sir L. *History of English Thought in the Eighteenth Century,* 2 vols. New York, 1927.

Strauss, L. *The Political Philosophy of Hobbes,* tr. E. M. Sinclair. Oxford University Press, 1936.

Turberville, A. S. *English Men and Manners in the Eighteenth Century.* Oxford, 1926.

— *The House of Lords in the Eighteenth Century.* Oxford, 1927.

— *Johnson's England.* Oxford, 1933.

Vaughan, C. E. *Studies in the History of Political Philosophy,* 2 vols. Manchester University Press, 1925.

Voltaire, *Œuvres complètes,* 97 vols. Paris, 1824–32.

— *Lettres philosophiques,* ed. G. Lanson, 2 vols. Paris, 1909.

Walpole, H. *Memoirs of the Reign of King George the Third,* 2 vols. London, 1845.

Williams, B. *The Whig Supremacy 1714–1760.* Oxford, 1939.

Winstanley, D. A. *Lord Chatham and the Whig Opposition.* Cambridge University Press, 1912.

— *Personal and Party Government.* Cambridge University Press, 1912.

INDEX

(Names and Titles)